Teach English in Korea: A Complete Step-by-Step Guide to Teaching English Abroad, Getting TEFL Certified, and Living in South Korea

By Bradley S. Brennan, Ph.D., MBA, B.Ed.

Teach English in Korea: A Complete Step-by-Step Guide

First Edition, 2026

ISBN: 979-8-234-00638-7

Published by Brennan Edu

www.teachenglishinkorea.org

This book was funded by grant #76351-1 from Inha University.

Dedication

For the woman in the coffee shop who asked me, "Have you ever considered teaching in Korea?" For without her, I would never have had my son, Jae.

Table of Contents

Introduction: Who This Book Is For and How to Use It

Navigation Tip

This guide is built so you can read it cover-to-cover or jump straight to the section you need right now. If you are just getting started, begin with Part One to understand the market and prepare your application. Already have a job offer? Skip to Part Three for the visa process. Have you just landed in Korea? Part Four will get you settled. Struggling in the classroom? Part Five has you covered. Keep the QR codes handy throughout; they link to updated forms, checklists, and guides hosted on TeachEnglishinKorea.org.

This guide is organized into six parts that mirror the natural arc of the teaching-in-Korea journey, from first curiosity through to career planning after your contract ends.

Part One

"Understanding the Opportunity" covers Chapters 1 through 4. Here you will get the full picture of Korea's ESL market, the types of schools, qualifications, pay, and TEFL certification, so you can decide if Korea is right for you and position yourself competitively.

Part Two

"Getting a Job" covers Chapters 5 through 8. This is where you build your application materials, find and evaluate job openings, ace the interview, and negotiate a contract you feel confident signing.

Part Three

"The Visa and Immigration Process" covers Chapters 9 through 11. These chapters walk you through every step of the visa application with country-specific guidance, and then help you prepare for the move itself, from packing strategies to mental preparation.

Part Four

"Arriving and Settling In" covers Chapters 12 and 13. Once you land, these chapters help you set up your apartment, banking, and transportation, and then navigate the cultural dynamics of your Korean workplace.

Part Five

"Thriving in the Classroom" covers Chapters 14 through 17. This section equips you with classroom management strategies, lesson planning skills, age-group-specific teaching techniques, and a deeper understanding of the cultural forces shaping Korean education.

Part Six

"Life Beyond the Classroom" covers Chapters 18 through 21. These chapters cover travel and food adventures, building a social life and community, managing your finances and legal obligations, and planning your next steps, whether you stay in Korea or move on.

Following Chapter 21, you will find the Bonus Resources section, which includes a sample cover letter, a self-introduction video script, a lesson plan template, a list of teaching job boards and general expat resources, and a Korean survival phrases cheat sheet. These are reference materials designed for quick access whenever you need them.

QR codes are sprinkled throughout the book, linking you to updated checklists, visa guides, and how-to blog posts hosted on TeachEnglishinKorea.org. That way, even if this book is printed or saved offline, you will always have access to the latest resources, downloadable documents, and insider updates.

Note: The Teacher Stories throughout this book are based on real people I have worked with over my twenty-plus years of recruiting and mentoring English teachers in Korea. Names have been changed to protect their privacy.

Part One

Understanding the Opportunity

Chapter 1: Why Teach English in Korea?

Chapter Summary

This chapter explores the personal and professional growth opportunities that teaching English in Korea offers, from cultural immersion and career development to financial stability and lifelong friendships. You will learn why thousands of teachers from around the world choose Korea each year, understand the current state of the E-2 visa market and who is making the move, and get a realistic preview of what your first year will look like month by month. You will also gain mindset strategies that separate teachers who thrive from those who struggle, and a clear overview of how this book is structured to guide you through every step of the process.

Why This Chapter Matters

If you are reading this book, you are at least curious about teaching in Korea, and possibly already committed to making it happen. Either way, this chapter sets the foundation for everything that follows. Before diving into resumes, visa applications, and classroom strategies, you need to understand what you are stepping into: the size and shape of the ESL market, the kinds of people who succeed in Korea, and the mindset that will determine whether your experience is transformative or frustrating. Think of this chapter as the honest conversation I wish someone had with me before I moved to Korea more than twenty years ago. It would have saved me months of confusion and a few embarrassing mistakes.

A Life-Changing Opportunity

Teaching English in South Korea is more than just a job; it is a life-changing opportunity for personal growth, cultural immersion, and professional development. It allows you to step outside your comfort zone, build meaningful relationships with students and colleagues, and explore one of Asia's most modern, dynamic, and culturally rich countries. At the same time, you will be gaining classroom experience, developing teaching strategies, and acquiring valuable cross-cultural communication skills that can serve you well whether you continue in education or pivot into another career path in the future.

Teacher Story: Trading Suits for a Chalkboard

Michael, a 27-year-old from Manchester, had been working in finance for five years. On paper, he was doing well, good salary, comfortable apartment, steady career path, but he described his life as "just rinse and repeat." A friend connected him to a former TEIK teacher who was back in the UK and "wouldn't shut up about Korea." Within three months, Michael applied, accepted a job in Daejeon, and packed up.

His first few weeks were a bit overwhelming to him: navigating a grocery store where nothing looked familiar, adjusting to 12 noisy 8-year-olds in his classroom, and remembering to sort his trash into recyclable and non-recyclable and to take out the garbage on the right day (after forgetting twice). He started to get more into a rhythm by the end of his second month in both his classroom and personal life.

By his third month, one of his Korean colleagues pulled him aside and said, "I think I know someone you should meet." Her name was Jiyeon, a Korean English teacher at another hagwon (학원) nearby, and the colleague thought they'd be a perfect match because they both loved hiking and the outdoors. Their first meeting was on a crisp autumn Saturday, joining a small group hike up Gyeryongsan Mountain with colleagues. Michael remembered being out of breath halfway up. Still, Jiyeon kept pace easily, pointing out wildflowers, temple rooftops peeking through the trees, and the best spots for mountainside bibimbap (비빔밥) and dongdongju (동동주) Korean unfiltered rice wine, made by grandmothers who dotted the trails. That hike turned into many more, from summer camping trips on the East Coast to winter treks through snow-dusted trails.

Jiyeon didn't just share his love of the outdoors; she became his cultural guide. She taught him subtle Korean workplace etiquette, explained why specific phrases made parents smile, and helped him avoid a few embarrassing faux pas with her gentle humor. She also introduced him to her favorite parts of Korean culture: lantern festivals, makgeolli after long hikes, and the quiet peace of temple tea ceremonies. They both learned about each other's cultures and even took a trip to the UK during one of the vacations for a week, so Michael could introduce her to his parents and show her his country.

By his sixth month, Michael had traveled to Busan, hiked Seoraksan, learned to read Korean menus, and built friendships with both locals and other expats. Two years later, he and Jiyeon were married and moved back to the UK, where he now teaches at an elementary school in his hometown, and Jiyeon teaches the Korean language at their church.

Takeaway: Sometimes, the biggest adventure isn't just moving abroad, it's meeting someone who helps you see a new country not as a visitor, but as part of a shared life.

The Current E-2 Visa Landscape

South Korea's demand for foreign English teachers remains strong. According to the Korean Immigration Service's Statistical Yearbook, the number of E-2 visa holders peaked in 2010 at 22,800 teachers during the height of Korea's "English Craze." By contrast, 2024 saw 13,676 teachers, a figure about 40% lower than the peak but significantly higher than pandemic lows.

To put the recent rebound into perspective, pre-pandemic 2019 saw approximately 29,200 E-2 visas issued. That number collapsed to 11,326 in 2020, a 61% drop, and bottomed out at 5,376 in 2021, the lowest in recent history. Recovery has been steady since then: 10,515 in 2022, 12,451 in 2023, and 13,676 as of the May 2024 Monthly Report. Based on our recruitment data and conversations with partner schools, 2025 numbers appear to be trending between the

2024 figures and the 2019 highs, especially as travel restrictions have fully eased and demand for in-person instruction has surged.

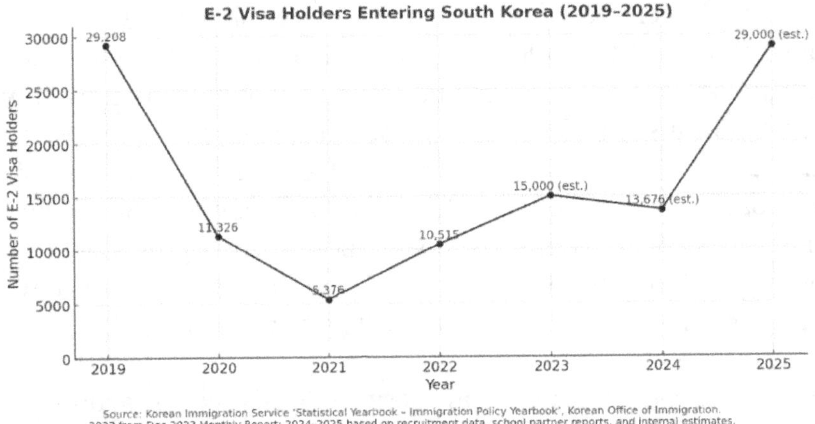

Source: Korean Immigration Service Statistical Yearbook – Immigration Policy Yearbook, Monthly Immigration Reports (Dec 2023, May 2024).

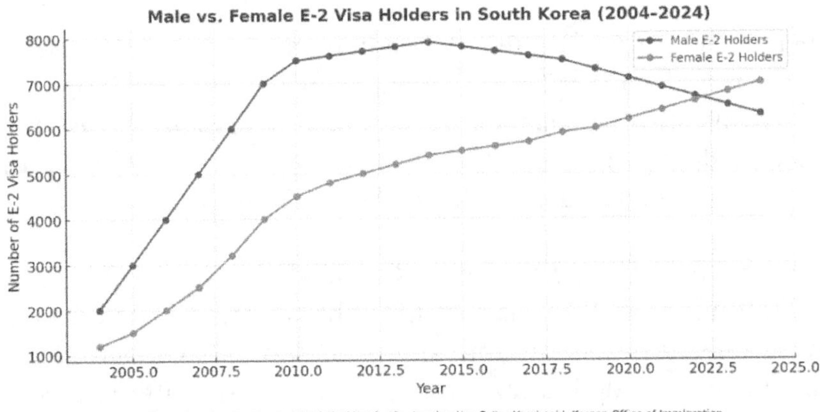

South Korea's demand for foreign English teachers remains strong. According to the Korean Immigration Service's Statistical Yearbook, the number of E-2 visa holders peaked in 2010 at 22,800 teachers during the height of Korea's "English Craze." By contrast,

2024 saw 13,676 teachers, a figure about 40% lower than the peak but significantly higher than pandemic lows.

To put the recent rebound into perspective, pre-pandemic 2019 saw approximately 29,200 E-2 visas issued. That number collapsed to 11,326 in 2020, a 61% drop, and bottomed out at 5,376 in 2021, the lowest in recent history. Recovery has been steady since then: 10,515 in 2022, 12,451 in 2023, and 13,676 as of the May 2024 Monthly Report. Based on our recruitment data and conversations with partner schools, 2025 numbers appear to be trending between the 2024 figures and the 2019 highs, especially as travel restrictions have fully eased and demand for in-person instruction has surged.

Source: Korean Immigration Service Statistical Yearbook – Immigration Policy Yearbook, Monthly Immigration Reports (Dec 2023, May 2024).

Teacher Story: From Corporate Boardroom to Korean Classroom

Consider the story of Emily, a Canadian university graduate who landed a coveted corporate job in Vancouver after finishing her degree. Within two years, she had bought a condo, enjoyed a comfortable salary, and checked all the boxes of conventional success, yet she felt unfulfilled and all of this by her early twenties.

Through a friend I had placed in Korea, who spoke highly of her experience, Emily learned about teaching abroad. She decided to take the leap, applied through my company, and moved to Korea to teach English. She had decided to try something completely different from her current life and to chase her desire to have a very different and exciting adventure.

To document her journey, Emily started a small YouTube vlog. At first, it was a way to keep in touch with friends and family. But one video about her transition to Korean work life unexpectedly went viral, attracting thousands of views. Her growing audience led her to interview me for one of her videos, which also took off, cementing her as a small but notable voice in the expat teaching community.

Over her contract term, Emily gained confidence in public speaking, developed new friendships, and became skilled at navigating cross-cultural communication. After several years in Korea, she decided to return to Canada, this time with a broader worldview, a stronger resume, and the confidence to pursue her next adventure.

Takeaway: Emily's experience mirrors that of thousands of others who come to Korea, not only to teach, but to reinvent themselves. The statistics show that despite a decline from the early 2010s, the E-2 teaching market remains vibrant and is now rebounding rapidly. For those who step into the role, the rewards extend far beyond a paycheck: they gain the resilience, adaptability, and cultural fluency that come from living and working in a foreign country.

South Korea's appeal lies in its unique blend of opportunity and lifestyle. Teachers often find themselves navigating a high-tech society, where you can pay for coffee with your phone and have groceries delivered in under an hour, while also engaging in centuries-old traditions, from temple stays to traditional markets. The contrasts keep life exciting: you might spend a Friday night enjoying live K-pop in Seoul and your Saturday morning hiking past ancient fortresses in the mountains. This combination of professional stability, cultural immersion, and adventure is why so many teachers call their time in Korea one of the most transformative periods of their lives.

Who Chooses to Teach in Korea?

Every year, thousands of teachers from English-speaking countries make the leap to live and work in South Korea. Based on our TeachEnglishinKorea.org (TEIK) recruitment data and feedback from our partner schools, the majority are recent graduates seeking an exciting first step after university. Others are career changers looking to escape the monotony of office life, and a smaller percentage are experienced, licensed educators wanting international exposure.

Based on TEIK internal data, roughly 72% of teachers we place are recent graduates, fresh out of university with degrees in education, English, communications, or unrelated fields, but with a strong sense of adventure. About 23% are career changers, professionals from fields such as business, hospitality, and customer service who are looking for a lifestyle change or an opportunity to travel while earning. The remaining 5% are experienced licensed educators with official teaching licenses and years of classroom experience, often drawn to the unique cultural experience and competitive compensation. Many in this last group are burned out with teaching back home and the lack of respect for teachers, which is the opposite in Korea.

Pro Tip

Before accepting any job offer, join online communities where current and former teachers in Korea share real experiences. Facebook groups like "English Teachers in Korea," the "r/teachinginkorea" subreddit, and long-standing forums such as Dave's ESL Café are excellent places to ask questions, read reviews, and gather honest feedback about specific schools, recruiters, and cities. These platforms can offer invaluable insights that job listings and recruiters may not disclose.

Top Motivations for Choosing Korea

There are a multitude of reasons why teachers choose to move 5,000+ miles away from home and teach in Korea. I broke it down into seven categories that cover the majority of the teachers I interviewed and spoke with. Of course, there are some very specialized reasons, like they met a Korean boyfriend or girlfriend in their home country and want to move to Korea, or Korean adoptees wanting to learn about their roots, but most people fall into these main groups.

For many, it comes down to adventure at the right time in life. Most are in a life stage where they are free from heavy commitments like mortgages or children but still seeking meaningful experiences before settling down. Others are driven by a passion for teaching and mentoring. Even if not formally trained, many are drawn to working with children and view teaching as a way to make a positive impact while exploring a new culture.

Financial opportunity is another major draw. The combination of competitive pay, free housing, paid airfare, and a low cost of living allows many to save significantly, often paying down large student loans while abroad. Cultural appeal also plays a significant role, as the global influence of K-dramas, K-pop, Korean food, and traditional culture inspires many to choose Korea over other destinations.

Some teachers describe Korea as a delayed dream. These are people in their late 20s to late 30s who had always wanted to teach abroad after graduation, but life circumstances, career paths, relationships, or other responsibilities delayed their plans until now. For career changers, Korea often serves as a reset button, a way to step out of an unfulfilling job, escape burnout, or recover from significant life changes like divorce, while gaining new skills and perspective. And for many, Korea is simply a gateway to Asia. With affordable flights and proximity to Japan, China, and Southeast Asia, Korea offers teachers the chance to explore the broader region during holidays.

Pro Tip

Not all teaching positions in Korea are created equal. Before signing a contract, take the time to research the school's reputation. Look for online reviews, ask your recruiter specific questions about staff turnover and work conditions, and, if possible, request to speak directly with a current foreign teacher employed at the school. Their perspective can give you a much clearer idea of what daily life and expectations will be like. A few hours of research now can save you from months of stress later.

Purpose of This Guide

This book was created to provide aspiring English teachers with a comprehensive, honest, and practical guide to every stage of the experience. Over the past decade, I have worked closely with thousands of teachers and school administrators through TEIK. I have reviewed resumes, answered late-night visa questions, helped teachers navigate contract disputes, and celebrated their successes. Along the way, I realized how many of the same questions and issues come up again and again. Teachers often told me they wished there were a clear, detailed resource that could walk them through everything, from the job search to classroom management to weekend travel. This book is my response to that need.

Why This Guide is Different

Unlike the scattered advice on forums and social media, this book is structured, up-to-date, and practical. It is not sugarcoated, nor is it weighed down by unnecessary academic jargon. Instead, it is a field guide grounded in authentic experiences, honest insights, and clear explanations. It gives you the tools to make wise decisions, avoid common mistakes, and thrive both inside and outside the classroom. Whether you are still weighing your options or you are already applying for jobs, this book is designed to support you every step of the way.

My Perspective from the Field

Over the past two decades of helping teachers start their journey in Korea, I've learned that every placement is more than just a job match; it's the beginning of a personal story. I've seen teachers arrive brimming with excitement, and others stepping off the plane with quiet uncertainty, unsure if they've made the right decision. In almost every case, those first few months are transformative. People discover new strengths, adapt in ways they didn't think possible, and often surprise themselves with how quickly they build a life in a completely new environment.

From my vantage point, the teachers who thrive most aren't necessarily the ones with the most experience or the best résumés; they're the ones who embrace adaptability, curiosity, and a willingness to learn. Korea will test these qualities, sometimes in subtle ways (like adjusting to a new work hierarchy) and other times in more immediate challenges (navigating banking or healthcare in a foreign language).

One thing I've learned that isn't in most other guides is the value of building connections early. Many teachers underestimate how much having even a small support network can shape their experience. Whether it's through school colleagues, other expats in your city, or events like our spring and fall networking dinners, having a circle of people to share meals, frustrations, and victories with makes the difference between simply working abroad and truly living abroad. These moments, meeting someone who helps you through your first Korean winter, or swapping lesson ideas over a bowl of kimchi jjigae (김치 찌개, kimchi stew), become the real highlights when you look back.

I've placed thousands of teachers in schools across the country, but I still approach each one as a unique match. Behind every contract is a person with hopes, goals, and sometimes a little nervousness about stepping into the unknown. Helping them navigate the complexities, before, during, and even after their contract, has been one of the most rewarding parts of my work.

What Your First Year Looks Like

Every teacher's experience in Korea is different, but after placing and mentoring thousands of teachers over the years, I can tell you that the emotional and professional arc of the first year is remarkably consistent. Knowing what to expect month by month won't eliminate the challenges, but it will help you recognize that what you're feeling at any given point is completely normal and almost always temporary. Here is an honest look at what the next twelve months will feel like.

Month one is pure sensory overload. You've just landed in a country where you can't read most signs, the food is unfamiliar, and your apartment has a washing machine with buttons entirely in Korean. Your school will hand you a curriculum, introduce you to your co-teacher, and point you toward your first classroom, sometimes with very little training. You'll spend your evenings figuring out how to use your gas stove, where to buy toilet paper, and why your floor is warm. You'll make mistakes constantly, ordering the wrong thing at a restaurant, bowing at the wrong moment, accidentally throwing your recycling in the wrong bin, and that's fine. Everyone does. By the end of the first month, you'll have a handful of landmarks memorized, a favorite convenience store, and the beginnings of a routine. You'll also be exhausted in a way that surprises you, because even simple tasks require twice the mental energy when everything around you is unfamiliar.

Month two is when the classroom starts to click. You're still figuring out your teaching materials, but you've taught each lesson at least once now, and the second time through is noticeably easier. You know which activities work with your students and which ones fall flat. You're learning your students' names, their personalities, and which ones need encouragement versus a firm hand. Outside of school, you've probably found a go-to restaurant near your apartment, downloaded Papago and KakaoTalk, and maybe made your first Korean friend, often a coworker who takes pity on you and shows you where to get decent coffee. Homesickness tends to peak around this time. The novelty has worn off just enough for you to miss the ease of daily life back home, but not enough for Korea to feel comfortable yet. Call someone from home, let yourself feel it, and then go eat something delicious. It passes.

Month three is a turning point. At most hagwons, students rotate into new classes every three months, which means you'll start teaching the same material you just finished to a fresh group of students. This is when teaching in Korea gets dramatically easier. Your lesson plans are already built, your timing is dialed in, and you know exactly which games and activities your students respond to.

The confidence boost is enormous. Socially, you've likely connected with other foreign teachers in your area, whether through your school, a local Facebook group, or one of the many expat meetups and events around the country. By the end of month three, the panic of month one feels like a distant memory.

Months four and five are when Korea starts to feel like home. Your morning routine is automatic. You know which subway exit to use, which banchan you like at your regular lunch spot, and how to navigate the self-checkout at the grocery store. Teaching is no longer the all-consuming challenge it was, and you have mental bandwidth to invest in things outside of work. This is when many teachers start exploring Korea more seriously, booking weekend trips to Busan or Gyeongju, discovering hiking trails near their city, or signing up for Korean language classes. It's also when your social circle starts to solidify. You'll naturally gravitate toward the people whose company you enjoy, and the friendships you form during this period often become the most lasting ones of your entire time in Korea.

Month six is the midpoint of your contract, and it often comes with an unexpected emotional dip. You're comfortable enough that the daily adventure of being abroad has become routine, but you still have six months left, which can feel like a long time if you're having a tough week at school or missing home. This is completely normal, and almost every teacher I've worked with describes some version of it. The teachers who push through it, usually by planning a trip, picking up a new hobby, or simply reminding themselves why they came, come out the other side feeling recommitted and energized. The ones who dwell on it tend to spiral. If you feel a slump around the halfway mark, recognize it for what it is: a predictable phase, not a sign that you made the wrong decision.

Months seven and eight are where many teachers hit their stride. Your teaching is confident and creative. You're improvising in the classroom, adapting lessons on the fly, and genuinely enjoying the time you spend with your students. Your Korean has improved enough to handle basic conversations, and you've accumulated a mental map of your city that makes daily life feel effortless. This is also the period when your social life outside of school becomes especially important. Make sure you have friends and outlets beyond your coworkers. Everyone needs to vent about work sometimes, and the healthiest way to do that is with people who don't share your staff room. Talking about colleagues with other colleagues is a fast track to a toxic workplace atmosphere, and I've seen it damage otherwise great experiences. Keep your school relationships professional and warm, and save the honest venting for friends outside the building.

Month nine is when your school will start asking whether you plan to renew your contract. For some teachers, the answer is obvious. They love their school, their city, and their students, and signing on for another year is an easy decision. For others, it's more complicated. Maybe the job is fine, but the city doesn't excite you anymore, or maybe you're ready for a new challenge but aren't sure what that looks like. This is the right time to start having honest conversations with your recruiter about your options. Many teachers choose to stay in Korea but switch schools or cities for their second year, and recruiters can help you explore what's available without committing to anything. Don't let anyone pressure you into a decision before you're ready, but don't procrastinate either, because the best positions for the next hiring cycle fill quickly.

Months ten and eleven often feel bittersweet. If you're leaving, every experience starts to feel like a "last." Your last cherry blossom season or your last autumn hike. Your last school festival. The last time your favorite student runs up to you in the hallway, yelling, "Teacher!" You'll start making mental lists of things you want to do before you go, restaurants you haven't tried, cities you haven't visited, and friends you keep meaning to meet up with. If you're staying, these months feel more like a bridge, wrapping up the current term while mentally preparing for a fresh start with new students and maybe a renegotiated contract. Either way, this is the time to take care of logistics. Confirm your severance details, get your pension paperwork in order, and start collecting written references from your director and co-teachers while you're still there, so they can hand them to you in person.

Month twelve is the home stretch. Your final weeks will be a mix of nostalgia, excitement, and administrative tasks. You'll say goodbye to students who have become genuinely important to you, and some of those goodbyes will hit harder than you expect. You'll pack up an apartment that felt impossibly foreign twelve months ago and now feels like the most familiar place in the world. And whether you're heading home, traveling through Asia, or walking into a new school for year two, you'll leave Korea with something you didn't have when you arrived: the knowledge that you can build a life anywhere, from scratch, and thrive.

The skills you develop over this year, adaptability, cross-cultural communication, creative problem-solving, patience, and the ability to connect with people across language and cultural barriers, are not just teaching skills. They're life skills. Employers in every industry value the resilience and perspective that come from thriving in a completely different cultural and professional environment, and you'll carry them with you long after Korea becomes a chapter in your story rather than your daily reality.

The Importance of Mindset

I always say that if you had two teachers with the exact same job, same students, same housing, and the same experiences, but one said, "I had a fantastic time in Korea," and the other said, "I didn't enjoy my time in Korea," the difference is 100% mindset. Teachers who can laugh at themselves and situations are the ones who can roll with the punches and the inevitable minor things that come up while you are adjusting to a new culture.

One teacher approached challenges as an enjoyable and rewarding part of living in another country, laughing at the mishaps, staying curious about cultural differences, and seeing each hurdle as part of the adventure. The other teacher took things personally, resisted change, and constantly compared life in Korea to "how it's done back home."

The truth is, Korea was built to be comfortable for Koreans, not for visiting foreigners. That's not a flaw; it's precisely how it should be. As expats, we're guests in their country, which means it's our job to adapt, not theirs. We need to be open to new ways of thinking, embrace unfamiliar routines, and remain flexible enough to fit into Korean culture rather than expecting it to bend to ours.

One teacher I placed put it perfectly, and they said something like: "The moment I stopped expecting Korea to work like my home country and started enjoying the differences, my entire experience changed for the better." These are not the exact words they said, but it is the gist of what they said to me at one of our events. I have made many mistakes in Korea, and I can laugh about them now, and I often tell teachers about my faux pas to save them from making the same.

Teacher Story: From Overwhelmed to Mentor

Amber arrived in Korea in March, full of energy but unprepared for just how steep the first-month learning curve could be. At our spring-hosted dinner, she pulled me aside, looking exhausted. She admitted she was feeling completely overloaded, juggling lesson planning, learning new materials, adjusting to life in a new country, and trying to keep up with her students' pace.

To make matters worse, Amber struggled with spelling and had been called out by her Korean head teacher for errors in students' journals after several parents complained. The criticism hit hard, and she felt she was letting everyone down.

I suggested a practical fix: start drafting her journal entries on her phone using Grammarly, and double-check tricky phrases with ChatGPT before writing in the students' take-home books. I also reminded her that the first two to three months are the toughest, but after the first "level-up" when students move into new classes she had already taught once, everything would feel easier. The second cycle would be smoother, and by the third, she'd have mastered her materials.

She took the advice to heart. By summer, Amber's confidence was growing, her classes were running more smoothly, and her head teacher began praising her progress. By the time we met again at our fall-hosted dinner, she was a different person, smiling, relaxed, and full of pride in how far she'd come.

Amber not only re-signed for a second year but also volunteered as a mentor for incoming teachers, helping them navigate the same rocky start she once faced.

Takeaway: The first months in Korea can be overwhelming, but if you push through and build systems to make your job easier, you'll come out stronger, and you might even become the person others look to for guidance.

Contract Renewal

Most schools will ask three to four months before your contract ends if you'd like to re-sign. By then, you'll be in a much better position to decide if you want to stay for another year, because you'll know that with the right mindset, the second year is almost always smoother than the first. At the end of year one, many teachers choose to stay in Korea but change their setting, sometimes moving to a new city, seeking higher pay, adjusting to better working hours, or simply looking for a different lifestyle fit. This is especially common for teachers who spent their first year in satellite cities around Seoul or smaller regional towns but originally had their sights set on Seoul itself. In these cases, it's normal to reach out to your recruiter to explore new opportunities, as they can help you find a position that better matches your evolving preferences and career goals. We will cover contract renewal in detail in Chapter 21.

Understanding Korea's Education System

Korea's approach to education is deeply rooted in its history and cultural values. The modern ESL market really began to boom in the early 1990s during what many call English Fever, a national push to improve English proficiency to compete in the global economy. Hagwons (private academies) expanded rapidly, public school programs brought in foreign teachers, and English became a central pillar of Korea's long-term development strategy. By the mid-2000s, teaching English in Korea had become one of the most sought-after jobs for young professionals from English-speaking countries.

Today, Korea's education system is known for its rigor, structure, and heavy focus on measurable results. Students typically attend public or private school during the day and then often attend hagwons in the evening for additional lessons, English being one of the most common. For foreign teachers, this means your work environment can vary greatly depending on whether you're in a public school or a hagwon. Public school teachers usually work during daytime hours and have larger classes, while hagwon teachers work in smaller class sizes but often into the evening.

Why Parents Invest So Much in Education

One of the most defining features of Korea's education culture is the extraordinary financial commitment parents make toward their children's studies. It is estimated that many Korean families spend over 50% of their monthly disposable income on extra education, private academies, tutoring, and enrichment programs. The reasons for this are deeply tied to Korea's economic reality: with few natural resources, the nation's greatest asset is its human capital. Korea has one of the highest rates of advanced degree holders in the world, creating what could be visualized as a diamond-shaped workforce distribution: a small base of unskilled labor, a large middle made up of highly educated professionals, and another small tip of elite specialists.

Because of this emphasis, most parents see supplemental education as non-negotiable. It is entirely normal for children to attend multiple private academies, including English, math, Korean language, music, sports, and more, after finishing their regular school day, sometimes even on weekends. For parents, this is not "extra," it is the norm, and it's part of a competitive arms race to give their children any advantage possible.

When I first moved to Korea, I told myself I would never be a tiger parent. I wanted my son to enjoy his childhood the way I grew up in the USA, spending afternoons outdoors playing sports with friends, riding bikes, exploring the neighborhood, and socializing without a rigid schedule. At the same time, I wanted to give him opportunities I didn't have. So, we let him try different activities and choose what he wanted to continue. Over the years, he has tried inline skating school (yes, they exist here), English academies, several math programs, Korean language and history classes, basketball, soccer, piano, violin, you name it. The twist? He enjoyed them all and wanted to do even more, partly because his friends were going too. Before we knew it, we found ourselves doing exactly what most Korean families do, spending significant amounts of money on extracurricular education, with weeknights often ending at 8 or 9 PM and weekends equally packed.

This commitment to education is one of the reasons Korean students can appear tired in class, not due to a lack of interest, but because their days are filled from early morning to late evening with structured learning. For foreign teachers, understanding this context can make a huge difference in how you approach and empathize with your students.

The Journey Ahead

One of the most rewarding parts of teaching in Korea is the personal transformation it sparks. You'll learn to think on your feet, adapt to new environments, and collaborate with people from vastly different backgrounds. By the end of your journey, you'll likely be more independent, empathetic, and confident than ever before, life skills that carry far beyond the classroom.

At times, the journey will stretch you. You may feel homesick, misunderstood, or overwhelmed by the pace of work or the structure of your school. But you will also experience joy, laughter, personal breakthroughs, and countless small wins, like mastering the subway system, ordering dinner in Korean, or hearing your students say "Teacher, I love English class."

Teacher Story: The Accidental Mentor

Rachel, a 25-year-old from Toronto, arrived in Korea with zero teaching experience and what she described to me later as a healthy dose of imposter syndrome. She told me during a pre-departure call before coming to Korea, "I'm worried I'll barely keep my own head above water. I'm not sure I will be a good teacher." I told her to keep a positive attitude, always listen to teaching advice from her school and seek advice from teachers at her school who she felt taught well. Her plan was obvious from our discussions: focus on surviving her first year, keep her head down, and avoid making waves at her school. I spoke with her a few times during her first six months to give her advice on specific classroom situations, but mostly it was general guidance, and I also gave her websites for teaching materials that she wanted to have access to.

But during her second semester, a new foreign teacher, Tom, who was placed at her school from Portland, Oregon, joined her hagwon. At first, he was struggling with the same challenges she'd once faced: late-night lesson prep, awkward cultural misunderstandings, and the constant worry of "Am I doing this right?" Without even realizing it, Rachel told me that she started sharing little tips she had learned in her first half of the year: how to organize lesson materials so prep took half the time, which coffee shop owners were friendly to foreigners, how to navigate the infamous Korean garbage sorting rules, where to buy things for his apartment, and where to eat.

One Friday night, while they were having chimek ((치맥chicken and beer, from the Korean word maekju (맥주)), Tom admitted to her that she had kept him from quitting twice already in his first few months. That's when it hit her. Somewhere along the way, she'd gone from overwhelmed newbie to a source of stability for someone else. Her coworkers noticed too and gave her praise when she would help other teachers. Her Korean manager began introducing her to incoming teachers as someone they could go to for questions and advice.

By the end of her contract, Rachel was training new hires formally, developing resource binders, and even helping the school improve its onboarding process. During her farewell dinner party, the director thanked her not only for her teaching but for making the foreign teacher team feel more comfortable. Rachel went back to Canada and started a master's course in education, determined to become a full-time teacher back home.

Takeaway: You might start your Korean teaching journey feeling like the least experienced person in the room, but growth sneaks up on you. One day, you'll look around and realize you've become the steady hand guiding someone else. In Korean workplaces, this quiet, dependable leadership is deeply respected and often opens unexpected doors for your career.

Final Thoughts

I hope that this chapter has given you a clear picture of what teaching in Korea looks like, who does it, and why it matters. This book is your guide, your roadmap, and your support system. Use it well, and let it remind you that you are not alone. Thousands have come before you, and many more will follow. Now, it is your turn.

Chapter 2: Types of Teaching Jobs in Korea

Chapter Summary

This chapter breaks down the main categories of English teaching jobs available in Korea, including public schools, private academies (hagwons), universities, international schools, and freelance tutoring. You will learn how salaries, schedules, benefits, and working conditions compare across these options, and how your visa type, qualifications, and personal preferences should influence your decision. Real teacher experiences throughout the chapter will help you set realistic expectations, and by the end, you will have a clear framework for choosing the job type that matches your goals, personality, and lifestyle.

Why This Chapter Matters

Around 80% or more of foreign teachers in Korea start in private language academies (hagwons), with roughly 15% or less joining public schools through programs like EPIK, and fewer than 5% landing specialized teaching positions (adults, companies, etc.), or university jobs. While hagwons offer year-round hiring, with main intakes for spring and fall (March 1st and September 1st) and urban availability, public schools follow seasonal intakes and typically have more structured schedules. University positions are the most competitive of all, often requiring advanced degrees in the subject taught, with two years of prior teaching experience in Korea, and strong professional networks. In recent years, these jobs have become even harder to find because of stricter qualification requirements, and because many rural and smaller universities have reduced staff or closed entirely due to the country's declining birthrate and ongoing migration toward major cities.

Understanding Your Options

If you have made it this far, you are probably seriously considering teaching in Korea. However, before you pack your bags and book your flight, it is essential to understand the different types of teaching jobs available. Korea offers a variety of options, each with its advantages and challenges. Whether you are looking for stability, high pay, or flexibility, there is a teaching job that fits your needs. In this chapter, I will break down the major teaching job categories, share personal experiences, and help you determine which option suits you best.

Teacher Story: From "Almost Missed" to "Dream Job"

In 2022, Melissa, a 24-year-old recent graduate from Toronto, was eager to start teaching in Korea. She'd been to Seoul once as a tourist and loved the energy of the city, but she had no teaching experience beyond tutoring her younger cousins. Her plan was simple: search online, send her resume, and wait for offers.

The problem? Melissa's resume was built for retail and hospitality jobs in Canada. It listed her part-time barista position, her university courses, and a short stint as a camp counselor. Still, it didn't frame any of that in a way that Korean school directors value: reliability, adaptability, and the ability to manage a classroom. Her cover letter was equally generic, opening with "Dear Hiring Manager" and focusing more on why she wanted to live abroad than on what she could contribute to the school and her potential students.

After three weeks and over 20 applications, she had received only one polite rejection and a lot of silence. Feeling discouraged, she contacted us. Together, we rebuilt her application from the ground up. We reframed her barista job as proof of punctuality, multitasking, and working under pressure, and her camp counselor role became evidence of leadership, child management skills, and creative activity planning. Her cover letter was personalized for Korean schools, addressing the principal directly, showing awareness of Korean classroom culture, and expressing her interest in being involved in after-school activities. We had her watch 10 to 15 self-introduction videos to benchmark them, so she could make a polished one-minute pitch to a school that showed her passion for teaching and her genuine love of children. She also highlighted various mentoring, coaching, and informal teaching she had done. Finally, we added a short paragraph about her previous visit to Seoul, mentioning the specific district she loved and her interest in learning Korean, small but meaningful details that show sincerity.

Within two weeks, Melissa had three interview requests. She accepted a position at a well-regarded hagwon in Gangnam with a higher-than-average salary and free housing five minutes from the subway. Six months later, she told us, "If I hadn't rewritten my resume, I might still be waiting for an email back. Now I walk to work in Seoul every day, and my students know me as Teacher Mel. It's the best decision I've ever made."

Understanding What Schools Look For

Whether you're aiming for a public-school placement through EPIK or a high-paying hagwon in Seoul, hiring managers in Korea tend to value the same three things: reliability, adaptability, and student engagement. The way you demonstrate those qualities, on paper and in interviews, often determines whether you get an offer or a polite "We'll keep your application on file."

Korean school directors and recruiters review hundreds of applications each hiring season. They're not just looking for someone who speaks English; they're looking for someone they can trust to stand in front of a classroom of 10 to 40 students, deliver engaging lessons, follow the school's rules, and represent the school positively to parents.

While qualifications matter, most entry-level teachers will need at least a bachelor's degree and a 120-hour TEFL certificate; schools also focus heavily on presentation. They'll notice if your resume is clean, professional, and free of errors. They'll see if your cover letter is specific to their school, instead of a generic copy-and-paste template.

And in your self-introduction video, they're looking at much more than your words. They're observing your energy, how you speak, and whether you project confidence and warmth. I've had many teachers denied an interview because of a few spelling errors on their resume, so be sure to proofread it before submission.

I once worked with a candidate named James, a 28-year-old from the UK who had solid credentials, a degree in English Literature, a TEFL certificate, and even volunteer tutoring experience. But his first self-introduction video was filmed in a dimly lit bedroom with a pile of dirty laundry in the background. He spoke too quickly, avoided eye contact with the camera, and never smiled. The content of what he said was acceptable, but the impression to schools was that he was unenthusiastic and unprepared.

We coached James to re-film in a bright, tidy space during the day, with a simple background like a wall. We suggested that he had a map of the world or a UK poster to add to the wall, to make it seem more like a classroom or education-themed. He slowed his pace, smiled naturally, and used a few hand gestures to emphasize points. He mentioned specific ways he could help students, like running an English conversation club or preparing them for speech contests. Those small changes made all the difference: within a week, he had two job offers, one of them from a top-tier hagwon in Seoul and one from a large school in Gyeonggi-do.

Pro Tip

Korean schools are not just hiring an English speaker; they're hiring a colleague, a role model, and in many cases, a "face" for their school. Every part of your application should communicate that you are approachable, dependable, and invested in your students' success.

Matching Your Skills to the Right Job Type

Choosing where to teach in Korea is not just about which job sounds the best; it's about finding the type of position that plays to your strengths, fits your personality, and aligns with your goals. Many teachers make the mistake of chasing salary or location without fully considering whether they'll thrive in that environment. The result? A mismatch that can turn what should be a life-changing adventure into a year-long struggle.

Think of it this way: a public-school position with a co-teacher might be perfect for a first-time teacher who thrives on structure and wants extra support. But the same job could frustrate someone who craves autonomy and creative freedom. On the flip side, a high-paying hagwon role might be ideal for a teacher who enjoys small classes and fast-paced work, but it could overwhelm someone who prefers a slow-and-steady environment.

Teacher Story: The Gangnam Reality Check

Emily had just graduated after spending a semester studying in Seoul, living in the upscale Gangnam district. She loved the cafés, nightlife, and convenience, and she had a strong circle of friends there. When it came time to find a teaching job, she was adamant about returning to Gangnam, convinced it would be the perfect place to live and work.

I advised Emily that teaching in Gangnam might feel very different from being a student there. The area's schools often cater to highly competitive families with very high expectations. But Emily was confident she could handle it, so I placed her in a reputable academy in the neighborhood.

Within three months, Emily called me in tears. While most parents and students were terrific, a few mothers, and even some students, had made blunt comments about her appearance, including her weight, clothing, and makeup. In a district known for its emphasis on image and achievement, these remarks were especially stinging.

Gangnam is an incredible place to live, but it's also one of the wealthiest areas in Korea's most prosperous city. Just like Beverly Hills in the U.S., prestige can come with pressure, and sometimes sharper social scrutiny. For Emily, the location she thought would make her happiest ended up being one of her most significant stressors.

Takeaway: When choosing a job location, consider more than just lifestyle perks. Ask yourself: Will I thrive in the social dynamics and expectations of this community? The answer may be just as important as the paycheck or the view from your apartment window.

Know Your Teaching Personality

Before accepting any position, it helps to think honestly about the kind of work environment where you do your best. Start by asking whether you prefer working independently or collaboratively. Independent workers often enjoy hagwons or university roles, while collaborative teachers may do better in public schools where co-teaching is common. Consider whether you prefer small, focused groups or large, diverse classrooms. Small groups allow for more personal interaction but may require more energy per student, while large classes require strong classroom management skills. Also think about whether you need variety in your workday or prefer a consistent routine. Hagwons can offer fast-changing schedules and curricula, while public schools usually have set timetables.

Beyond teaching style, factor in your lifestyle and long-term goals. If you are an early riser, public schools, which typically start early and end mid-afternoon, may suit you well. If you are a night owl, hagwons that run into the evening might be a better fit. Consider whether summers and winters off for travel or study matter to you. University jobs offer the longest breaks, followed by public schools, while hagwons usually have shorter vacation periods. If career progression in education is important to you, international schools and universities provide the clearest advancement paths, particularly if you pursue further qualifications.

Finally, play to your strengths. If you have strong academic credentials, consider aiming for international schools or universities. If you're high-energy and adaptable, hagwons might be your sweet spot. If you're patient and structured, public schools can be an excellent match. And if you have specialized skills like business English or test prep, private tutoring and corporate teaching can be lucrative options, especially with the proper visa.

I once mentored two teachers, Emma and James, who both came to Korea the same year. Emma loved variety and independence, so she thrived at an independent hagwon (a non-chain hagwon run by a Korean American teacher) where she could design her lessons and move quickly between student levels. James preferred structure, a pre-made curriculum, and a clear daily routine, so he felt at home in a public school with a supportive co-teacher. Both earned similar salaries (Emma made 200,000 KRW more than James), but because they each chose a role that fit their personality, they were far more satisfied and less stressed than peers who had chased location or pay without thinking about job fit.

If yes, international schools and universities provide the clearest advancement paths, primarily if you pursue further qualifications.

Pro Tip

Before accepting a position, picture your average Tuesday in that role. If the thought of waking up early to teach 35 students with a co-teacher excites you, public schools might be perfect. If you'd rather work with small groups into the evening, hagwons could be the better choice. The more your day-to-day reality matches your preferences, the more successful and happier you'll be.

Public Schools (EPIK)

One of the most well-known and stable ways to teach in Korea is through the EPIK (English Program in Korea) system. This government-run program places native English teachers in public schools across the country. Contracts typically run for one year, starting in either February or August.

Salary & Benefits

The salary ranges from 2.0 to 2.7 million KRW per month, depending on experience, qualifications, and location. Most teachers with only a bachelor's degree and a TEFL certificate start around 2.1 to 2.4 million KRW monthly. In comparison, those with an education or master's degree typically begin at 2.3 to 2.6 million KRW or higher.

Schedule & Work Environment

Working in a public school means a predictable schedule, usually from 8:30 a.m. to 4:30 p.m., with weekends and holidays off. You will be teaching large class sizes, often with a Korean co-teacher. The benefits are tremendous: free housing, a settlement allowance, pension contributions, and paid vacation days, typically around 18 to 26 days per year. However, it's important to note that even with these longer vacation periods, many schools require teachers to conduct extra mandatory classes during these breaks. While these additional classes come with extra pay, their frequency depends on the school, so checking your contract for details before signing is essential.

Orientation & Placement

Your first week as an EPIK teacher is an intense introduction to the job and the country. All new teachers must undergo a one-week orientation, which includes approximately forty hours of training. This orientation covers classroom management, cultural adaptation, lesson planning, and Korean language basics. While beneficial, the training can also be exhausting, especially since most teachers have just arrived from overseas and are still adjusting to the time difference. At the end of the orientation, teachers are assigned to their schools, meaning they have no control over where they will be placed. Most placements are in rural locations because when the program was established in 1995, it aimed to improve English proficiency in less developed areas. Over the years, as major cities like Seoul and Busan developed their own English education programs, EPIK placements in those areas became increasingly rare.

The Co-Teacher Dynamic

Many of my friends taught in the EPIK program, and their experiences varied wildly depending on their school placement and co-teachers. One friend was assigned a much older co-teacher who had been teaching for decades. She was strict, followed the textbook to the letter, and essentially reduced my friend's role to that of a parrot, repeating vocabulary words while she controlled the classroom. He found the experience frustrating, as he had little freedom to engage with the students meaningfully. On the other hand, another friend had a co-teacher who was just a few years older than him and had recently graduated from college. Feeling unsure of herself, this co-teacher gave him complete control of the classroom, letting him plan and execute lessons as he saw fit. He loved the independence but also felt the pressure of being entirely responsible for the students' progress.

The co-teacher dynamic can truly be a double-edged sword. If you get along well with your co-teacher, your work-life balance is excellent, and contract renewal is easy. However, if the relationship is tense, the job can become miserable, and getting a contract extension can be difficult. This was a lesson my most unfortunate friend learned the hard way. Most EPIK jobs are rural, and you could end up teaching at two to three different schools so that you could have two or three different co-teachers. The worst case I saw was a teacher in a rural town who taught at five schools in the same district and had five different co-teachers who evaluated him.

Teacher Story: When the Co-Teacher Relationship Goes Wrong

One foreign teacher I knew started his EPIK year full of excitement. During orientation, he hit it off with his assigned Korean co-teacher, and one thing led to another. He thought it was just a one-night stand. She, however, believed it was the start of something much more serious.

I asked him if he wanted to have a relationship with her. When he said no, I told him bluntly that he was an idiot. As I expected, when he didn't return her feelings, the atmosphere shifted fast, from cordial and fun to hell in a handbasket. She became cold in meetings, uncooperative in lesson planning, and even started undermining him in front of students during lessons. The tension was unbearable, and within months, he had to request a transfer to another school.

When we spoke afterward, I told him, "There's a reason why dogs poop in other people's yards. You don't want to make a mess in your own space, especially the one you have to show up to every single day."

Takeaway: Keep your work relationships professional. In a co-teaching setup, crossing personal boundaries can quickly turn your dream job into a nightmare.

EPIK: The Pros and Cons

That being said, EPIK can be an excellent choice for first-year teachers without prior experience. Because the role often leans toward that of a teacher's assistant, new teachers can ease into the profession rather than being thrown into a classroom without guidance. The structured schedule and formal school setting make it a comfortable transition for those familiar with public school life back home. However, the larger class sizes, typically 25 to 50 students, can be challenging. Unlike hagwons, where students are grouped by skill level, public school students take the same English classes regardless of ability. Teachers must navigate classrooms where some students are nearly fluent while others struggle with introductory phrases. Many Korean students also attend hagwons after school, so their proficiency can be significantly higher than their peers, making differentiated instruction an essential skill for public school teachers.

Another challenge with EPIK is the possibility of being assigned to multiple schools. Some teachers work at just one school, while others rotate between up to five different locations each week. This means more commuting and less consistency with students, making it harder to establish strong relationships and a structured teaching routine. While EPIK offers excellent benefits and stability, these factors can make it less ideal for those who prefer certainty and autonomy in their teaching experience.

Pro Tip

If you are considering EPIK, there are several important things to keep in mind. Do not lie on your application, as EPIK will terminate your contract if it discovers the truth. Disclose any tattoos and avoid facial or excessive ear piercings during your interview, as failure to do so may result in termination. Complete your documents well in advance, because any issues with paperwork can result in your application being declined. Learn more than survival Korean, since your co-teacher can assist you with most things, but it is best to avoid being entirely dependent on them, as many school staff members have limited English proficiency. And if you do not want to be placed in a rural location, then do not apply through EPIK, because you have no say in where you will be placed, and most positions are in small to tiny cities and towns.

Private Academies (Hagwons)

Hagwons are private after-school academies that provide supplemental English instruction, often focused on test prep, conversation skills, or specialized subjects like business English. They operate as businesses first, schools second, meaning parent satisfaction, student retention, and profit margins are major drivers.

Types of Hagwons

Corporate chains are large, prominent brand-name academies such as Poly, Rise, SLP, YBM, and Maple Bear, with extensive curriculum, professionally trained management, and standardized contracts covering salary, vacation days, and benefits. They usually provide one to two weeks of paid training, making them ideal for first-year teachers who want structure and clear expectations. However, their rigid systems can feel restrictive for experienced teachers who prefer to adapt lessons and teaching style.

Franchise operations are individually owned schools operating under a corporate brand. Some franchises mirror corporate chains exactly, with the same curriculum, schedules, and training, while others feel entirely different, depending on the owner's management style. This means your experience can vary dramatically, even if the school's name is identical to another location in the next city. These schools may have more freedom about curriculum, schedules, and other details based on the owner's goals or character. You can think of anyone with $100,000 to $200,000 who can buy a franchise, regardless of their teaching or management experience or English ability.

Independent schools are typically just one school or a small group of two or three. They range from small expat-run schools to mid-sized operations with a few foreign teachers. Independent schools often serve niche markets such as adult conversation, business English, or specialized exam prep, and can be wonderful for teachers who value classroom freedom. The trade-off is that their curriculum may be limited, so teachers often need to create a moderate to significant portion of their teaching materials.

Hagwon Working Environment

Hagwon environments can be highly competitive, and teachers must be able to accept constructive criticism. Many hagwons will strive to provide the best training and support to help you improve as a teacher. They will often sit in on your classes to observe, which can be daunting for some but is an opportunity for others to showcase their passion for teaching. Some classrooms have CCTV installed, which can be off-putting, but it is also a safety feature that can protect teachers in the event of classroom accidents. Hagwons prioritize high test scores and student retention, which can pressure instructors to deliver results quickly. I once had a boss who would observe my classes unannounced, and his feedback was often direct and occasionally harsh. Some teachers thrive under this pressure, while others find it overwhelming.

Hagwon experiences can vary dramatically. While everyone knows a horror story about specific schools, far more positive stories exist. A new teacher's workload will be much greater than a second-year teacher's due to a steep learning curve. For the first three to six months, you will spend countless hours learning your teaching materials and preparing for classes, which is unpaid prep time. However, as students cycle through classes every three months, you will teach the same courses multiple times a year, and each time, it becomes easier, resulting in less time spent on preparation.

The relationships between teachers can also create toxic work environments. With 5 to 25 native English teachers at a single school, it can be a great way to make friends and build a social network. However, with larger groups, there will always be cliques and drama. My advice is to steer clear of negative people. You can easily spot them because they often say, "Back in (their home country), we do things like (insert action), but in Korea, they do it like..." These individuals tend to be ethnocentric and resent that Korea is not like their hometown. They should be avoided because they are unhappy and tend to share their unhappiness with those around them. Instead, focus on making friends with like-minded, positive people. Additionally, try to make friends with other expats and locals who do not work at your school. This is the best way to avoid potential drama and significantly expand your social circle.

Hagwon Work Culture and Management Style

Workplace culture in hagwons also varies dramatically. There is potential for conflict or disagreements due to differences in management styles and cultural or language barriers. Korean managers, especially male managers, often believe in a hierarchical management style, a belief that stems from the fact that all able-bodied men serve in the Korean military. On the other hand, many female managers adopt a more family-oriented approach. During your interview and follow-up conversations with a current teacher, you should ask about their experiences working at the school. Specifically, ask what they like and what challenges they face. Some academies treat their teachers well, offering support, training, and fair policies. Others, however, can be disorganized or mismanaged, with unpaid overtime, sudden schedule changes, or unfair contract alterations. I once had a friend who arrived in Korea only to discover that the hagwon he signed with had gone bankrupt. He had to scramble to find a new job while living in temporary housing. These horror stories are not the norm, but they do happen. To avoid such situations, always check reviews and ask to speak with current teachers before accepting a position.

Why the Majority of Teachers Work at Hagwons

Despite the challenges, many teachers prefer hagwons because they generally offer higher pay, the ability to choose a preferred working and living location, smaller class sizes, and more control over teaching methods. Hagwon students also tend to have stronger English skills, which allows for a more interactive classroom experience and greater flexibility in lesson planning. Additionally, having a built-in social network of other native English teachers is a huge plus. These factors make hagwons appealing to those who enjoy an engaging, fast-paced teaching environment and appreciate greater flexibility in their teaching approach.

Pro Tip

Have a few interviews with different schools (two or three)
so that you can compare them. They can be slightly different
based on pay, schedules, management styles, and atmosphere.

Universities and International Schools

University Teaching Positions

Ten or more years ago, some Korean universities would hire
foreign native English-speaking lecturers with just a BA degree and
years of teaching experience. Those days are long gone. Most
universities now require at least an MA degree in the subject being
taught, plus at least two years of teaching experience at the university
level. If you want to get hired by a university, you should focus on
searching for an English department position, as these offer the
largest pool of expat lecturing jobs. It is often better to take any
university lecturing position available and then, after two years, try to
move to a more prominent university once you have the necessary
experience. Additionally, many regional universities are closing due
to Korea's declining birthrate, making it increasingly difficult for
candidates outside of Korea to get hired by a university.

University Pay and Benefits

Foreign university teachers (non-tenure track lecturers) earn
between 2.5 and 5.0 million KRW per month, with housing included,
although most fall within the 3.0 to 4.0 million KRW range. Teachers
interested in these jobs should pursue an MA or PhD degree in the
subject they wish to teach. The real perks are the long vacations, up
to four months of paid leave sometimes. International school salaries
range from 3.0 to 6.0 million KRW monthly but require full-time
hours and proper teaching credentials. However, some university
teaching jobs are termed "Unigwons," which is a play on a university-
level hagwon, so they are run like English academies and are usually
the lowest-paying university jobs, with the least benefits. However,
these jobs are good stepping stones to better university teaching
positions.

If you are thinking long-term, consider pursuing an MA or PhD degree while teaching in Korea. Several prominent English-language programs are tied to major universities in the United States and offer all classes in English, taught by American and Korean professors. I received my MBA through one of these joint programs (Sejong University and Syracuse University, now partnered with Arizona State University), and I later completed my PhD at Kyung Hee University's Hospitality and Tourism Management Program. These programs are designed for working professionals, with classes offered at night, on weekends, and during vacations, and they cost a fraction of what the same degree would cost in the United States. An advanced degree dramatically expands your career options, both in Korea and internationally.

International School Teaching Positions

International schools do not typically hire E-2 visa holders and prefer to employ F-type visa holders, such as those with an F-1, F-2, F-3, F-4, F-5, or F-6 visa. The F-4 visa is for individuals of Korean heritage, granting them work flexibility similar to that of a Korean citizen. The F-5 visa is a permanent residency visa, and the F-6 visa is for foreigners married to a Korean national. Most teachers at international schools hold a teaching license from their home country, an education degree, or a specialized degree in their subject. These schools prioritize stability and long-term commitments, making them more inclined to hire teachers who do not require visa sponsorship.

Why Teach at Universities and International Schools

Universities and international schools are the golden ticket for experienced teachers. These positions offer higher pay, lighter schedules, and more prestige. University positions provide the longest vacations, ranging from 8 to 20 weeks, and typically have the lightest workload, with teaching hours averaging between 12 and 18 hours per week. On the other hand, international schools usually operate on a 9:00 a.m. to 4:00 p.m. schedule, incorporating planning periods, breaks, and lunch, similar to public schools back home. Both types of schools typically provide housing, a housing stipend, or higher pay and often offer additional perks such as free or reduced tuition for dependents, medical insurance, and pension contributions.

Over my first four years in Korea, I taught full-time at two different hagwons and worked part-time at dozens of teaching jobs. Then, I completed an MBA through a joint program in Seoul. Earning my MBA helped me secure a position with the Korean Tourism Organization (KTO) at its headquarters in Seoul. I worked there for almost two years before moving to Chicago to serve as their Marketing Manager for six years. I later secured a university position in the College of Business at a Korean university, where I continue to teach full-time. The freedom of a university position is incredible. I designed my own Business English curriculum and spent my 12-week summer and winter vacations focusing on my English teacher recruitment business. The trade-off is less job security since contracts are often renewed every two years. If you meet the requirements, this is one of the best teaching jobs in Korea.

Private Tutoring and Freelance Teaching

While technically not permitted under an E-2 visa, private tutoring is a common practice. Many teachers make extra money giving one-on-one lessons to business professionals, children, or university students. Hourly rates range from 30,000 to 75,000 KRW, depending on location and demand. Of course, most schools do not want you to teach outside of their institution, so you should refrain from mentioning it. However, teaching online through various platforms, such as VIP Kids, should be no problem since you are not technically teaching in Korea.

Freelance teaching is another option for individuals with a different visa type, such as an F-series visa. Some teachers run their tutoring businesses or work part-time at multiple locations. If you want to teach Business English, I recommend completing a Business English specialty TEFL course. It is comprehensive, inexpensive, and looks great on your resume. You can complete a 40-hour BE course online in a week or two for approximately $100 to $150.

I once tutored a businessman who needed help with presentations. He paid well, but last-minute cancellations were frustrating. If you go this route, establish clear policies to protect your time and income. Always have your private students pay you in advance and in cash; the little white envelopes stuffed with money are the norm. To save time and increase your pay, it is better to try 1.5 hours twice a week rather than one hour three times a week, as this reduces travel time and costs.

Pros and Cons of Each Option

Job Type	Pros	Cons
Public Schools (EPIK)	Stable, benefits, cultural immersion, vacation time	Lower salary, large classes, co-teacher dynamic
Hagwons	Higher pay, small classes, more independence	Unpredictable work environment, fewer vacation days
Universities	Light workload, high salary, long vacations	Competitive, requires experience, yearly contracts
International Schools	High salary, structured work environment	Requires teaching credentials, full work schedule
Private Tutoring	High hourly rate, flexible schedule	Legally restricted for E-2 visa holders, inconsistent income

Teacher Story: Building a Side Income the Smart Way

After his first year in Korea, James realized that his hagwon hours left him with free mornings. On an F-4 visa, he was allowed to work outside his main job, so he began offering private business English lessons to professionals in his area. Instead of charging hourly and dealing with constant cancellations, he created a policy: students had to book in four-week blocks, paid in advance. He also set a 24-hour cancellation rule; missed lessons weren't refunded. This system kept his income steady and reduced last-minute schedule changes. Within six months, his side income equaled his primary salary, and he had complete control over when and where he worked.

His approach shows that in Korea, setting clear boundaries is just as crucial as teaching skills when freelancing.

Choosing the Right Path

Every teaching job in Korea comes with its own blend of advantages and drawbacks. What feels like the perfect fit for one teacher may be entirely wrong for another. The key is understanding these differences in advance so you can choose a role that aligns with your professional goals, personal preferences, and lifestyle needs.

As you've seen, public schools tend to offer stability, structured schedules, and generous vacation time. At the same time, hagwons provide higher earning potential, more flexible locations, and smaller class sizes, but often at the cost of longer hours and tighter performance expectations. Specialized positions, though rare, can be the most rewarding for teachers with unique skills, niche experience, or advanced degrees.

Pro Tip

As you evaluate your options, keep four priorities in mind: know what matters most to you, whether that is stability, high pay, creative freedom, or career progression. Consider your long-term goals, because if you plan to stay in Korea for several years, a university or international school job is a worthwhile target. Network with other teachers, since many of the best jobs are found through word of mouth. And read your contract carefully, looking for clauses about working hours, vacation time, and severance pay, to avoid surprises.

Final Thoughts

Choosing the right path isn't about finding the "best" job in an objective sense; it's about finding your best fit. Your personality, teaching style, and adaptability will play as much of a role in your success as the school itself. Spend time reflecting on what matters most to you: Is it a predictable schedule? A high salary? Freedom in the classroom? A vibrant social scene? Once you know your priorities, you can evaluate offers with clarity and confidence.

Remember, no job is perfect, but the right job for you will challenge you in the best ways, help you grow professionally, and give you the stability to enjoy all the cultural experiences Korea has to offer.

In the next chapter, we'll explore the eligibility requirements and qualifications you need to teach in Korea, including visa requirements, background checks, health screenings, and what to do if your situation doesn't fit neatly into the standard mold.

Chapter 3: Eligibility and Requirements

Chapter Summary

This chapter covers the basic legal requirements for teaching English in Korea, including citizenship, education, and TEFL certification. You will learn the differences between native and non-native English teacher eligibility, get step-by-step guidance for criminal background checks and health screenings by country, and understand what to expect from Korea's drug testing and prescription medication rules. You will also learn how physical and mental health factors may influence your visa application and what strategies teachers use to navigate these sensitive areas.

Why This Chapter Matters

So, you are seriously considering teaching in Korea? Before you daydream about temple stays and tteokbokki, you must ensure you are eligible to teach here. This chapter will guide you through the fundamental requirements, the differences between native and non-native applicants, and provide you with everything you need to know about background checks, health screenings, and the realities of physical and mental health expectations in Korea. Although this may not be the most exciting chapter, it is essential for legally working and thriving here.

Who can teach in Korea?

Every year, thousands of people apply to teach English in Korea, and while the process isn't overly complicated, it is rigorous. Korea has developed a well-regulated system for hiring foreign teachers with little room for error. Failing to meet even one requirement, like submitting the wrong kind of background check or arriving without proper documentation, can delay your job start or disqualify you entirely. Additionally, Korea has cultural expectations regarding health, appearance, and professionalism that may differ from those in your home country. Understanding these expectations can help you prepare mentally and practically for a successful start.

Core Requirements for the E-2 Visa

Citizenship

The basic requirement to teach English in Korea legally under the standard E-2 visa is straightforward: you must be a citizen of one of the seven designated English-speaking countries, the United States, Canada, the United Kingdom, Ireland, Australia, New Zealand, or South Africa. You must also hold at least a bachelor's degree in any field from an accredited university in one of those seven countries.

Education

This detail often catches many applicants off guard. Over the years, I have seen multiple candidates denied because their degree came from a university in a non-eligible country, even if the curriculum was entirely in English. I have also seen applicants from Quebec, Canada, get rejected because their degrees were from French-speaking universities. While their English was excellent, the Korean immigration office was strict about the degree's origin and language of instruction. That said, I have also seen cases where applicants were approved despite earning their bachelor's degree in a non-English-speaking country, as long as they followed up with a master's degree from a university in one of the seven designated English-speaking countries. This shows that sometimes it comes down to the discretion of the immigration officer and the strength of the relationship between the hiring school and the local immigration office. Smaller regional immigration offices tend to be more lenient and flexible than the larger ones in Seoul, Gyeonggi-do, or Incheon.

Teacher Story: The Quebec Degree Dilemma

Marie, a 29-year-old from Montreal, thought she had everything lined up for her move to Korea. She held a bachelor's degree from an

English-speaking university in Quebec, spoke fluent English, and was raised bilingual. She had also completed a 120-hour TEFL course. Confident, she applied to a well-known hagwon chain, impressed the director, and received a verbal job offer.

But when her documents reached immigration, things stalled. The immigration officer pointed out that her degree was from a university in a French-speaking province, even though her program was entirely in English. In Korea, immigration rules for the E-2 visa focus strictly on where your degree is from and the primary language of instruction for that institution. While Marie's English skills were undeniable, the officer wasn't obligated to accept her degree.

In this case, I suggested she create a 3 to 5-minute self-introduction video in English for the school director to show the immigration officer. Sometimes, this extra step can sway an officer's decision; it's 100% up to their discretion. I've seen this work before, but I've also seen it fail. Over the years, I've had American, Canadian, and British teachers with degrees from places like the American University of Paris, the American University of Cairo, and Stockholm University, all programs taught entirely in English, denied visas simply because the universities were located in non-English-speaking countries.

For Marie, the officer still said no. Instead of giving up, she enrolled in a one-year accelerated MBA program in Vancouver, Canada. A year later, she reapplied, submitted both degrees, and a different immigration officer approved her application immediately. This time, she was on a plane to Korea within weeks.

Takeaway: In Korea, "fluent English" isn't enough; immigration cares about the origin of your degree and the official language of instruction. If you're in a gray area, a well-made self-introduction video might help, but having a qualifying degree is the surest path. If you don't meet the requirements now, plan a way to meet it; your detour could open even better opportunities later.

If you hold dual citizenship, I suggest not listing it on your visa application, especially if one of the countries is not an English-speaking country. Immigration cannot check if you are a dual citizen (unless it is Korean citizenship), but if they see it, they may doubt your English ability, and they will probably ask you to provide a criminal record check with an apostille from both countries, even if you have never lived in the second country. I have seen this cause multiple-week delays in visa processing. In two recent cases, teachers from Northern Ireland who held Irish passports were required by immigration to obtain an Irish criminal record check, even though they had never lived in Ireland. The Irish police couldn't issue one because they had no record of residence, so the teachers had to visit a police station across the border to get a letter confirming this, then get those letters apostilled and notarized. Both teachers eventually received their visas, but the process was a significant hassle that could have been avoided entirely.

TEFL/TESOL/CELTA Certification

In addition to a degree, most employers now prefer or require a TEFL, TESOL, or CELTA certification, especially for first-time teachers. The industry standard is a 120-hour TEFL certificate, with bonus points awarded if it includes a practicum or classroom component. While a TEFL certification is not a requirement for the E-2 visa itself, it is necessary for EPIK and most large school chains. Getting a specialized add-on course, like a Young Learners certificate, can also be a smart move. Since more than 90% of hagwon jobs involve teaching kindergarten and elementary students, this certification can make you more competitive and better prepare you for the day-to-day classroom environment. If you are applying for more competitive jobs, such as positions in public schools through EPIK or university roles, having an education degree or teaching experience can help you stand out.

If you are already in Korea on a different visa, such as an F-6 (spouse visa), F-4 (overseas Korean), or F-5 (permanent resident), your options open up significantly. These visas allow you to work without employer sponsorship and are not restricted to the seven English-speaking countries. However, schools will still typically require a bachelor's degree or some form of TEFL certification, and you must still provide a clean, apostille-notarized national criminal record check.

Native vs. Non-Native English Teachers

This is one of the more sensitive areas in Korean ESL hiring practices. By law, the E-2 visa is restricted to citizens from the seven English-speaking countries. This excludes many highly qualified teachers from countries where English is widely spoken or taught to a high standard. Most non-native English teachers hold F-type visas and secure jobs through in-person interviews, networking, and job searches in smaller cities and towns.

Even with the legal right to work, some schools and hagwons still prefer native speakers. This is not always fair, but it is the current reality and a requirement for an E-2 visa. If you are a non-native speaker with an F-4, F-5, or F-6 visa, your best chances lie in building a strong resume, getting a master's degree, gaining teaching experience, and securing glowing references. Some schools, especially international schools or specialized academies, are more open to hiring non-native English-speaking teachers, particularly if you have subject matter expertise.

There is also the matter of accent. While Korean schools do not officially list "accent neutrality" as a requirement, many hiring managers have preferences. Teachers with strong regional accents may be unfairly judged, while those with neutral, international, or Americanized accents may receive preferential treatment. Korean schools overwhelmingly prefer North American accents because most curricula are designed around American English, and college entrance exams heavily emphasize North American pronunciation and usage. If you have a strong accent, you should make a concerted effort to speak more slowly, use standard terms, and communicate as clearly as possible. I lived in the UK for two and a half years, and the spectrum of accents ranged from crystal-clear and easy to understand to almost a different language being spoken. Even my ex-English girlfriend from Northern England had difficulty understanding other British English speakers from various regions of the UK.

To improve your chances of getting hired, one essential tool is the one-minute self-introduction video. This is often the first impression you give an employer and can make or break your chances of getting an interview. Upload your video to YouTube, either as Public or Unlisted, to showcase your personality, communication skills, and classroom presence. Make sure your camera is positioned at eye level on a stationary surface rather than held in your hand. Use a neutral or teacher-friendly background and light your face from the front, never from behind, with natural sunlight being ideal. Dress business casual, be well-groomed, and speak clearly in complete sentences. Avoid visible tattoos and remove facial piercings, and keep any facial hair well-groomed. We will cover self-introduction videos in much more detail in Chapter 5.

If you are a non-native speaker looking to break into the market, networking and personal recommendations can be potent tools. Attending local TESOL events, conferences, or online forums like Dave's ESL I and local Facebook teaching groups can help connect you with open-minded employers. I have worked with several non-native English teachers who were outstanding educators, far more passionate and prepared than some native speakers. They brought a strong work ethic, creative ideas, and multilingual advantages into the classroom. While the market can be more challenging, it is not impossible. With persistence, qualifications, and a good support network, non-native speakers can and do succeed here.

Criminal Background Checks

Korea takes its background checks seriously, and you should too. For E-2 visa applicants, a national-level criminal background check is mandatory and must be clean, with no exceptions. The report must also be sent to the appropriate government office in your home country for an apostille. The process can take anywhere from a few days to several weeks, depending on your country of origin, so plan accordingly. Your background check must be recent, typically issued within six months of your visa application.

Teacher Story: Clearing the Record

Sally, a 25-year-old from Seattle, thought her dream of teaching in Korea was within reach. She had a bachelor's degree, a TEFL certificate, and glowing references. But when her FBI Criminal Record Check came back, there it was, a mark from when she was 18 and in college: an arrest for possession of marijuana. The charge had never gone to court, and there was no conviction.

Back home, she'd almost forgotten about it. But in 2024, Korean immigration had tightened its rules. Even arrests without convictions were now grounds for denial. Sally provided a detailed two-page apology letter, explained the situation clearly, apologized repeatedly, and hoped for the best. The immigration officer was sympathetic, but firm. The answer was no.

Determined not to give up, Sally hired a lawyer and spent several thousand dollars petitioning the courts and the FBI to have the arrest expunged. The process was grueling: multiple petitions, nine months of waiting, and countless follow-up calls. Even after the court approved the expungement, it took another three to four months for her record to update in the FBI system, finally.

More than a year after her first application, Sally submitted a brand-new Criminal Record Check, clean this time. With the expungement in place, her E-2 visa was approved without issue. The delay had been costly and frustrating, but Sally said it taught her the value of dealing with potential visa problems before applying.

Takeaway: Even a minor, years-old arrest with no conviction can derail your application in today's stricter immigration climate. If there's anything on your record, work to clear it before you apply; it could save you thousands of dollars and a year of waiting.

How to Obtain a Criminal Record Check (CRC) by Country:

For the United States, request a national criminal background check through the FBI's official website. For faster processing, you can use an approved FBI Channeler, which can provide results as a PDF via email within a few hours to two days. Once received, the report must be apostilled by the U.S. Department of State.

For Canada, apply for a certified criminal background check through the RCMP. Fingerprints are required. The results must then be apostilled.

For the United Kingdom, apply for a Basic Disclosure through the Disclosure and Barring Service (DBS). Afterward, have it legalized with an apostille through the UK Legalisation Office.

For Ireland, request a Police Certificate from your local Garda station. The Department of Foreign Affairs should then authenticate the document.

For Australia, obtain a National Police Check through the Australian Federal Police (AFP). Once issued, it must be apostilled by the Australian Passport Office.

For New Zealand, apply for a Criminal Record Check from the Ministry of Justice. The Department of Internal Affairs must then authenticate it.

For South Africa, obtain a police clearance certificate from the South African Police Service (SAPS). The Department of

International Relations and Cooperation (DIRCO) must then authenticate it with an apostille.

Do not try to gloss over anything. I knew one teacher who had a minor theft charge from college and wanted to hide it. It caught up with him, and he lost the job offer, forcing him to leave Korea. Korea doesn't take kindly to any criminal history, even misdemeanors. If you have something on your CRC, you need to write a lengthy, detailed apology letter explaining what happened, how you learned from it, and how you will be an outstanding teacher in Korea.

Before 2025, we assisted some teachers with minor offenses on their CRCs in obtaining E2-1 visas. However, from 2025, immigration has become stricter, denying most applicants who do not have a clean CRC. This includes being arrested and not convicted of a crime. Since the decision is up to the individual immigration officer's judgment, there may be a chance to get the visa approved, but a higher chance that it will be denied. Therefore, if you have something on your CRC, it is better to apply to have it expunged, if possible, before applying.

Health Screenings and Drug Tests

Once you arrive in Korea, you must undergo a health screening within 90 days to legally validate your visa. This includes a basic physical exam, a drug test (urine sample), and a chest X-ray for tuberculosis. HIV/AIDS tests are also standard. The results of this exam are sent directly to immigration and your school. You must pass all parts of this exam to complete your Alien Registration Card (ARC) and begin teaching.

Once you arrive in Korea, you must undergo a health screening within 90 days to legally validate your visa. This includes a basic physical exam, a drug test (urine sample), and a chest X-ray for tuberculosis. HIV/AIDS tests are also standard. The results of this exam are sent directly to immigration and your school. You must pass all parts of this exam to complete your Alien Registration Card (ARC) and begin teaching.

Be warned: Korea has a strict zero-tolerance policy for illegal drugs. Even if a drug is legal in your home country, such as marijuana in certain U.S. states or Canada, it is considered a serious offense in Korea. A positive drug test, regardless of where or when the substance was consumed, will lead to immediate contract termination, deportation, and an immigration ban. There have been multiple cases of teachers failing the drug test even though they had not used drugs in Korea.

Teacher Story: The Edible That Ended It All

Kevin, a 29-year-old from Toronto, had been looking forward to starting his new life in Korea. He'd already quit his job, sublet his apartment, and said his goodbyes. A week before his flight, he attended a farewell party where a friend offered him a THC gummy. In Canada, it was legal, no big deal, he thought.

Kevin assumed the effects would wear off in a day or two. What he didn't realize was that THC can stay in the body for weeks, especially for occasional users who don't actively detox. Within days of landing in Korea, his school sent him for the standard medical exam. A week later, the results came back: positive for marijuana.

Immigration moved quickly. His contract was terminated, his E-2 visa cancelled, and he was told to leave the country immediately. There was no second test, no appeal, no grace period. Kevin was back on a plane within two weeks of arriving, thousands of dollars poorer and devastated at the lost opportunity.

If Kevin had told me about consuming the gummy, I would have suggested to the school that they delay the drug test for several weeks. That way, he could have vigorously exercised, drunk loads of water, and hoped the THC level dropped low enough to pass. Unfortunately, he didn't mention it until after the positive drug test came back. Once that result is in, there's nothing anyone can do to reverse it.

Takeaway: Korea has a zero-tolerance policy for drugs, including marijuana. THC can linger in your system for weeks. If you've consumed it in any form, give yourself plenty of time, four to six weeks minimum, to detox before your medical exam.

Pro Tip

If you have consumed THC in any form (flower, gummy, pill, etc.), make sure to exercise vigorously daily and drink copious amounts of water for at least four to six weeks before coming to Korea. Most teachers take the drug test the week they arrive, but you can delay the test for a few weeks after arriving to give yourself more time to pass.

Keep in mind that Korean authorities do not take foreign legal systems into account when it comes to drugs. They reason that you were aware of the drug test and still chose to risk it. Even traces of marijuana, which can stay in the system for days or weeks depending on usage, can lead to failure. There is no second chance, no retest, and no appeal.

Prescription Medications

Prescription medications can also be tricky. Some common ADHD medications (like Adderall), certain anti-anxiety drugs, and strong painkillers are either banned or require special permission from the Korean Food and Drug Administration. If you plan to bring prescription medication, you must carry a valid prescription, a signed doctor's note, and, preferably, a translated copy in Korean. You should also declare the medication at customs when entering Korea and check in advance with your nearest Korean consulate to ensure it is permitted. Failure to follow these steps can lead to your medication being confiscated or, in rare cases, your entry being denied. Preparing in advance is always better than being caught off guard.

Take the medical exam seriously. Get good sleep, stay hydrated, and avoid any medications or supplements that could result in a false positive. Double-check with your recruiter or school if you're unsure about anything in advance. The medical exam is the final hurdle before you're fully legal to work, and it's one you definitely don't want to stumble on.

Pro Tip

If you take prescription medication, verify its legality in Korea before you arrive. You can refill most prescriptions in Korea or find a similar name-brand equivalent to what you currently take back home.

Mental & Physical Health Considerations

Korea doesn't officially discriminate based on mental or physical health, but the truth is a little more complicated. During the visa health check, if any issues are detected, whether it's a chronic condition or a mental health issue, it could impact your job status. Some schools are more understanding than others, but unfortunately, stigma around mental health is still present.

Since 2025, many visa applications have been denied when applicants disclose taking mental health medications such as antidepressants, anti-anxiety drugs, or ADHD prescriptions. While some visas have still been approved, this depends on the school's support and the discretion of the immigration office. Due to this inconsistency, two common strategies have emerged. The first is to answer "No" to all mental health-related questions on the medical questionnaire, temporarily stop taking prescribed medications one to two weeks before flying to Korea, complete the visa medical exam, and then resume afterward.

While this method can work, it can be risky, especially if the abrupt discontinuation of medication affects your well-being. It's also ethically and legally questionable. The second approach is to be fully transparent on the questionnaire, check "Yes," list your medications, and provide a formal doctor's note explaining the diagnosis, its purpose, and how the condition is successfully managed. These documents are submitted to the immigration office, but this approach also comes with a significant risk of rejection. It is up to the teacher to decide which route is best for them.

Teacher Story: The One-Week Pause

Lena, a 31-year-old teacher from Portland, had been managing ADHD for years with a prescribed medication. When she accepted a job in Seoul, she planned to be fully transparent about her medication use. Her recruiter warned her that while immigration once accepted many mental health prescriptions with a doctor's note and the school's support, the rules had tightened significantly since 2024.

In the past, applicants who checked "Yes" to taking mental health medications, ADHD meds, antidepressants, and anti-anxiety drugs could still get approved with proper documentation. But now, more often than not, the visa was denied outright, regardless of medical proof or the school's backing. Immigration officers had become much stricter, and the risk of rejection was high.

After weighing her options, Lena chose to stop taking her medication one week before flying to Korea. She checked the half-life of her two prescriptions and confirmed they were both one to two days, meaning the medication would be entirely out of her system within a week. She answered "No" to the medication question on the health check form, passed her drug test without issue, and resumed her medication the day after her results came back clear.

This strategy isn't without risks; abruptly stopping certain medications can affect mood, focus, and overall well-being, but it has an almost zero chance of triggering a visa denial. Many teachers who take this route later refill their prescriptions in Korea or find a similar alternative through local clinics. Lena was able to continue her treatment without disruption and complete her one-year contract without any problems.

Takeaway: If you take prescription medication for mental health, understand that being honest on the medical questionnaire can lead to a high chance of visa denial. Many teachers choose to temporarily stop their medication before arrival, pass the health check, and then resume treatment in Korea. Still, this decision should always be discussed with your doctor first. You can also ask your recruiter about their experiences and their suggestions before you make a final decision. I have this discussion dozens of times per year with prospective teachers who are grappling with this issue.

Chronic Conditions

Another area of concern involves chronic conditions, particularly Type 1 diabetes. While Type 2 diabetes is typically not an issue for visa approval, several teachers with Type 1 diabetes have been denied E-2 visas recently. Some Korean immigration officers perceive this condition as a potential liability, believing the teacher may be at greater risk for a medical emergency in the classroom. While not an official policy, this viewpoint can influence visa decisions. If you have Type 1 diabetes or another chronic condition, speak with your recruiter or a visa specialist to determine the best approach. A detailed doctor's note outlining your management plan and medical stability may help support your case, but results are not guaranteed.

Ultimately, this is a personal decision that should not be taken lightly. If you're currently taking any mental health medications or have a history of treatment, it's vital to consult with your physician before making any decisions. Additionally, please discuss with your recruiter or school whether they have successfully sponsored teachers in similar circumstances.

Physically, the job isn't too demanding, but you will be on your feet for much of the day, especially in hagwons. Most schools do not want their teachers sitting behind the desk while they teach. They want the teacher to go around the room and work with students and to be in front of the class when they are delivering new material or reviewing previous lessons.

It's common to get sick in your first few months in a new environment, with new germs. It is even harder to avoid getting colds with so many children around you sneezing and coughing. Basic health insurance (which your employer should provide) and a good self-care routine go a long way.

Final Thoughts

Meeting the eligibility criteria isn't just a box-ticking exercise; it's the foundation for a smooth job search and successful start in Korea. Prepare early, double-check all documentation, and avoid last-minute surprises that could jeopardize your plans. Teaching in Korea is a life-changing opportunity, but only if you're ready for the realities behind the glossy brochures and vlogs. If you meet the requirements, prepare your documents early, and become open-minded, you're already ahead. In the next chapter, we will look at TEFL certification in detail, how to choose the right program, and how it impacts your job prospects and salary.

Chapter 4: Getting TEFL Certified

Chapter Summary

This chapter explains what TEFL, TESOL, and CELTA certifications are and why they matter in the Korean job market. You will learn about the 120-hour standard that most schools require, when it makes sense to invest in advanced or specialized modules like Young Learners or Business English, and how to compare online, in-person, and hybrid courses for cost, flexibility, and employer preference. You will also learn how to identify reputable programs, avoid low-quality certifications, and understand how your TEFL choice can directly impact your job opportunities, salary, and location options.

Why This Chapter Matters

If you're thinking about teaching English in Korea, getting TEFL certified is one of the most important steps you can take. TEFL stands for Teaching English as a Foreign Language, and it's more than just a box to check for your résumé; it's a signal to employers that you've invested in learning how to teach, not just speak, English. Across Korea, from public schools to private academies, directors often scan applications specifically looking for a TEFL certificate.

Even though TEFL certification is not an official visa requirement for the E-2 teaching visa, in practice, most reputable schools expect it, and in a competitive city like Seoul, not having one can easily move your résumé to the bottom of the pile. It's also your first real introduction to lesson planning, classroom management, and strategies for teaching students whose English level may range from absolute beginner to near-fluent.

I've seen plenty of new teachers arrive in Korea with no formal teaching background. Still, with a solid TEFL course under their belt, they were able to walk into the classroom on day one with a toolkit of ready-to-use activities, a better understanding of Korean classroom culture, and the confidence to handle 20 curious faces staring back at them. Without that preparation, the first few months can feel like trial by fire.

Think of TEFL certification as both a hiring advantage and a survival guide. It opens doors to better schools, higher salaries, and more desirable locations, but it also helps you avoid the stressful feeling of "making it up as you go" once you're standing in front of your students.

Understanding the Acronyms

Before you start looking at courses, you'll see a mix of acronyms in job postings: TEFL, TESOL, and CELTA, and it's easy to get confused about which one you "need." Here's what they mean and how they apply to teaching in Korea.

TEFL: Teaching English as a Foreign Language. This is the most common certification for teachers heading to Korea. It's aimed at preparing you to teach English in countries where English is not the primary language. TEFL courses focus on lesson planning, teaching techniques for different skill levels, classroom management, and cultural awareness. In Korea, nearly all private academies (hagwons) and many public-school programs list "TEFL" as their preferred or required qualification for teachers who don't have an education degree or teaching license.

TESOL

Teaching English to Speakers of Other Languages. TESOL is more of an umbrella term. It includes both TEFL (teaching abroad) and TESL (teaching English in an English-speaking country, such as teaching recent immigrants in Canada, the U.S., or the UK). The content of most TESOL courses is very similar to TEFL, and in the Korean job market, the two are treated as interchangeable. A Korean school director won't care which one you have as long as it's 120 hours, accredited, and reputable. Some universities and training providers choose to call their course "TESOL" instead of "TEFL" because it sounds broader and more academic, but for Korea, there's no practical hiring advantage.

CELTA

Certificate in English Language Teaching to Adults. CELTA is a specific, brand-name TEFL program created and accredited by Cambridge University. It's considered one of the most rigorous and globally recognized certifications in the ESL world, and it's highly respected by employers, particularly in Europe, the Middle East, and for jobs teaching adults. However, CELTA courses are expensive (often $2,000+), require about a month of full-time, in-person study, and focus heavily on adult learners. If you plan to teach kindergarten or elementary students in Korea, which is the case for most foreign teachers, much of the CELTA content won't be directly applicable. Still, some teachers choose it because of its prestige and portability if they plan to teach in multiple countries later.

When it comes down to it, for Korea: For 99% of applicants, a solid 120-hour TEFL or TESOL course from a reputable, accredited provider is all you need. Whether your certificate says TEFL or TESOL matters far less than whether employers recognize the course and whether it gives you the skills to manage a classroom full of energetic Korean kids. CELTA is an excellent option if you want a high-prestige credential for future international teaching jobs, but it's usually overkill for starting in Korea. I've had teachers say they are CELTA certified, so they expect much higher pay, and I have to tell them that schools in Korea look at the three TEFL certificates as almost identical.

The 120-Hour Standard

In Korea, a 120-hour TEFL or TESOL certificate is the gold standard for applicants who don't already hold a degree in education or a teaching license from their home country. This requirement isn't written into Korean immigration law for the E-2 visa, meaning technically, you can still get a visa without one, but in practice, most schools expect it. They won't even interview candidates who don't meet the 120-hour benchmark.

Why 120 hours? In the ESL industry worldwide, 120 hours is widely seen as the minimum amount of professional training needed to prepare a new teacher for the classroom. This isn't just about clocking time. A proper 120-hour course should cover core areas such as lesson planning and curriculum design for different levels and age groups, classroom management techniques for non-native English speakers, pronunciation and phonics instruction, teaching the four skills of speaking, listening, reading, and writing, cultural awareness and adapting lessons for different learning environments, and assessment and feedback methods. The key is that the course should include contact hours, meaning structured lessons, assignments, and feedback from a qualified tutor, rather than simply being a stack of PDF readings with a quiz at the end.

While you'll see TEFL courses advertised as 40, 60, or 80 hours, most Korean schools will treat these as incomplete. Anything less than 120 hours may be seen as "dabbling" rather than serious training. Employers want to know that you've put in the effort to gain a well-rounded foundation before you face a room full of eager and sometimes restless students.

It's also worth noting that the "hours" in TEFL courses aren't always created equal. A legitimate 120-hour program should require meaningful study time and assessments, not just clicking through slides. If a course feels suspiciously quick or cheap, employers may suspect it's not rigorous, and that can hurt your application. A part of the 120 hours includes time spent going over materials, but it also includes the hours spent doing discovery learning while conducting research about different aspects of the course to complete assignments.

Pro Tip

Before enrolling, email the TEFL provider and ask if they offer any discounts for early enrollment, group registration, or bundled specialization modules. Many providers run seasonal promotions or partner discounts that are not advertised on their website. If you are applying through a recruiter or a program like TEIK, ask whether they have a negotiated rate with a preferred TEFL partner. It never hurts to ask, and the savings can be meaningful.

Specialization Modules

Some teachers go beyond the standard by adding specialization modules to their 120 hours, and this is where you can really set yourself apart. The most popular add-ons are Young Learners (YLs) and Business English (BE), and they typically take an additional 20 to 40 hours to complete at a cost of $75 to $150.

Why does this matter in Korea? Most private academies run a split schedule, kindergarten classes in the morning and early afternoon, then elementary students in the late afternoon and evening. That means having formal training in teaching young learners is a huge plus. If you're aiming for a kindergarten-heavy school, being able to discuss specific child-centered activities, classroom management strategies, and developmental needs during your interview can set you apart. The Business English TEFL certification is valuable if you want to teach high-paying private classes to professionals.

This is precisely where specialized TEFL modules pay off, especially if your background doesn't naturally align with teaching children. You might have strong communication skills or a customer service background, but without something concrete that ties you to the world of education, your résumé might look generic. A targeted certificate can bridge that gap, giving you not just talking points for your interview but also the confidence to walk into your first class prepared.

Teacher Story: TEFL Specialization Certificates

One of my teachers, Emily, had spent her entire working life in the service industry, restaurants, retail, and hospitality, both during and after college. She had no formal teaching experience and had never worked with young children. Still, she was determined to land a job in Seoul and had just completed her 120-hour TEFL program. The challenge was obvious: she needed a way to stand out in a highly competitive market, especially for positions that involved teaching kindergarten.

We suggested she take an additional 40-hour Young Learners TEFL course designed specifically for teaching Korean kindergarten-aged students. The difference was remarkable. Not only did she gain practical ideas and age-appropriate teaching techniques, but she was also able to speak at length in her self-introduction video about what she had learned and how it applied to Korean English kindergartens.

At the same time, we encouraged her to rework her résumé to highlight related informal experiences she had never considered as "teaching." These included being a camp counselor when she was a senior in high school, teaching Taekwondo (태권도) to children, babysitting for her neighbors' young kids all through middle and high school, and even volunteering for six months at a Head Start program as part of a sociology course in college. Suddenly, her profile painted a much richer picture of someone with a long history of working with children, even if it wasn't in a formal classroom.

By the time she finished her application package, Emily came across as warm, energetic, and genuinely enthusiastic about working with young learners, exactly what schools look for in kindergarten teachers. That extra investment in specialized training, paired with reframing her past experiences, didn't just fill gaps on her résumé; it gave her the confidence and credibility she needed to secure a position in her dream location.

Takeaway: If your background doesn't obviously connect to teaching, a specialization module and some creative résumé framing can transform how schools see you. The investment is small, but the payoff in job options and confidence is significant.

Online vs. In-Person vs. Hybrid

One of the first major decisions you'll make when choosing a TEFL program is whether to study online, in-person, or through a hybrid model. Each option comes with its own advantages and drawbacks, and the right choice for you will depend on your budget, schedule, learning style, and career goals.

Online TEFL courses are by far the most popular choice for teachers heading to Korea because they allow you to study from anywhere in the world at your own pace. This flexibility makes them ideal for those who are working full-time or traveling before the move. Accredited online courses can be very affordable, often ranging from $200 to $500, though some higher-end options cost $1,000 or more. Since they are self-paced, you can complete them in as little as a few weeks. However, they don't provide hands-on teaching practice, and the quality of online TEFL courses varies widely; some are excellent, while others are little more than "pay-and-print" certificate mills. If you choose this route, you'll need to be self-motivated and selective about the program you enroll in.

In-person TEFL courses are held in a physical classroom, often in the country where you plan to teach or in major ESL training hubs like Thailand, Spain, or Vietnam. These courses offer the most significant advantage in terms of hands-on teaching practice. You'll typically teach real ESL students under the supervision of experienced trainers, follow a structured daily schedule, and receive immediate feedback on your lessons. In-person programs are also great for networking, as you'll be surrounded by other aspiring teachers who share your goals. However, they are significantly more expensive, often $1,000 to $2,500 or more, and require you to commit four to six weeks full-time. If you plan to take one in Korea, you'll likely need to enter on a tourist visa before switching to an E-2 visa, which adds extra planning.

Hybrid TEFL courses combine the flexibility of online study with a short in-person practicum, usually lasting one to two weeks. The online portion covers the theory, grammar, and lesson planning, while the practicum allows you to apply what you've learned with real students. Employers generally respect hybrid courses, and they are a good middle ground for those who want some classroom experience but can't commit to a full in-person course. They tend to cost more than fully online programs, often $600 to $1,500, but are still cheaper than most in-person options. The main challenge is scheduling the practicum, which may require travel to another city or country, depending on the provider's training locations.

In the Korean job market, most hagwons and many public schools do not require in-person teaching practice, meaning an online TEFL certificate is often enough to secure a position. However, for complete beginners or those who feel nervous about classroom management, a hybrid or in-person program can provide valuable confidence before stepping into a Korean classroom. Being able to walk into your first day already familiar with lesson planning, pacing, and managing groups of energetic students can make a big difference, not only in how your employer views you, but also in how comfortable you feel during those crucial first weeks on the job.

How to Choose a Reputable Program

Once you've decided to pursue TEFL certification, the next big question is which program to choose. Not all TEFL courses are created equal, and the wrong choice could leave you with a certificate that employers in Korea don't take seriously, or worse, one that immigration officers' question.

A reputable TEFL program will typically be accredited by a recognized body such as ACCET, DEAC, Ofqual, or TQUK. Accreditation is more than just a stamp of approval; it means the program has met strict educational standards, offers a legitimate curriculum, and provides qualified instructors to guide you through the material. It also signals to employers that your certificate wasn't earned through a "pay-and-print" operation. Keep in mind, though, that accreditation often comes with a higher price tag. While unaccredited TEFL courses can sometimes be good, you should always check in advance if your target schools accept them.

A good rule of thumb is to run the course through your recruiter before you enroll. Recruiters have firsthand knowledge of which certificates their partner schools value and which ones get dismissed outright. This step can save you from investing time and money in a program that won't help you land a job.

When evaluating TEFL programs, watch out for several red flags. Be cautious of unrealistic promises, like "guaranteed job placement" without an interview, since no reputable school in Korea hires teachers they haven't screened. Avoid programs with no instructor feedback, grading, or assessments, as a good course will include interaction with experienced trainers who review your assignments and offer practical tips. Pay attention to transparency: a poorly designed website, missing contact details, or vague curriculum information are all warning signs, and if you can't find independent, third-party reviews from former students, you should be cautious. Finally, beware of programs that hand out certificates after just a few hours of reading material or a handful of quizzes. Korean schools are increasingly savvy about identifying low-quality certificates, and a "fast and easy" course may end up hurting your credibility rather than helping it.

As a general rule: if it seems too good to be true, it probably is. The effort you put into your TEFL course will be reflected not just in your certificate, but in your teaching ability, and in the confidence schools have when they hire you.

Teacher Story: The Tale of Two TEFL Programs

A few years ago, two first-time teachers, Brian and Sophie, were applying for jobs in Seoul. Sophie chose an expensive ten-week online 120-hour TEFL program that cost around $1,600, attracted by the structured modules, job placement assistance, and a half-day tour of Seoul with dinner included. Brian, on the other hand, went through TEIK's TEFL partner and completed a 120-hour online course with tutor support for about $250. His program also gave him the chance to attend TEIK's free-hosted networking dinner in Seoul twice.

In the end, both teachers were hired at the same school in Seoul, started on identical salaries, and received the same benefits. The school didn't distinguish between their TEFL certificates. Both approaches worked, but they came with very different costs and experiences.

Takeaway: For many employers in Korea, having a TEFL certificate matters more than where it comes from. That said, if a TEFL course is unbelievably cheap, there's usually a reason; it often means the quality is low, the training is minimal, and the program's reputation is weak. The sweet spot is a reputable, accredited course at a reasonable price that gives you real skills along with the certificate.

How TEFL Boosts Your Job Prospects

A TEFL certification does more than meet the minimum requirement for most teaching jobs in Korea; it can directly impact the quality of the job offers you receive, the salary you start on, and even the locations available to you. In competitive markets like Seoul and Gyeonggi-do, where schools can choose from dozens of qualified applicants, a strong TEFL certificate can be the factor that tips the scales in your favor.

Some hagwons and public schools even offer salary bonuses or higher pay tiers for candidates with a TEFL that includes a practicum component, since it signals that you have actual classroom experience. For example, two teachers applying for the same position may have identical degrees. Still, the one with a TEFL practicum might secure a higher starting salary or a preference for prime locations near Seoul because they have at least 20 hours of teaching practicum.

Beyond the hiring stage, TEFL training can have a day-to-day impact on your confidence and performance. A solid course will teach you how to create lesson plans that are both engaging and culturally appropriate, manage mixed-ability classrooms, and adapt your teaching to different learning styles. These skills are especially valuable in Korea, where a single class may include students with vastly different levels of English ability.

Even experienced educators benefit from TEFL training because it's tailored to teaching English as a second language, which is different from teaching in a native English environment. For instance, I've worked with teachers who had a decade of experience in their home country but struggled in Korea until they learned strategies for simplifying instructions, building vocabulary in context, and keeping lessons interactive without overwhelming beginners.

Employers also notice when a TEFL certificate comes from a reputable, well-structured program. I've received applications where the "certificate" was clearly from a low-quality provider, with no contact hours, no assignments, and no real curriculum. Schools dismiss those immediately because they know the training was superficial. On the other hand, when they see a TEFL from a recognized, accredited provider, it signals professionalism, effort, and a genuine interest in teaching.

Finally, a TEFL isn't just for Korea; it's a portable qualification that can open doors around the world. Teachers often use their experience in Korea as a springboard to positions in other countries, international schools, or even online teaching businesses. In that sense, it's not just a ticket to your first job abroad, it's an investment in your long-term career.

Final Thoughts

In the world of English teaching in Korea, a TEFL certification is far more than a formality; it's a professional foundation. It shows schools that you've taken the time to prepare, that you value your role as an educator, and that you're committed to giving students the best possible learning experience. Whether you choose a $250 online program with tutor support or a $1,600 structured course with added extras, what matters most is that your TEFL is reputable, accredited, and genuinely equips you with skills you'll use in the classroom.

That said, not all TEFLs are created equal. Some teachers enroll to "check the box" for employers, while others use it as an opportunity to specialize, add practicum hours, or focus on a niche like Young Learners. Your decision should reflect your goals: Are you aiming for Seoul's competitive market? Do you want to feel confident walking into a kindergarten classroom on day one? Are you hoping to use Korea as a launchpad for an international teaching career?

Ultimately, the TEFL you choose should give you more than a certificate; it should provide you with confidence. Confidence to manage a classroom, to adapt to Korean cultural and educational norms, and to communicate your value to employers. A quality TEFL program will prepare you not only for the logistics of teaching but also for the unpredictable, rewarding reality of life in a Korean school.

With your TEFL certification in hand, you'll be ready for the next big step: putting together an application package that gets noticed, gets interviews, and gets you hired. In the next chapter, we'll break down exactly how to prepare your resume, self-introduction video, and supporting documents so you can turn your new qualification into a job offer in Korea.

Part Two

Getting a Job

Chapter 5: Preparing Your Application Materials

Chapter Summary

This chapter walks you through the five key components of a successful application package for teaching in Korea: a Korean-ready resume, a tailored cover letter, a personal statement for programs like EPIK or TaLK, a professional self-introduction video, and a sample lesson plan. You will learn how to format each document for the Korean market, avoid the most common mistakes that cause directors to pass on otherwise strong candidates, and present yourself as someone who is approachable, dependable, and genuinely invested in teaching.

Why This Chapter Matters

Applying to teach English in Korea is not just about meeting visa requirements; it's about competing in a hiring process that is both fast-moving and highly selective. Korean school directors and recruiters make quick judgments based on how polished and professional your application materials look. Often, they only scan a resume for a few seconds before deciding whether to move forward. If your resume is cluttered, your photo is unprofessional, or your self-introduction video feels unprepared, your application may never even reach a school director's desk.

Recruiters, who act as the first filter, play a significant role in shaping outcomes. They are constantly reviewing dozens of applications per day, and their job is to eliminate candidates who appear disorganized, unqualified, or uncommitted. For this reason, your application needs to be recruiter-friendly: concise, culturally appropriate, and consistent across all documents. When your package is easy to read, free of red flags, and tailored to the Korean market, you not only increase your chances of being recommended but also make the recruiter's job easier. And in practice, recruiters remember and prioritize applicants who make their work smoother.

From the employer's perspective, application materials do more than prove your eligibility; they signal who you are as a person and a teacher. Korean schools place a high value on professionalism, adaptability, and personality fit. They want to see signs that you'll handle cultural differences respectfully, work well within a structured hierarchy, and connect with young learners in the classroom. Your resume, cover letter, and video all serve as proxies for these qualities. Strong application materials communicate warmth, responsibility, and a genuine interest in teaching, which are often the deciding factors when two candidates have similar qualifications.

In short, this stage sets the tone for your entire job search. Well-prepared materials can lead to faster interviews, better job offers, and placements in more desirable locations. Poorly prepared ones can stall your progress before it even begins. Treating this stage seriously is the foundation of a successful teaching career in Korea.

Your Korean-Ready Resume

When applying to teach in Korea, your resume is often the very first thing a recruiter or school director will see, and sometimes it's the only document they review in detail before deciding whether to move forward. Unlike in many Western job markets, where resumes are minimalist one-page summaries, Korean schools expect something more tailored, polished, and visually professional. Think of your resume as a snapshot of who you are as a teacher, not just a work history.

One key difference is the expectation of a professional headshot. While photos are not included on resumes in North America or Europe, they are standard in Korea and not considered discriminatory. A clean, well-lit headshot with professional attire gives hiring managers immediate reassurance that you understand cultural expectations. Applicants who leave the photo off often find their resumes dismissed without review. Recruiters typically will add your headshot to the resume if you do not.

Formatting also matters. Korean directors often glance at resumes for less than 15 seconds, so make yours easy to scan. Use clear section headings like Education, Teaching Experience, Certifications, and Other Relevant Experience. Place the most important qualifications, such as your degree, TEFL certification, and any teaching-related work, near the top. Schools consistently tell me that messy, overly long resumes with cluttered designs are red flags that suggest disorganization. A clean, well-structured document communicates reliability before you even say a word.

Equally important is how you frame your experience. Don't underestimate informal roles such as tutoring, babysitting, summer camp counseling, coaching, or volunteering, especially if they involve working with children. In Korea, those experiences are seen as highly relevant because they demonstrate patience, leadership, and an ability to connect with young learners. Working with children in many capacities develops similar transferable skills that teachers need to be successful. Instead of vague statements like "Strong communication skills," be specific. For example: "Tutored two elementary students in reading comprehension, creating weekly lesson plans tailored to their progress," or "Served as a camp counselor for 25 children, leading group activities and ensuring student safety." Schools value applicants who can demonstrate both initiative and care when working with children. By reframing informal experiences into concrete, teaching-relevant skills, you show directors you already have the foundation they're looking for.

Pro Tip

Use specific, action-oriented descriptions like "Designed and delivered weekly ESL lessons for beginner learners (ages 6–9)" rather than vague statements like "Strong interpersonal skills."

Common Resume Mistakes to Avoid

Casual or inappropriate photos are one of the most common issues. A selfie, a cropped vacation shot, or a blurry image suggests you don't take the process seriously. Always use a professional headshot, or at minimum, use a white wall as a background and take a well-lit photo during the day with natural lighting while smiling. Overly vague language is another problem; avoid generic statements like "Good with kids" or "Team player" and instead be specific about what you actually did and achieved. Cluttered formatting with long paragraphs, unusual fonts, or decorative designs makes resumes hard to skim, so stick to a clean, modern format with consistent headings. Don't waste space listing every duty from an unrelated job; instead, highlight transferable skills that show leadership, responsibility, or communication. Many candidates also leave out teaching-adjacent experiences like babysitting, coaching, tutoring, or volunteering with youth, which gives schools the impression that you lack experience with kids. Finally, watch for typos or grammar errors, as directors expect English teachers to model correct language, and even small mistakes can raise doubts about your professionalism.

Pro Tip

Have your resume reviewed for typos, flow, and overall look by a friend or someone you trust. I've had many schools pass on well-qualified teachers because of resume typos, poor quality formatting, or a poor-quality photo.

Writing a Tailored Cover Letter

Your cover letter is your chance to move beyond the bullet points of your resume and show schools who you are as a teacher and as a person. Korean hiring managers, especially hagwon directors, often read dozens of resumes a day, and many look nearly identical. A well-crafted cover letter can be the detail that makes you stand out.

A strong Korean teaching cover letter typically follows three parts. The introduction should clearly state who you are and what position you're applying for, mentioning how you learned about the opportunity, whether through a recruiter, job board, or referral. The middle section is where you connect your background to what the school is looking for, highlighting transferable skills like leadership, childcare, tutoring, and coaching, while showing enthusiasm for working with Korean students. The closing should reinforce your excitement for the role, signal your readiness to begin the visa process, and thank them for their time.

Here is an example of a strong opening paragraph:

> "Dear Hiring Manager, my name is Sarah Johnson, and I am excited to apply for the English teaching position at your academy. With a bachelor's degree in communications, a 120-hour TEFL certification, and experience mentoring children through volunteer tutoring and youth programs, I am confident in my ability to create engaging and supportive lessons for your students. I am particularly drawn to your school's emphasis on interactive learning and student confidence, values I strongly share as an educator."

This type of opening works well because it is polite and professional (important in Korean culture), specific in referencing qualifications directly, and aligned with the school's mission, showing the applicant researched the role.

For the middle section, show that you've researched Korea and the school type. Instead of saying "I like Korean culture," write something like: "I admire the value Korean families place on education and look forward to contributing to that tradition by creating engaging lessons that help students feel confident using English." Include any informal but relevant experiences, such as babysitting, tutoring, coaching, or volunteering, since Korean schools value a demonstrated comfort with children even if it wasn't in a classroom. Keep it sincere and avoid clichés like "teaching is my passion" unless you back it up with a concrete example.

Here is an example of a strong closing paragraph:

"I am eager to bring my energy and adaptability to your students, and I am fully prepared to relocate, complete the visa process, and participate in training as needed. Thank you very much for your consideration, and I look forward to the possibility of contributing to your school community."

This ending shows commitment, readiness, and humility, three traits that Korean directors appreciate.

Teacher Story: The Cover Letter That Made the Difference

Alicia, one of the teachers I worked with a few years ago, didn't have much formal teaching experience. She was worried that her résumé alone wouldn't stand out, especially since she was applying to schools in Seoul, one of the most competitive markets. Instead of writing a generic cover letter, she spent an evening studying the school's website. She noticed they ran several after-school cultural clubs, including a cooking program where students practiced English while making simple Korean dishes.

In her cover letter, Alicia didn't just say she "loved teaching"; she wrote about how she wanted to contribute to those cultural clubs. She explained that she enjoyed cooking herself and looked forward to helping students use English in hands-on, creative ways. That small detail made a big impression. The school director later told me that her enthusiasm for their program convinced them she would fit in perfectly, even more than her degree or TEFL certificate did.

Takeaway: In Korea, directors want to see not just your qualifications but your genuine interest in their specific school. Even a single thoughtful reference to a program, activity, or value they highlight can set you apart from dozens of other applicants. If you have anything that you are passionate about that can be interesting for your students, you should share it.

Teacher Story: The Copy-Paste Cover Letter

Not every application makes a good impression. One teacher I worked with, Daniel, had solid qualifications, a degree, a 120-hour TEFL, and tutoring experience. Unfortunately, his cover letter held him back. He used the same generic letter for every job he applied to, only changing the school's name at the top. The body of the letter was vague, full of statements like "I am passionate about teaching" and "I would be a great fit for your school," without a single reference to the specific school or its programs.

Directors noticed. In Korea, hagwon owners and public-school coordinators often skim dozens of applications in a single day. A bland, cookie-cutter letter signals that the candidate hasn't put in effort, and worse, that they may not be serious about the job. Daniel applied to nearly twenty schools and didn't get a single interview offer. Only after we reworked his cover letter to highlight what he could offer each school, tailoring it to mention student age groups, curriculum style, and location preference, did he start getting positive responses.

Pro Tip

Directors want to see your passion for teaching and children, and a positive, friendly, and energetic mindset. A few personalized sentences about their specific school can be the difference between rejection and an interview.

The Personal Statement (EPIK, TaLK, etc.)

When applying to government-run programs like EPIK (English Program in Korea) or TaLK (Teach and Learn in Korea), you'll usually be asked to submit a personal statement in addition to your résumé and cover letter. Unlike the cover letter, which markets you to a specific school, the personal statement is meant to show who you are, why you want to teach in Korea, and how you will contribute as a teacher and cultural ambassador. Think of it as your chance to "connect the dots" between your personal experiences, your teaching potential, and your adaptability in Korea.

Recruiters and coordinators are looking for several things in a strong personal statement. They want to see your motivation: why Korea, and why now? They want evidence of suitability, meaning that you can work with children and adapt to new environments. They look for cultural sensitivity, an acknowledgment that Korea is different from your home country and that you're ready to embrace those differences. And they want to understand your teaching philosophy, even if you've never formally taught. How do you imagine yourself in the classroom? Are you patient, energetic, and creative?

Instead of writing something generic like "I love working with kids, and I am passionate about teaching," try something specific. For example: "During my final year of university, I volunteered twice a week at a local Head Start program, helping preschoolers with early literacy skills through songs and picture books. That experience taught me how to make learning both fun and accessible, even for students with limited language ability. I look forward to bringing that same energy and creativity into a Korean classroom." This kind of detail makes your application memorable and believable.

There are a few common pitfalls to avoid. Generic statements like "I want to teach because I love kids" are too vague; you need to show, not just tell. It's fine to mention if Korean culture initially sparked your interest through K-pop or K-drama, but make sure you balance it with deeper reasons, such as education, cross-cultural experience, or long-term goals. And don't pretend Korea will be "easy." Better to admit you know there will be cultural and language barriers and that you see them as growth opportunities. Pretending otherwise suggests you haven't thought it through.

Teacher Story: Marcus's Rural Placement

Marcus, an American teacher I worked with, wrote a personal statement that stood out precisely because it was honest and grounded. He had previously volunteered in rural Peru, where he taught English at a community center with limited resources. In his statement, he didn't gloss over the difficulties; he described the challenge of improvising lessons without a textbook and finding ways to keep students motivated despite long days of farm work. Then, he connected that directly to Korea:

"I know that teaching in a small Korean town may bring similar challenges, such as fewer resources or students who are tired from long school days. But I've already learned how to adapt in those situations, and I'm confident I can bring creativity and patience to my future classroom."

That combination of real-world experience, honest reflection, and adaptability made his application stand out. He was ultimately placed in a rural Korean middle school, where he thrived and even extended his contract.

Takeaway: Honesty and specificity beat polished generalities every time. Programs like EPIK want to know you've actually thought about what teaching in Korea will be like, not just that you want to live abroad.

Creating a Self-Introduction Video

For many schools, your self-introduction video is the very first impression they'll have of you, often watched before your résumé is even opened. Directors use it to assess three things immediately: clarity of speech, including your accent, pacing, and pronunciation; personality and presence, meaning whether you are warm, confident, and approachable; and professionalism, including your dress, demeanor, and environment. A strong video can make up for a thin résumé. Conversely, a sloppy or uninspired video can sink an otherwise competitive candidate.

How to Structure Your Video

A good self-introduction video follows a simple four-part flow. Start with a brief introduction of about 15 to 20 seconds where you state your name, nationality, degree, and TEFL certification. Then spend 15 to 30 seconds on your motivation, sharing why you want to teach in Korea while avoiding clichés like "I love K-pop" unless you frame them within a broader cultural interest. Next, use 20 to 30 seconds to highlight your teaching qualities, focusing on specific skills or experiences like working with children, tutoring, mentoring, or coaching, and use examples where possible. Close with about 10 to 15 seconds of warmth, something like "I look forward to meeting you and creating a fun, supportive classroom together." Keep it under two minutes; shorter is often better, and about one minute is ideal since directors watch dozens per week.

For presentation, film in a quiet, well-lit room with a clean background, using natural light whenever possible. Place the camera at eye level on a stable surface, with no low-angle shots or handheld shakiness. Dress as you would for an interview, with business casual being perfect. Speak clearly, smile, and project positive energy. Schools consistently hire the candidate who looks energetic and approachable over the one with the longest list of qualifications.

There are a few common pitfalls to avoid. Speaking too quickly or mumbling makes it hard for directors to assess your English clarity. Filming in a messy bedroom, noisy café, or dim lighting creates a bad first impression. Overloading with hobbies unrelated to teaching wastes valuable time, as schools don't need to hear your entire travel history. And monotone delivery kills enthusiasm, which matters as much as content, so be sure to smile.

Teacher Story: How One Video Sealed the Deal

One British teacher I worked with, Sarah, had a degree in robotics and had spent nearly seven years designing and building robots for a leading tech company. On paper, she was far from the typical ESL candidate, highly technical, introverted by nature, and used to working alone. I honestly wasn't sure how well she would transition into teaching.

But when we spoke, she lit up as she described her favorite part of her robotics career: explaining how the machines worked, sharing the design process, and teaching others about the technology behind them. She didn't love working by herself; what she loved was talking about her passion and helping others understand it.

That same spark came through in her self-introduction video. She used her technical skills to create the most polished, professional-looking video I've ever seen from an applicant. More importantly, she conveyed genuine enthusiasm for teaching and learning. As she described how she explained robotics concepts to colleagues and school groups, she radiated energy and passion, exactly what schools want to see in someone who will stand in front of a classroom full of curious kids.

Her video turned what looked like a technical, non-teaching background into a decisive advantage. It highlighted her communication skills, her creativity, and her love of helping others learn, all of which transferred beautifully to teaching English in Korea. She was quickly hired, and her director later told me it was her video that convinced them she was the right fit.

Takeaway: Your background doesn't have to be in education. What matters is that your video shows warmth, energy, and a genuine love of helping others learn. Directors choose personality over pedigree every time.

Pro Tip

Show warmth and energy; directors often choose the most engaging personality over the most decorated resume.

Here are more than a dozen excellent self-introduction videos for you to benchmark. I would watch all of them since they are mostly only one minute long. Here is the link: https://www.teachenglishinkorea.org/videos.

Teacher Story: When a Video Works Against You

Not every introduction video hits the mark. One teacher I worked with seemed like a genuine, caring person during our calls, but he was very introverted. I gave him clear advice before filming: don't script and read word-for-word. Instead, focus on being warm, positive, and showing enthusiasm for children. After all, he had a great story to share, nearly 20 hours volunteering at a community center, tutoring kids one-on-one.

Unfortunately, his first attempt was precisely what I warned against. He read directly from a script, and it showed. His eyes darted left to right as he followed the text; his voice was monotone, and his delivery felt robotic. It came across flat and lifeless, the exact opposite of what Korean schools are looking for. He looked like someone making a hostage video instead of a self-introduction video, since he seemed so nervous, uncomfortable, and uptight.

He remade the video four more times, each one only slightly better. At the end of each attempt, he forced an awkward smile, which highlighted how uncomfortable he felt. By the fifth version, it became clear that no number of retakes would solve the problem. He couldn't project the warmth and energy schools want to see on camera, so I didn't share his video with schools, and I just sent his resume and photo. He had three to four interviews, but he didn't receive any job offers.

I always give constructive criticism to teachers, because my job is to help them become as marketable as possible. In his case, I suggested benchmarking by watching multiple sample videos to understand what works, and practicing casually before recording. Most people don't realize how self-conscious they become in front of a camera; they laugh, giggle, or stiffen up because of nerves. Practicing first helps smooth this out. Unfortunately, he never reached that point of confidence, and I eventually decided not to send his video to schools, since it risked hurting his chances more than helping them.

Takeaway: A strong résumé will only take you so far. If your video doesn't show warmth and personality, schools will pass. Be open to constructive feedback, watch great examples, practice a few times, and let your natural enthusiasm shine.

Creating a Sample Lesson Plan

Not every application will ask you for a sample lesson plan, but including one can give you a significant advantage. Korean school directors love to see proof that you've thought about how to teach in a real classroom. Even if you've never taught before, a simple, well-structured lesson plan shows initiative, preparation, and a willingness to step into the role with confidence.

Think of the lesson plan as your way of answering the director's unspoken question: "What would this teacher actually do in front of my students?" If your plan is practical, age-appropriate, and easy to follow, it immediately reassures the school that you'll be effective once you arrive.

Lesson Plan Basics

A strong sample lesson plan demonstrates not only that you can structure a class but also that you understand how Korean classrooms actually work. Schools want to see that you can balance clarity, engagement, and cultural expectations. A polished plan should read like a roadmap: easy to follow, outcome-based, and realistic for the age and level of your students.

The starting point is always the objective. This is where many first-time applicants stumble. A vague statement like "students will understand introductions" doesn't mean much to a hiring director. A specific, measurable goal does: "By the end of this lesson, students will be able to introduce themselves using 'My name is ____' and ask, 'What is your name?'" Think of it as a promise you're making to the director that the lesson won't just be busywork but will deliver a clear learning outcome. Korean schools are very results-driven, so your ability to phrase objectives in practical, student-centered terms sets you apart.

Next comes the warm-up activity, which is often underestimated. Korean students are used to long days and multiple classes back-to-back, so a fun, short warm-up isn't just an icebreaker; it's a reset button that grabs their attention. A classic "Name Ball Game," where students toss a ball and introduce themselves, works well with young learners. For slightly older groups, you might project a funny cartoon image of two kids meeting and ask, "What do you think they're saying?" For kindergarten, songs or chants are gold; directors love seeing teachers who can blend play and learning. One master teacher I was observing once told me, "If a teacher can make a five-year-old laugh while practicing English, I know they'll succeed." Keep the warm-up to under five minutes, and always tie it to the day's target language.

The presentation stage is your chance to introduce the new language point in a way that's simple, visual, and memorable. Directors will be watching to see how you model language. Instead of explaining grammar rules, show and repeat. If the target is "My name is...," write it on the board, point to yourself, say the phrase with a smile, and encourage students to echo. Props, puppets, and even short video clips can enhance this step. One practical example: showing a 15-second clip of a cartoon character introducing themselves. This not only contextualizes the phrase but also grabs students' attention immediately. In Korea, talking less about English and demonstrating more in English is what sells you as a teacher.

After that, the practice phase allows students to try the language in a structured setting safely. Pair work is perfect here. For example, students can practice short dialogues with partners:

A: "Hi, my name is Jisoo."

B: "My name is David. Nice to meet you!"

As the teacher, your role is to circulate, listen, and gently correct. Korean schools appreciate teachers who encourage shy students to participate without being harsh. A simple tip: start with choral repetition (the whole class speaking together) before breaking into pairs. This reduces anxiety and builds confidence. Some teachers use role cards (with names and countries) to make practice feel like a game. If your sample plan shows variety, not just drills, you'll score big points.

The production stage is where students use the language more creatively and independently. This is the moment directors lean forward, because they want to see if you can genuinely get kids talking. A strong example for a beginner class might be to have each student stand up, introduce themselves, and then introduce a partner: "This is my friend Hana. She is from Korea." You can add props like flags, country cards, or even simple drawings. For older students, you might design a role-play scenario, like two students meeting at a school event. The point is that students should feel ownership of the language, and you should show the director you know how to step back and let students shine.

Finally, a wrap-up and review ensure the lesson doesn't just fade out. Korean schools value routine and closure, so end on a high note. You might quickly review key phrases by pointing to yourself and prompting, "My name is...?" or tossing the ball back to a student for a final round. Then ask a few individual students follow-up questions: "Where are you from?" "Can you say that in a full sentence?" Finish with positive reinforcement and an explicit sign-off, like "Great job today! See you next class!" A good wrap-up not only helps retention but also builds classroom routine and discipline, both of which are highly valued in Korean schools. A quick homework suggestion, like drawing a family tree and writing "This is my mom. Her name is ____," can also show that you understand continuity in learning.

This is also the point where I personally made every review into a short game. Gamifying the lesson gave students a burst of energy at the end and turned review into something they looked forward to. I would set up a quick three-to-five-minute activity, keep score on the board, and give out high-fives as rewards for each correct answer or point scored. It was my "carrot" part of carrot-and-stick classroom management, and it worked wonders. Korean children spend long hours in school, private academies, and at-home study, so even a brief, playful competition at the end of class feels like a huge treat. The promise of a game became a powerful motivator for good behavior during the lesson, and it ensured students left the classroom smiling and excited to return the next day.

When schools evaluate sample lesson plans, they aren't just checking whether you can write one; they're imagining how you'll perform in front of their students. A plan with clear objectives, age-appropriate activities, and a smooth flow from warm-up to wrap-up tells them you'll walk into class prepared, organized, and capable of engaging Korean learners. Recruiters often tell me that applicants who submit a thoughtful sample plan, even when not required, are automatically moved to the "yes" pile because it shows initiative and professionalism.

Teacher Story: Making Room for Games in a Packed Curriculum

One teacher I worked with was frustrated because their school, a large, well-known hagwon chain, had such a comprehensive curriculum that they felt chained to the teacher's manual. Every class was crammed with exercises, drills, and workbook pages, leaving no space for even a five-minute review game at the end. The result? Their students were restless and bored, and classroom management became an uphill battle.

When they came to me for advice at one of our networking dinners, I suggested two simple changes. First, during the practice stage, instead of assigning work individually, they had students complete the tasks in pairs or small teams. This doubled the pace and created more energy in the room. Second, instead of modeling just one or two examples and then letting students grind through the rest, I encouraged them to work through the bulk of the examples together as a class, keeping the pace brisk while still reinforcing the content. These tweaks meant the class finished the core material faster, freeing up five to ten minutes at the end for a quick game.

When I saw this teacher again at our next networking dinner, they were excited to tell me how much of a difference it made. Their students were more engaged, discipline problems dropped, and the teachers themselves were enjoying lessons more. That slight shift, creating time for a short, playful review, transformed not just the vibe of the classroom but also the teacher's confidence. For both teachers and students, fun can be a powerful motivator.

Takeaway: Don't be afraid to adapt the manual. Korean school directors ultimately care more about student engagement and parent satisfaction than whether you finish every single page of the workbook.

Adapting for Age and Level

One of the easiest ways to make your application stand out is to show you can adapt lesson content to different ages and proficiency levels. Recruiters and school directors immediately notice when a sample plan feels "cookie-cutter" or mismatched to the age group. For example, kindergarten students thrive on movement, songs, and repetition (think action songs like Head, Shoulders, Knees and Toes combined with gestures). Elementary students enjoy visual aids and interactive activities such as role-play dialogues or card games. Middle schoolers tend to be self-conscious, so group projects or pair-work debates work well, giving them structure while allowing expression. High schoolers respond best to real-life scenarios, like ordering food, planning a trip, or giving short presentations, that link English to their future goals.

Showing this flexibility doesn't require multiple complete lesson plans; sometimes, just one strong plan with a short note like "This activity can also be adapted for younger learners by adding gestures and visuals" is enough to signal your versatility. Schools want teachers who can adjust on the fly and keep students engaged at any level.

For instance, one candidate applying for a highly competitive private hagwon job in Daechi-dong, Gangnam, created a lesson around ordering food at a restaurant in English. The plan included menu vocabulary, a short role-play skit, and a group activity where students designed cafés. The lesson was simple but practical, and the school later told me it was a primary reason he was offered the job. Another teacher went even further by tapping into a real-world connection. One of his students worked at McDonald's, so he borrowed an actual McDonald's uniform, menus, and props from the restaurant. He transformed the classroom into a mini fast-food counter where students practiced ordering, paying, and serving food entirely in English. This approach was both fun and highly practical, and the students loved it. For the director observing, it was a perfect demonstration of creativity, adaptability, and student-centered teaching.

That kind of lesson sticks in people's memories, for students, because it felt real, and for school directors, because it proved the teacher could make English not just an academic subject, but a usable, engaging skill.

Final Thoughts

Your application package isn't just paperwork; it's your first demonstration of teaching ability. The way you write your resume, cover letter, personal statement, and sample lesson plan communicates to schools whether you'll be clear, engaging, and organized in the classroom. Directors don't expect perfection, but they do expect to see initiative, adaptability, and evidence that you understand how Korean classrooms operate.

The strongest candidates are those who treat their applications like a teaching audition. A well-prepared lesson plan shows that you can engage students. A polished video demonstrates warmth and confidence. A thoughtful cover letter proves you're motivated to live and work in Korea. Put these together, and your application becomes more than just paperwork; it becomes a compelling portrait of who you are as a teacher.

Most importantly, remember that schools value engagement more than rigid perfection. Directors want to know that their students will enjoy learning from you, not just that you can check every page of a workbook. If your application shows that you can make lessons both practical and enjoyable, you'll stand out from the crowd.

In the next chapter, we'll look at how to find and evaluate job openings, work with recruiters, and navigate the process of choosing the right school for your goals.

Chapter 6: Finding the Right Job

Chapter Summary

This chapter covers how to search for ESL teaching jobs in Korea using recruiters, direct applications, and networking. You will learn how to evaluate contracts carefully for salary, housing, working hours, and benefits, and how to spot red flags in job offers that could lead to poor placements. You will also gain practical tips for negotiating salary and housing in a culturally appropriate way, and understand how building a support network early leads to better opportunities and a smoother adjustment.

Why This Chapter Matters

Once your resume, cover letter, and application materials are polished, the next crucial step is finding the right teaching job in Korea. Many new teachers assume that landing a position is simply a matter of luck or timing, but in reality, it's about strategy, discernment, and preparation. The Korean ESL market is vast, with thousands of opportunities advertised every year. However, not all schools are equal, and not all contracts are created with the teacher's best interest in mind.

Korean school directors and recruiters receive an overwhelming number of applications, often reviewing dozens before selecting a candidate. To stand out, you need more than basic eligibility; you need to understand how directors think. Most directors aren't just looking at your degree or TEFL certificate; they are evaluating whether you'll bring stability, energy, and a positive presence into their school. They are asking themselves: Will this person be dependable? Will they work well with parents and co-teachers? Will students enjoy their classes and want to keep coming back every month?

Recruiters act as an initial filter. They know what schools are looking for and will often eliminate applications with sloppy resumes, vague cover letters, or lackluster introduction videos before they ever reach a director's desk. This means that every part of your application isn't just a formality; it's the evidence schools use to decide if you're worth the investment of a 12-month contract, airfare, housing, and training. Schools invest a lot of time, energy, and resources to hire, train, and mentor new teachers, so they want to be sure they are choosing the right person for the job.

The good news is that teachers who take the time to research, ask questions, and compare opportunities are the ones who consistently secure the best positions. Finding the right job is not a gamble; it's the result of informed choices. By learning how to read contracts critically, evaluate schools, and build supportive networks, you can avoid the common pitfalls that lead to burnout or frustration and instead secure a role that allows you to thrive both inside and outside the classroom.

Recruiters vs. Direct Hire

Recruiters are often a good starting point, as they can streamline the process by matching your qualifications with multiple openings and handling much of the communication. However, relying on them can limit your options to only the schools they partner with. Conversely, applying directly allows you to explore a broader range of schools and potentially negotiate a better salary. Still, it requires more time and effort to find openings and manage applications yourself. It is not uncommon to see teachers use a recruiter for initial interviews, while also proactively applying to schools they find on job boards.

Using Recruiters

For most first-time teachers heading to Korea, working with a recruiter is the natural starting point. Recruiters act as intermediaries between schools and applicants, helping to match candidates with openings, set up interviews, and guide them through the visa process.

The most crucial point to understand is that teachers do not pay recruiters. Schools are the ones who pay them a placement fee, which means you get free access to their services. Done right, this relationship can save you enormous time, reduce stress, and even provide a built-in support system once you arrive in Korea.

A good recruiter is far more than a job broker. They help coordinate interviews, walk you through every step of the documentation process, and explain details like how to get your degree apostilled or what to expect at the health check. They also prepare you for interviews by explaining what specific schools are looking for and what questions directors tend to ask. Once you land a job, they usually help with housing arrangements, airport pickup, and the Alien Registration Card (ARC) process. For new arrivals, having someone explain Korean systems, from banking to cell phone contracts, can be invaluable.

Recruiters can also serve as advocates. If you run into a conflict with your school, such as unclear vacation days or unexpected schedule changes, a recruiter can step in as a mediator. Schools value their long-term relationship with recruiters, so your concerns are often taken more seriously when relayed through that channel. Some recruiters even go further, hosting networking events or dinners that connect new teachers, giving you an immediate community when you arrive. For example, TEIK hosts biannual dinners in Seoul, where dozens of teachers share stories, advice, and contacts, a simple but powerful way to avoid the isolation that can hit hard during the first months abroad.

How to Evaluate Recruiters

That said, not all recruiters are equal. A trustworthy recruiter will answer your questions clearly, be upfront about both the positives and negatives of a school and respond to messages promptly. They will also be willing to connect you with teacher testimonials or allow you to speak with someone they have successfully placed before. If a recruiter is transparent, responsive, and patient, that's a good sign they are prioritizing your interests alongside the school's.

On the other hand, some recruiters treat candidates as numbers. Warning signs include vague or evasive answers about contracts, delays or silence when you ask follow-up questions, and pressure to accept a job quickly without sufficient time to review. Sometimes recruiters also push jobs that don't match your original preferences, for example, offering rural placements after you've clearly said you only want Seoul. This kind of bait-and-switch tactic is a red flag that the recruiter is more interested in filling vacancies than finding the right fit for you.

Teacher Story: Jamie's Search for the Right Recruiter

Jamie's job search began the way many teachers' do: she posted her résumé on Dave's ESL Café, a long-standing job board for ESL teachers in Korea. Within just a few days, she was contacted by more than ten different Korean recruiters, each requesting her headshot and basic job preferences. At first, she felt excited at the response, but the enthusiasm quickly turned into frustration. After submitting her details, only two or three recruiters actually followed up, and those conversations were brief and impersonal. Instead of asking about her goals or preferences, they immediately pushed her toward interviews in smaller towns and remote cities far from Seoul, the one place Jamie dreamed of living and working.

Feeling ignored and pressured, Jamie sensed that these recruiters were not acting in her best interest. She later stumbled upon an interview I had given on YouTube with Catherine (Cat) Young, a former teacher I had placed in Seoul who had become a popular vlogger. Cat's story resonated with Jamie, and she reached out to me directly. During our first conversation, Jamie admitted she wondered if being Asian American played a role in why recruiters weren't following up with her. I explained honestly that, while her fluency and qualifications were excellent, bias in the Korean ESL market is real. Some parents cannot easily distinguish between native and non-native speakers by listening. Still, they can visually differentiate between Asian and non-Asian teachers, leading some schools to favor non-Asian candidates. On top of that, schools often show a preference for North American accents (due to Korean exams being based on American English) and sometimes even prefer female candidates for kindergarten classes.

With this context in mind, we focused on strategy. I encouraged Jamie to highlight her strengths, craft a strong self-introduction video, and remain open to interviews in and around Seoul. Within a short time, I arranged several interviews for her in the capital. Eventually, however, Jamie chose a position in Gyeonggi-do, just outside Seoul. She connected immediately with the director during the interview, and the school offered her a higher salary than the Seoul placements. In the end, she landed a job that gave her the lifestyle she wanted, close enough to Seoul to enjoy the city, but with the added benefit of supportive management and a higher paycheck.

Takeaway: Don't settle for recruiters who don't listen to your goals. Reliable recruiters will ask detailed questions, communicate clearly, and respect your preferences. If you feel pushed into a school or city that doesn't align with what you want, step back and reassess. The right recruiter will not just find you a job; they'll help you find the right job where you can thrive.

Applying Directly

For teachers who prefer to have more control over their job search, applying directly to schools can be an effective route. Direct applications allow you to explore a broader range of opportunities beyond what recruiters present, and they give you a chance to negotiate directly with schools. Job boards such as Dave's ESL Café, Gone2Korea, WorknPlay, and ESLROK are still widely used, while Facebook groups like ESL Jobs in Korea or Teaching Jobs in Seoul post openings daily. Many teachers also find positions by browsing regional job boards, expat forums, or even school websites.

The most significant advantage of applying directly is that you see the job posting exactly as the school intended, with no middleman filtering the details. You also maintain more negotiating power, since you can communicate directly with the hiring director or head teacher. For instance, one teacher I worked with, Anthony, found his job by messaging a director on Facebook after seeing a posting in an expat group. Because he wasn't routed through a recruiter, he was able to negotiate a housing allowance that was higher than the standard and get clarification on his schedule directly from the school.

However, applying directly also comes with its challenges. Schools in Korea receive hundreds of applications for popular locations like Seoul and Busan. Without a recruiter to advocate on your behalf, your materials need to stand out even more. You'll be responsible for managing the entire application process: sending your résumé, scheduling the interview, securing visa paperwork, and following up with immigration. Missteps, such as sending the wrong type of background check or failing to notarize a diploma, can delay or even derail your application.

Another risk is that you won't always know which schools are reputable. A posting might sound perfect on paper, but unless you ask to speak to a current foreign teacher, you may not uncover issues such as high turnover, unpaid overtime, or poor housing until it's too late. Recruiters often act as a filter for these red flags, but when applying directly, you have to do that due diligence yourself.

Still, direct applications can be rewarding. Teachers who are proactive, organized, and willing to ask the right questions often find that they can secure slightly better salaries or more desirable housing arrangements. Direct communication also helps build a relationship with the school from the beginning, which can set the tone for a stronger working relationship later.

Pro Tip

For detailed, country-specific guides on visa processing times and procedures, visit https://www.teachenglishinkorea.org/blog/categories/e2-teaching-visa-process-for-korea. These walkthroughs cover each step for the United States, Canada, the United Kingdom, Australia, and other eligible countries, and are updated regularly as requirements change.

Teacher Story: When Going Direct Backfires

One teacher I worked with, let's call her Sarah, initially hit it off with me during our first conversation. I set up several interviews for her, and she received multiple job offers that matched exactly what she was looking for in terms of location, salary, and school size. But instead of accepting one, she turned them all down. She asked for more interviews, which I arranged, and again she received several offers. This time, however, some schools started rescinding their offers after days passed without a response.

Soon after, I learned that other recruiters had also submitted Sarah's résumé to the same schools, which made directors suspicious. From their perspective, she appeared to be "shopping around" too much, trying to leverage one offer against another. Eventually, after eight or nine interviews through me, she informed me that she had accepted a position directly with a school she had found herself. I wished her well, and she promised to recommend me to her friends.

But a few months later, Sarah started contacting me again, first for help obtaining an apostille for her FBI background check, then for guidance on completing her visa at the Korean Consulate, since her school wasn't providing any support. After she arrived in Korea, she reached out once more because she had fallen out with her school and wanted my help finding a new job. I had to explain that she could only change jobs if her school issued her a Letter of Release (LOR), which schools rarely provide unless there are extreme circumstances. Without it, she had to finish her contract before applying elsewhere.

Looking back, it was clear that most of her frustration stemmed from common cultural differences and standard working conditions that could have been smoothed over if she'd had someone to guide her. Without that support, her relationship with the director soured, making her situation much more complicated than it needed to be. Working with a recruiter would not guarantee success, but it would have significantly reduced the chances of something spiraling out of control if she had someone knowledgeable to ask questions before making a scene at her school with her management and ruining her work environment.

Takeaway: Applying directly can give you freedom and choice, but it also means you're on your own when issues arise. Without the buffer of a recruiter to mediate with schools or explain cultural norms, even minor misunderstandings can spiral into bigger problems. If you go direct, make sure you're ready to navigate every part of the process yourself.

Reading and Evaluating Job Contracts

Once you receive an offer, the most important thing you can do is slow down and carefully evaluate the contract before signing. Korean teaching contracts are legally binding documents, and while many schools are reputable, some cut corners or take advantage of new teachers' inexperience. A rushed decision here can shape your entire year abroad.

Salary Expectations

As of 2025, most first-year hagwon teachers earn between 2.4 and 2.6 million KRW per month. Teachers with experience, an education degree, or additional TEFL certifications may push that to 2.6 to 2.8 million KRW. At the top end, some elite hagwons and international schools pay over 3.0 million KRW, but these roles are competitive and often come with higher demands. During the pandemic, salaries temporarily increased because there were fewer applicants, and some of that competitiveness remains today.

Be cautious if a school offers significantly less than the market average. For example, I once saw a contract offering 2.1 million KRW with no housing benefits. That's well below standard and usually a sign of a struggling school. On the flip side, if a school offers a salary much higher than usual without a clear explanation (like longer hours or additional duties), it's worth asking why.

Housing Terms

Most contracts include free housing, usually a one-room studio apartment close to the school. This is a substantial financial benefit, but the quality varies widely. Some apartments are modern and comfortable; others are old, small, or poorly maintained. Always ask for photos of the actual apartment before you sign.

Often, schools offer a housing allowance instead (typically 400,000 to 600,000 KRW per month). While this can sound attractive, I strongly advise against it for first-year teachers. Renting in Korea is complex and often requires a large deposit ("key money") of thousands of dollars. Unless you already have local support, it's safer to take the housing provided.

Working Hours and Hidden Time

Many hagwon contracts state "30 teaching hours per week," but leave out the preparation, grading, and administrative work that isn't counted. A typical hagwon schedule runs from 9 a.m. to 6 p.m. (for kindergartens) or 2 p.m. to 10 p.m. (for elementary and middle school programs). New teachers often feel overwhelmed during the first three months, spending long, unpaid hours planning lessons. However, as I remind teachers, this gets easier because most hagwons cycle students every three months, meaning you'll reuse lesson plans and activities.

Public school contracts (via EPIK) usually require 22 to 25 teaching hours per week, with more downtime for planning. The hours are often more predictable (9 a.m. to 5 p.m.), but public schools may offer less flexibility in teaching style.

Vacation Policies

Vacation time is another critical area. Public schools generally offer 18 to 21 paid vacation days, plus national holidays. Hagwons, however, often provide only 11 days, and they are usually fixed according to the school's schedule. Watch for vague phrases like "vacation upon mutual agreement." In practice, that often means "whenever the director allows it," which could leave you with little control over your time off.

By contrast, large, well-organized chains like POLY publish an annual calendar through their headquarters, so vacation and holidays are clearly set in advance. That makes planning trips much easier. The red flags usually come from smaller schools that decide vacation days at the last minute, which frustrates teachers trying to plan travel.

Termination Clauses

Always check how termination is handled. A fair contract will require both parties to give 30 to 60 days' notice. Some schools include one-sided clauses that allow them to dismiss a teacher without notice or withhold the last month's salary; both are unfair and should be questioned.

I had a teacher once whose contract stated that "early termination by the teacher results in a penalty of one month's salary," while the school could terminate at any time with no penalty. That's a red flag and a reason to push back before signing.

Pro Tip

Don't gloss over the fine print. Schools expect you to read carefully. If something feels vague, ask for clarification and insist on details in writing. Once you arrive, verbal promises don't hold weight in disputes with immigration or labor boards.

Red flags to watch out for in job offers

Not all schools in Korea are equal. While many hagwons and public schools are professional and supportive, some schools cut corners, mislead teachers, or operate with poor management. Your contract and the way a school handles the hiring process can reveal a lot.

Vague or Missing Contract Terms

One of the most common red flags is when essential details like salary, working hours, or vacation days are vaguely written or omitted. If a contract says "vacation upon mutual agreement," it often means the director will decide when (or if) you get days off. That makes it impossible to plan trips or family visits. Large chains like POLY avoid this problem by publishing a yearly headquarters calendar for all branches. Teachers know precisely when their vacations and holidays are set. Smaller schools, on the other hand, may only tell you your vacation dates a few weeks before, a headache if you were hoping to travel outside Korea.

High Turnover Rates

Turnover among foreign teachers in Korea is common and, to a certain extent, expected. Many teachers come with the intention of staying just one year before returning home, traveling elsewhere, or moving on to graduate school or other careers. Others stay longer, two or three years is not unusual, but even these teachers may change schools once or twice to explore a new city, secure a higher salary, or improve their working conditions. In this sense, turnover by itself is not automatically a bad sign.

Where turnover becomes a red flag is when a school has a pattern of teachers leaving before finishing their contracts. This usually points to deeper issues such as poor management, late or missing salary payments, an unsupportive work environment, or excessive workload. If a school has cycled through multiple foreign teachers mid-year, it's a sign that the problem lies not with the teachers but with the school itself.

A good way to investigate is to ask how many foreign teachers currently work at the school, how long the longest-serving teacher has been there, and how many have left before finishing their contract in the last two years. For example, if a school has employed ten teachers over the last two years but six of them quit mid-contract, that's a red flag. On the other hand, if a school has a steady core of teachers who stay for two or three years before moving on, it likely means the school is at least reasonably well-run.

Always ask to speak with a current teacher, and not just the "Head Teacher" who may be acting as a buffer for management. A trustworthy school will have no problem connecting you with a couple of its current or recent foreign teachers. If they hesitate or dodge the request, that's a warning sign in itself.

Pressure to Sign Quickly

Another warning sign is when a school or recruiter pushes you to accept a contract immediately. Yes, schools may be under time pressure because visa processing takes four to six weeks, but you should never feel rushed. Take time to ask questions, review carefully, and compare with other offers. A recruiter or director who pressures you without allowing space for due diligence is usually hiding something.

Split Shifts and Unclear Scheduling

Some contracts, especially for adult-only academies, include split shifts (for example, 6 to 9 a.m. classes and then 7 to 10 p.m. classes). This leaves teachers with long, awkward breaks in the middle of the day and very little work-life balance. Unless you specifically want this schedule, be cautious.

Missing Legal Benefits

By Korean labor law, full-time foreign teachers are entitled to National Pension contributions and National Health Insurance. Some schools try to avoid these obligations by claiming teachers are "independent contractors." If your contract doesn't mention pension and health insurance, or if the school says they'll pay you "extra" instead of enrolling you, that's a red flag. Not only is it illegal, but it leaves you without essential protections.

Communication and Transparency

Finally, pay close attention to how the school or recruiter communicates with you. Delayed responses, evasive answers, or constantly changing details are all signs of poor management. I had a teacher once who noticed the director dodged her questions about housing three times. When she pressed harder, the truth came out: the school intended to house her with another foreign teacher in a shared apartment, something that was never mentioned in the original posting.

Pro Tip

If something feels "off," trust your instincts. A good school won't shy away from your questions. Ask for photos, speak to current teachers, and don't ignore vague or inconsistent answers. The schools that get defensive when you ask for clarity are the ones you'll regret signing with.

Teacher Story: When Higher Pay Came with Hidden Costs

One teacher I worked with decided to take a job offer from another recruiter because it promised slightly higher pay and was closer to central Seoul. At first, it seemed like a win. However, just three or four months into the contract, the teacher contacted me again, this time asking for help finding a new job.

It turned out that the "higher salary" was not what it seemed. The extra money was tied to teaching additional classes on top of the regular teaching load, which stretched the workday far longer than expected. On top of that, the contract required unpaid duties that weren't clear during the hiring process. For example, the teacher had to ride the kindergarten bus five mornings a week, helping pick up students for 45 minutes before classes even began. The school also provided free lunch, but teachers were required to eat with their kindergarten students, supervising them during lunch instead of having a proper break. What initially looked like a slightly better financial package quickly turned into a heavier workload and less downtime, leaving the teacher burned out and frustrated.

The moral of the story is simple: always read the contract carefully and ask the right questions before signing. When speaking with current teachers, avoid yes-or-no questions that don't reveal much. Instead, ask open-ended questions like, "What do you like and dislike about working at your school?" or "Can you describe what a typical day looks like for you?" These kinds of questions give teachers the chance to share both the positives and negatives of their experience, allowing you to make a more informed decision.

Takeaway: Higher pay can sometimes mask heavier workloads or hidden obligations. Don't just look at the numbers; dig deeper by asking current teachers about their day-to-day reality.

How to Interpret Teacher Feedback

When you reach out to current teachers about a school, the answers you get may not always be straightforward. Some schools are genuinely supportive, while others gloss over problems. Here's how to interpret what you hear, with examples of what counts as a reassuring response versus a red flag.

When you ask what someone likes most and least about working at their school, a balanced answer is a good sign. A teacher who says the kids are great and management is generally supportive, but that workload spikes around report-writing time, is giving you a realistic picture. Similarly, hearing that the curriculum is very structured and doesn't require much lesson planning, even if it feels a bit rigid, suggests a manageable environment. On the other hand, if you hear that the director doesn't communicate much and expectations change at the last minute, or that the workload isn't just heavy during certain times but heavy all the time with no help, those are signs of deeper problems.

Asking about a typical workday is equally revealing. A teacher describes teaching five or six classes a day with prep time between them, a consistent schedule, and roughly 30 teaching hours per week, which describes a standard hagwon environment. However, if you hear that the hours on paper are 30 per week but the teacher ends up working from morning to night because of extra duties, or that they're expected to ride the kindergarten bus every morning and supervise lunch without additional pay, that suggests the contract understates the real workload.

Questions about late pay, housing, and management issues can surface the most critical problems. Hearing that pay is always on time, the apartment was clean and ready upon arrival, and the director is approachable are all reassuring. But if pay is sometimes late by a week or two, if the apartment had mold and the school took months to address it, or if the director avoids talking about problems, those are serious warning signs that your experience will likely be similar.

Finally, asking what someone would change about their job reveals whether complaints are normal frustrations or systemic issues. Wishing for a bit more vacation time while acknowledging the school sticks to the contract is a reasonable gripe. Wanting smaller class sizes, while recognizing it's beyond the school's control, is normal. But if a teacher says they would change the management because they don't respect the contract, or that teachers often quit before finishing their contracts, or that the atmosphere is stressful and people don't usually stay long, those are the answers that should make you seriously reconsider.

Pro Tip

No school is perfect, and every job will come with regular teacher duties like grading, lesson prep, or writing student reports. What you're really listening for are the uncommon issues that signal deeper problems: late pay, poor communication, contract violations, or a generally toxic work environment. A good teacher reference should sound balanced, with both positives and some minor drawbacks. If the feedback is all negative, or oddly too positive, it's worth digging deeper before signing.

Negotiating Your Offer

Negotiation in Korea works a little differently than in many Western countries. While you should always be polite and professional, it's normal to ask clarifying questions and even request modest improvements. Salaries are often the most flexible area, especially if you have teaching experience, a TEFL certificate, or multiple offers. For example, if one school offers 2.5 million KRW per month and another offers 2.6 million KRW, you can tactfully say, "I'm really interested in your school, but I do have another offer at 2.6. Would it be possible to match that?" This isn't considered rude if phrased professionally; it shows you know your value.

Housing, however, is less open to negotiation. Most schools either provide a free studio apartment or offer a housing stipend (usually 400,000 to 600,000 KRW). Some schools own their apartments, and in those cases, there's little room for alternatives. Shared housing is rare unless you're married, and even then, not every school is willing to arrange it. For unmarried couples or same-sex couples, it may be wiser to accept two separate studios, as Korean directors can be conservative and may worry that hiring couples could create management complications. If you are able to negotiate a one-bedroom apartment instead of two studios, be prepared to contribute a little extra each month, since larger housing is typically more expensive. Schools located outside of Seoul and Gyeonggi-do tend to be more flexible when negotiating.

Vacation time, prep hours, and extra duties are also worth clarifying. Contracts sometimes bury additional responsibilities (like attending school events or riding the kindergarten bus) without listing them as official teaching hours. You may not be able to eliminate these duties, but asking current teachers how the school handles them can help you decide if the trade-off is acceptable. Similarly, if a director makes verbal promises, like extra vacation days or bonuses, always insist on having them written into the contract before signing. In Korea, if it isn't on paper, it doesn't exist.

The most effective way to approach negotiation is with curiosity rather than demands. Ask questions like, "Is there flexibility on the salary for someone with TEFL training?" or "Could you clarify how prep hours are handled at your school?" Directors appreciate teachers who communicate clearly and respectfully, and you'll gain a clearer picture of whether the job is genuinely a good fit.

Teacher Story: Negotiating for Pets

One of my teachers, April, was determined to bring her two cats with her to Korea. This is becoming increasingly common, but it poses challenges — more than 70% of schools cannot allow pets because they don't own the apartments they provide; instead, they lease them from landlords, who typically forbid animals. In April's case, the school really wanted to hire her, but the landlord of their contracted housing had a strict "no pets" rule. At first, it looked like the school would have to rescind its offer.

Instead of giving up, I suggested a compromise: April offered a $600 pet deposit to reassure the landlord that any potential damages would be covered. The school took this proposal to the landlord, who agreed, and the problem was solved. I then drafted a simple pet deposit addendum for the school to attach to April's contract. This not only secured her job but also allowed her to bring her cats without jeopardizing her placement.

Takeaway: Negotiation in Korea isn't just about salary or housing; it's often about creative problem-solving. If something is important to you, whether it's bringing a pet, arranging a different housing option, or clarifying duties, don't assume it's impossible. Schools and landlords can sometimes be flexible if you approach the issue with a practical solution that protects their interests as well as yours.

Teacher Story: Negotiating Couple Housing in Daejeon

I once worked with a teaching couple placed in Daejeon, a city about 45 minutes from Seoul by KTX or 1.5 hours by bus. Their school offered them two brand-new studio apartments in a modern officetel. Each unit came with built-in appliances like an oven/microwave, a washer, and closets. Everything was clean and contemporary. But there was one problem: the spaces were too cramped for them to live together comfortably. The school gave them the option to either take both studios or share one while collecting a 400,000 KRW stipend for the second unit.

Instead, the couple requested something different: a one-bedroom apartment with a separate sleeping area. Because they often went to bed at various times, they needed two distinct spaces in their home. The school took their request seriously and found a one-bedroom unit nearby. The catch was that it was 200,000 KRW more per month than the combined cost of two studios, and the deposit was higher as well. To make it work, the school proposed that the couple contribute an extra 100,000 KRW each per month. The couple happily agreed.

What impressed me most was how the school handled the process; they did a walk-through of the one-bedroom unit, filmed it, and even provided the blueprint from the real estate office so the couple could clearly visualize the space. This small compromise on both sides resulted in a much better living arrangement for the teachers, while keeping the school's budget reasonable.

Takeaway: If you have specific housing needs, it never hurts to ask. Schools may not always say yes, but when you present your request reasonably and offer to share part of the cost, many are willing to work with you.

Final Thoughts

Negotiation is not about squeezing every possible benefit out of a school; it's about ensuring clarity and fairness. Salary is sometimes flexible, housing usually isn't, and everything must be written into the contract. Remember, no teaching job in Korea will be perfect; every role comes with routine responsibilities like lesson planning, grading, and reports. What you want to identify are the less common red flags: unclear contracts, poor management, stressful work culture, or schools that won't follow through on promises.

If you approach this stage with patience, professionalism, and the willingness to ask thoughtful questions, you'll not only protect yourself from future headaches but also position yourself as the kind of thoughtful, reliable candidate schools want to hire. Whether it's bringing a pet, negotiating housing as a couple, or simply asking for details about workload, the key is to frame your requests as practical solutions rather than demands. Schools and directors appreciate it when a candidate brings a thoughtful, win-win approach to the table. You're not just asking for something; you're showing that you care about making the placement work smoothly for everyone involved.

In the next chapter, we'll cover the interview process itself, what to expect, how to prepare, and how to present yourself in a way that makes directors confident you're the right hire.

Chapter 7: Acing the Interview Process

Chapter Summary

This chapter prepares you for the interview stage of teaching in Korea. You will learn what Korean school directors and recruiters are really looking for, how to prepare for common interview questions and deliver strong, detailed answers, how to showcase key traits like teamwork, adaptability, and enthusiasm, and how to avoid common pitfalls that cause strong candidates to lose offers. You will also learn the cultural nuances of communicating effectively with Korean interviewers and how to set up a professional video interview.

Why This Chapter Matters

Your resume may open the door, but your interview determines whether you get to walk through it. In Korea, interviews carry enormous weight because schools aren't just hiring an English teacher; they're inviting someone into their community. A polished application shows that you are qualified on paper, but the interview reveals whether you can bring energy, professionalism, and warmth into the classroom.

For many directors, the decision is made in the first one to two minutes. If you appear disinterested, stiff, or unprepared, the interview will be short, often ending with a polite "We'll be in touch." On the other hand, if you greet the interviewer with a warm smile, clear communication, and genuine enthusiasm, many directors will quickly feel confident they've found the right teacher.

It's also important to understand that Korean interview styles differ from those in the West. Some directors may ask very few questions, focusing instead on how you present yourself, how clearly you speak, and whether your personality matches their school culture. Others may conduct long, detailed interviews that even include a school tour. Both approaches are standard, and the variation often depends on the director's personality and experience.

Another crucial distinction is between hagwon and public-school interviews. Hagwon interviews tend to be personality-driven: directors want bubbly, outgoing, and approachable teachers, especially for kindergarten and elementary levels. EPIK interviews, by contrast, are more structured and formal. They emphasize professionalism, lesson planning ability, and cultural adaptability rather than just energy and friendliness.

Pro Tip

The key takeaway here is simple: in Korea, interviews are not just about verifying your resume; they are about evaluating whether you can fit into the school environment. Your ability to project positivity, adaptability, and teamwork will matter just as much as your qualifications.

Understanding What Schools Are Looking For

While your resume may have secured the interview, it's your presence, attitude, and communication skills that will ultimately earn you the job. Korean private school directors are not just hiring an English teacher; they are inviting someone into their school community. They're looking for teachers who are not only competent in the classroom but also contribute positively to the school culture, get along well with local staff, and connect with students and parents. You must keep in mind that Korean directors will choose a person with a more outgoing, talkative, and friendly character over a teacher who is better qualified, because they want teachers whom they can mold and shape, but who will, more importantly, not cause problems at their school. Teacher skills can be taught, but changing a person's character is not easy, even if it is possible to do.

Team Spirit

Team spirit is one of the most highly valued traits. Directors want to know that you can collaborate effectively with Korean co-teachers and fellow foreign staff. Be ready to share specific examples of successful teamwork from your past, whether from a university group project, a previous job, or volunteer work. For instance, you could describe a time you worked with a co-teacher to modify a lesson on short notice. You might explain, "My co-teacher and I realized a planned activity wasn't working, so we quickly brainstormed a new game using flashcards. It not only salvaged the lesson but made it even more fun and effective." This kind of flexibility and cooperation is exactly what Korean schools are looking for. They want to see that you are a positive, solutions-oriented person who can be a part of the team.

Adaptability

Adaptability is equally essential. Teaching in Korea will involve unexpected changes in your schedule, curriculum, or classroom dynamics. Highlight moments in your past where you successfully adjusted to change. Did you travel or live abroad and have to navigate a new environment? Did you have to modify a teaching plan on the fly or take on new responsibilities in a prior role? These experiences show that you can handle the cultural and professional transitions that come with teaching overseas. An example could be, "When I was working at a summer camp, our schedule was completely changed due to a rainstorm. I had to quickly pivot from outdoor games to an indoor craft project, which taught me the importance of being flexible and prepared for anything.

Enthusiasm and Friendliness

Enthusiasm and friendliness should shine through naturally during the interview. Smile genuinely, speak clearly, and maintain a warm and open demeanor. Korean schools often look for teachers who can energize a room, even when the students are shy or hesitant. If you appear cold, disinterested, or flat, schools may worry that you'll struggle to engage students, especially younger learners who need a vibrant and interactive teacher. This is especially true for hagwon positions, where a teacher's energy is a key selling point to parents.

Growth Mindset

Another desirable quality is a growth mindset. Make it clear that you're not only ready to teach but also eager to learn about Korean education, their curriculum, classroom expectations, and teaching methodologies. Expressing a willingness to grow professionally helps reassure schools that you'll take feedback well and remain committed to improvement. This is particularly comforting to a school director who will be investing a significant amount of time and resources into you.

Love for Children

Perhaps most importantly, communicate your genuine love for children. Korean private schools, especially kindergartens and elementary hagwons, want teachers who care deeply about their students' learning and well-being. You might say, "One of the things I find most rewarding about teaching young learners is seeing their faces light up when they understand something new. I love building those positive relationships and helping students feel confident using English, even when it's difficult." Showing passion for students' development makes a lasting impression.

During the interview, avoid giving vague or overly short answers. Korean interviewers tend to appreciate detail and clarity. When you respond to a question, take your time and provide a complete explanation, even if that means speaking for a full minute or two. This shows that you are communicative, thoughtful, and engaged in the conversation

Teacher Story: Switching Into "Teacher Mode"

One of my favorite teachers, Alexis, really impressed me when I first met her seven or eight years ago at one of our teacher networking dinners. Over dinner, she told me about her journey before Korea and how her first six months had gone so far. By nature, she described herself as more reserved and introverted, having worked in IT where she rarely had to interact with people. Yet, she had always been fascinated by Korea and Korean culture and dreamed of becoming a teacher.

When she arrived in Korea, she discovered something remarkable: she could switch into what she called her "Teacher Alexis" mode. In the classroom, she became outgoing, fun, bubbly, and chatty, the complete opposite of how she felt in her private life. She told me it wasn't stressful because she treated it as a role she could step into. On weekends, she recharged by spending time alone so she could bring her full energy back into the classroom each week.

Her approach worked beautifully. Within her first year, she became one of the school's best teachers, and by her second year, she was promoted to head teacher. I admired not only her positive energy but also the way she mentored new teachers. She became a regular at our networking dinners, where she always took time to meet newcomers, share advice, and check in on how they were adjusting.

Today, Alexis is still in Korea, married to a Korean national, and has started a family. Her story shows that being naturally introverted doesn't mean you can't succeed as a teacher in Korea. If you can find your own version of "teacher mode," and balance it with self-care outside of work, you can thrive in the classroom and beyond.

Takeaway: You don't have to change who you are to succeed in Korea. Instead, learn to channel your best qualities in the classroom and give yourself the time you need to recharge.

Thriving as an Introverted Teacher

If you're naturally introverted, don't assume that will hold you back in Korea. Many successful teachers, like Alexis, learn to step into a more energetic "teacher mode" during class while still protecting their downtime outside of school. The key is balance.

Think of your classroom energy like a performance: enthusiastic, animated, and engaging, but only for a few hours at a time. Schedule recovery time by planning quiet weekends, solo hobbies, or nature walks so you can recharge before Monday. Use structure to reduce stress by building solid lesson plans and reliable routines, which means you can save energy for connecting with students rather than improvising. And leverage your natural strengths, since introverts often excel at listening, observing, and connecting one-on-one, skills that help build strong relationships with students and co-workers.

Korean schools don't expect every foreign teacher to be a comedian or an extrovert. They want consistency, warmth, and student engagement. If you can manage your energy wisely, being introverted can actually be a hidden strength. Like Alexis, many successful teachers learn how to flip into a more outgoing, high-energy version of themselves when teaching. This doesn't mean being fake; it means projecting warmth, positivity, and engagement for the sake of your students. Schools don't expect you to be "on" all the time, but they do expect you to bring energy to the classroom.

Common Interview Questions and How to Answer

One of the most significant advantages you can give yourself in an interview is preparation. Korean school directors and recruiters tend to ask predictable questions, but they are evaluating more than just your words; they are gauging your energy, clarity, attitude, and cultural fit. Below are the most common interview questions, along with guidance on what directors are really listening for and how to deliver answers that stand out.

"Why do you want to teach in Korea?"

This question appears in nearly every interview, and it's your chance to show sincerity. Avoid shallow answers like "I love K-pop" or "I want to travel in Asia." While those may be true, schools are hiring teachers, not tourists. A strong answer puts teaching, growth, and children first, with culture and travel as secondary motivations. You might say something like, "I've always been passionate about teaching and working with children. Korea stood out to me because of its strong commitment to education, and I want to be part of that learning environment." Or you could frame it around personal growth: "I want to challenge myself professionally and personally. Teaching in Korea allows me to grow as an educator while immersing myself in a new culture." Directors want to hear that you've thought seriously about the role, not just the lifestyle.

"How do you handle a class with mixed ability levels?"

This is very common, as Korean classrooms often include students at widely different proficiency levels. A weak answer would be something vague like "I try to help the weaker students when I can," because it shows no clear strategy. A much stronger response is to explain that you design activities with different levels built in. For example, you might use differentiated tasks where higher-level students get extension activities or act as peer helpers, while beginners receive more scaffolding like sentence frames and visuals. Another practical approach is pairing strong and weaker students together so both benefit: the advanced student reinforces what they know, while the other gets peer support. You could also mention using grouping strategies, sometimes mixing levels so students can learn from each other, and sometimes grouping by ability so you can give tailored instructions. Directors love hearing this because it shows you're not going to leave anyone behind and that you understand the reality of Korean classrooms.

"How would you deal with a disruptive student?"

This question is less about discipline and more about emotional control. Discipline is handled differently in Korea than in many Western countries, and Korean directors expect teachers to remain calm, respectful, and solution-focused. If you answer "I'd discipline them quickly so the lesson isn't disrupted," it can sound too harsh and rigid. A better response is to talk about starting with subtle, non-verbal cues like eye contact, moving closer to the student, or tapping a desk to redirect behavior quietly. If the issue continues, you can calmly remind the student of the rules or speak to them privately instead of embarrassing them in front of classmates. Mentioning that you'd consult with your Korean co-teacher for cultural context is also a strong move. Directors want to know you won't yell, lose your temper, or show disrespect; keeping harmony is valued in Korean classrooms.

"What is your teaching style or philosophy?"

Directors want to hear that you can engage students and that you prioritize participation over lecture. They don't want to hear "I just follow the book," because that suggests passivity. Instead, you might say, "I focus on creating a student-centered classroom where children are speaking and active rather than just listening. I like using games, role-plays, and songs to make lessons fun and memorable." Another strong angle is to emphasize confidence-building: "I believe students learn best when they feel safe to make mistakes. My priority is helping them build confidence, because once they're willing to try, their skills improve naturally." Directors don't need you to reference educational theory; they want to know parents will see their children speaking more English because of your teaching. Keep your answer short, clear, and enthusiastic.

"How do you stay organized and plan your lessons?"

This question separates professionals from those who might "wing it." A vague answer like "I just go with the flow" is a red flag. A stronger reply is to say that you use structured lesson plan templates with clear objectives and timing for each stage, and that you keep backup activities ready in case a lesson ends early. You could mention that you maintain a binder or digital folder of flashcards, worksheets, and games you can quickly adapt. The key is to show you have systems in place, because Korean schools prize reliability and preparation as much as charisma. Schools fear teachers who "wing it," so show that you are systematic, dependable, and punctual.

"What are your long-term goals?"

Sometimes directors ask about your long-term goals. This is not a trap, but it's not the place to say "I just want to travel for a year." That makes you sound unserious. A better approach is to explain that you want to grow as a teacher and see where the experience takes you. For example: "In the short term, I want to become an effective classroom teacher in Korea. Long term, I'd love to develop professionally, whether that means staying in Korea longer, mentoring other teachers, or pursuing graduate study in education." Schools know most teachers only stay a year, but they prefer hearing that you're at least open to staying longer and investing in the role.

In all these questions, the pattern is the same: avoid short, vague, or overly casual answers. Directors appreciate clarity, detail, and evidence that you've thought carefully about teaching in Korea. They don't expect perfection, but they want to see preparation, professionalism, and personality.

Teacher Story: Mark the Rambler

Mark, one of the most positive and outgoing teachers I've ever met, showed me both the strengths and pitfalls of enthusiasm during interviews. In his very first mock interview with me, I asked the standard question: "Why do you want to teach in Korea?" He leaned forward, smiled, and dove into a five-minute response that started strong but quickly went off track.

At first, he highlighted his love of adventure, his passion for travel, and the fact that he had minored in Asian Studies, all excellent points that schools would appreciate. But then his answer spiraled into commentary about the job market in the U.S., his frustrations with the current political climate, and how his major hadn't opened many doors. By the time he wrapped up, he hadn't let me interject once, and the core of his message had been lost.

Afterward, I gave him some tough but constructive feedback: keep the chatty, positive energy, that's one of his best assets, but cut out the rambling. I told him to imagine his answers like mini-stories, with a clear beginning, middle, and end. I also suggested he avoid overloading on coffee or energy drinks before an interview, since he admitted those made him even more prone to nervous rambling. He laughed and confessed that when he was anxious, he had a hard time stopping once he started talking.

To his credit, Mark took the coaching seriously. His second interview was tighter, and by his third, he was nailing it, focused, confident, and still warm and engaging. He learned that schools love passion, but they want it packaged in a clear, professional response.

Takeaway: Enthusiasm can win interviews, but only when it's balanced with structure. Keep answers clear and concise, and remember, sometimes less really is more. However, it is always better to say too much than not enough.

Teacher Story: When Being Professional Came Across as Cold

Jasmine, a licensed teacher from the UK with a Bachelor of Education degree and several years of middle school experience, seemed like a dream candidate on paper. She had strong credentials, a crystal-clear accent, and the polished look schools often like. Yet, after three interviews, she received no job offers. Frustrated, she asked me why.

The feedback from directors was surprisingly consistent. While Jasmine came across as professional, they described her as cold, strict, and not particularly friendly. Two interviewers said bluntly that she might be excellent in a middle school, but she wasn't suited for teaching kindergarten, which is where most foreign teachers in Korea are placed. Another director noted that Jasmine asked no questions at the end of the interview, which they took as a sign she wasn't really interested in their school.

Jasmine was shocked. She believed she had "nailed" the interviews by being concise, formal, and focused on her credentials. What she didn't realize was that by giving short, serious answers, she had failed to show warmth, enthusiasm, or any love for children, the very qualities schools prize most. She also hadn't mentioned her passion for teaching or working with young learners. Instead, she emphasized her certifications and her experience teaching older students, which reinforced the impression that she wasn't a good fit for kindergarten.

After hearing this feedback, Jasmine adjusted her approach. She practiced smiling more during interviews, allowed her personality to come through, and made sure to explain that her primary motivation for teaching was her love of children. She also registered for a 40-hour Young Learners TEFL course, which gave her practical strategies and talking points tailored to Korean kindergartens. In her following two interviews, she came across as warm and eager, and both resulted in job offers.

Takeaway: Professionalism is essential, but in Korea, directors hire people who seem friendly, approachable, and passionate about working with kids. Even experienced, credentialed teachers need to show warmth and enthusiasm, not just qualifications.

Cultural Communication Tips

When interviewing with Korean schools, it's important to remember that you are not only communicating across languages, but across cultures. The interviewer will almost always be Korean, and their English ability will range from conversational to near-native. That means clarity is far more valuable than complexity. Avoid using academic or overly technical English in an attempt to impress. Instead, speak slowly, clearly, and with warmth. Simple, confident sentences carry far more weight than jargon or convoluted explanations.

Interviews in Korea also vary widely in length and style. Some directors prefer to keep things short, finishing within 15 to 20 minutes. In these cases, they usually know within the first minute whether they want to hire you. Small details, your accent, how much you smile, and whether you seem friendly and approachable can outweigh the content of your answers. Other directors may hold much longer interviews, sometimes 60 to 90 minutes, which can include a school tour, introductions to staff, or even time spent observing classes. The goal in these longer sessions is not just to evaluate your answers, but to see if you fit into the school's culture and environment.

The biggest cultural expectation to understand is that Korean schools, especially hagwons, want teachers who appear happy, smiley, bubbly, and energetic. This isn't superficial; it's rooted in how parents evaluate teachers. Directors know that parents often judge the quality of a school based on whether their child's foreign teacher seems friendly, approachable, and good with children. If you appear too serious, cold, or disengaged during the interview, a director may worry that you'll struggle to connect with students, no matter how strong your qualifications are.

Another cultural nuance is the balance between humility and confidence. In Western interviews, it's common to "sell yourself" boldly. In Korea, schools prefer candidates who show confidence but balance it with respect, gratitude, and humility. Saying things like, "I'm very excited to learn from your school's curriculum while also contributing my own ideas" demonstrates both confidence and adaptability.

Finally, don't underestimate non-verbal communication. Maintain steady eye contact with the camera, nod slightly to show attentiveness, and smile naturally throughout. These small cues go a long way in communicating warmth and sincerity, qualities that are often weighted just as heavily as your teaching skills.

Teacher Story: When Qualifications Aren't Enough

Tom looked perfect on paper. He had a secondary education degree, a 120-hour TEFL certificate, and years of one-on-one tutoring experience both online and offline in Canada. He also volunteered regularly, building up plenty of hours working with learners. On the surface, he was the kind of candidate most recruiters would be thrilled to present.

But during my interview with him, I noticed something concerning: he struggled to make eye contact with the camera. Even after I gave him feedback, this carried over into his school interviews as well. His answers were satisfactory, but his delivery was flat, and his lack of eye contact came across as distant and unconfident. Directors later told me that while he was qualified, they worried about how he would handle a classroom of energetic children when he couldn't project presence even in a one-on-one interview.

When I pressed him further, Tom admitted that it wasn't just shyness. He struggled with imposter syndrome and had long felt uncomfortable speaking in front of groups. He preferred tutoring because it felt safe, but a classroom of ten to fifteen Korean students felt daunting. I told him honestly that teaching in Korea might not be the right path, not because he lacked intelligence or heart, but because the demands of a Korean hagwon would likely push him into situations he wasn't ready for. Parents in Korea expect visible energy, warmth, and engagement from foreign teachers, and repeated complaints about a teacher's demeanor often led to non-renewals or even early dismissal.

A few months later, Tom contacted me again. He had taken a position in a small school in Gwangju through another recruiter. By the fourth month, the school had decided to let him go, citing his inability to connect with the students. Although he had a letter of release, I could not in good conscience recommend him to another one of my partner schools, because I knew the same issues would repeat.

The hard truth is that teaching in Korea is not for everyone. It's not just about surviving 5,000 miles from home or meeting the minimum visa requirements; it's about thriving in a lively, sometimes demanding classroom environment. Before applying, you need to know yourself and be honest about whether you have the confidence, resilience, and presence to succeed in a Korean classroom.

Takeaway: Qualifications get you in the door, but personality and presence keep you in the classroom. If you struggle with self-confidence or group settings, it's essential to work on these skills before committing to a year-long teaching contract in Korea.

Building Your Presence Before You Arrive

Not everyone is naturally bubbly or extroverted, and that's okay, but in Korea, schools expect teachers to project warmth, confidence, and energy in the classroom. If you're shy or worried about your stage presence, you can prepare ahead of time. Record yourself filming a one-minute practice introduction on your phone and watch it back, noticing your tone, eye contact, and body language, then repeat until you look and sound confident. Role-play with friends by practicing explaining simple concepts or leading a short activity with friends or family, since the more you simulate a classroom, the more natural it will feel. If possible, start small by volunteering with a small group of kids or tutoring a few students before heading to Korea, as building confidence in smaller groups helps prepare you for full classrooms. And remember the mindset shift: "Teacher You" doesn't have to be the same as your private self. Many successful teachers, like Alexis, flip into a more outgoing "teacher mode" in class, then recharge afterward. Korean directors don't expect you to be a stand-up comedian, but they do expect you to show enthusiasm and engage students. Confidence and presence can be learned with practice, so start building those habits now.

How to Prepare for Video Interviews

Since nearly all interviews for teaching positions in Korea are conducted online, your video call setup is as important as your resume. Many school directors will meet you once and base their entire hiring decision on that short conversation. That means small details like your background, how you hold your phone, or whether you smile can make or break the offer.

Platforms You'll Encounter

Most schools today use Microsoft Teams (which replaced Skype), KakaoTalk (카카오톡), Google Meet, or Zoom. My schools primarily use Teams since it makes it easy for me to set up three-way calls between the teacher and the school. For smaller or more traditional schools that haven't fully transitioned, Kakao is still common. Before your interview, always check which platform will be used, test it ahead of time, and make sure your audio and video are working correctly.

Camera Setup and Professionalism

Never hold your phone in your hand or prop it at a bad angle. I've seen teachers rest their phone on a desk, pointing upward at their chin, or walk around during the interview while holding it; both look unprofessional and distracting. Use a stationary setup, ideally a laptop on a desk, or if you're using a phone, secure it in place at eye level. Keep the camera steady, frame your head and shoulders, and look into the lens as though you're speaking to the director directly.

Background and Environment

Your background should reinforce the idea that you're teacher-ready. Directors notice everything. Messy laundry piles, unmade beds, or cluttered desks distract from your professionalism. The best option is a clean, neutral wall. A world map, a poster, or even a tidy bookshelf can give off a "teachery" vibe. One of my favorite setups was a candidate who used a simple poster with English phrases behind her; it made her look like she was already in a classroom.

Lighting and Sound

Light should face you, not come from behind. Sitting in front of a bright window will put your face in shadow. Position a lamp or sit near a window with natural light in front of you. For sound, headphones with a microphone usually work best; they reduce echo and ensure the director hears your answers clearly. Test this in advance so you're not fumbling during the actual interview.

Attire

Dress business casual, not overly formal. Men should wear a collared shirt without a tie; women can wear a blouse or a collared shirt. If you overdress in a suit, you may come across as strict or too uptight. Schools want teachers who are approachable, not intimidating. Cover tattoos if possible, remove facial piercings, and if you insist on wearing a nose ring, choose a small stud instead of a hoop. Remember, schools are conservative, and parents often sit in on demo lessons, so your first impression matters. Schools prefer clean-shaven men. If you are willing, shave off your beard, have the interview, then grow it back. If you do not want to shave your beard, keep it short, tight, and well-groomed.

Delivery and Demeanor

Smiling is non-negotiable. Many directors have told me they decide in the first minute of an interview based on whether a candidate seems friendly and outgoing. Teachers who look stiff, unsmiling, or too quiet are almost always passed over. At the same time, don't overdo it with nervous chatter or coffee-fueled energy. Keep answers clear and focused, usually about one to two minutes. Speak slowly, at a steady pace, and give specific examples rather than vague generalities.

There are several common pitfalls I've seen that are worth avoiding. Teachers walking around while holding their phones looks unprofessional, as do untidy bedrooms or piles of laundry visible behind them. Reading directly from a script, with eyes darting side to side, is immediately obvious and off-putting. Speaking in monotone or never smiling once makes directors assume you'll be flat in the classroom. Dressing too casually in hoodies or T-shirts suggests you don't take the role seriously, while dressing too formally in a three-piece suit can make you seem unapproachable. Wearing excessive makeup, visible piercings, or extreme hairstyles can also work against you, as Korean schools tend to be conservative. Each of these distracts from your strengths and suggests you may not adapt well to a Korean classroom.

Pro Tip

Think like a school director. They are imagining you in front of their students. If your interview environment is clean, your smile is warm, and your personality is engaging, they will assume your classroom will be the same. If you seem distracted, messy, or flat, they'll assume that's what their students will see too.

Teacher Story: When Flexibility Isn't What It Seems

A few years ago, I worked with a couple, Mark and Stacy, who looked great on paper. They were friendly and qualified, and during my initial conversation with them, they stressed how flexible they were. They knew that being placed as a couple, especially in Seoul, was a challenge, so they assured me repeatedly that they would be adaptable to whatever situation arose.

During their interview with a school director, however, that supposed flexibility quickly unraveled. Stacy dominated most of the conversation, speaking about 70% of the time, while Mark contributed about 30%. When the director asked if they could adapt to Korean culture, they both eagerly insisted that they could. But then came the question that derailed the entire interview: the director asked Mark if he could shave his beard. It wasn't a long or scruffy beard, just a week's worth of neatly trimmed stubble. Mark responded immediately that he would not shave his beard for any reason. Stacy quickly jumped in, doubling down, saying his beard was part of his identity and that he hadn't shaved since his college days.

Instead of leaving it there, both Mark and Stacy launched into what felt like a lecture on personal identity and individualism, explaining that his beard was who he was and asking why it should matter. The director listened politely, then ended the interview soon after. Later, he told me, "If they are this stubborn about a beard, imagine how stubborn they will be about other things." Needless to say, they weren't offered the position.

I relayed the feedback to them, and Mark was visibly offended. I tried to soften it by sharing my own story. When I arrived in Korea years ago, I too had a short stubble beard. On my very first day, the staff presented me with a gift: a shaving kit. When I laughed and explained that I usually kept my beard short, the head teacher smiled and said, "We understand, but your face looks dirty." I took it in stride, shaved that evening, and moved on. To me, a beard was like a shirt; I could change it at any time, no big deal. But for Mark, it was a non-negotiable. More than that, he took offense to even the suggestion and, instead of saying something like, "OK, I will consider that," finishing the interview and then declining an offer if given, he decided to lecture the interviewer.

Takeaway: While schools appreciate individuality, Korean employers place a high value on appearance, professionalism, and cultural fit. A small compromise, like shaving or covering tattoos, can be the difference between landing a job and losing one. Inflexibility over minor issues signals to schools that you may struggle to adapt in more significant areas. Save your energy for things that truly matter, like workload expectations or contract terms, not a five-minute shave.

Avoid These Common Mistakes

One of the most frustrating ways to lose an otherwise solid opportunity is by making small but preventable mistakes during your interview. These aren't about lacking experience or credentials;

they're about how you present yourself in those critical first minutes with a school director.

Overly Short or Vague Answers

Many teachers sabotage themselves by giving answers that are too short or vague. If you're asked, "Why do you want to teach in Korea?" and you respond with, "I like kids and I want to travel," you've already lost the chance to stand out. Korean directors value detailed, thoughtful answers that show genuine preparation. A stronger answer would be: "I enjoy working with young learners because I find their energy and curiosity inspiring. I'm also fascinated by Korean culture and history, and I see teaching in Korea as both a professional opportunity and a chance to immerse myself in the culture long term." Notice the difference; it's specific, personal, and professional.

Sounding Too Stern or Serious

On the flip side, some teachers believe professionalism means being overly formal, serious, or "all business." Several of my directors have told me they passed on candidates because they "looked too strict" or "seemed cold." Smiling naturally, using an enthusiastic tone, and showing warmth are crucial, especially for kindergarten and elementary positions. Professionalism doesn't mean rigidity; it means showing that you can lead a classroom and engage children in a way that makes learning fun.

Poor Engagement with the Interviewer

Another common pitfall is failing to engage with the interviewer. Korean interviewers expect you to show curiosity about their school. If you don't ask any questions at the end, they may assume you're uninterested or only focused on getting "a job" rather than this job. I've seen excellent candidates rejected because they failed to ask a single follow-up question. At a minimum, ask about the curriculum, class sizes, or what qualities they look for in successful teachers at their school. This not only shows genuine interest; it also gives you insight into whether the school is a good fit for you.

Talking Too Much or About the Wrong Things

Rambling is another issue. I've had teachers talk for five minutes straight about unrelated topics like politics, the economy back home, or their personal frustrations. Directors lose interest quickly when you go off-topic. Be concise, stay focused on teaching, and save the rest for conversations after you've built rapport in Korea. If you tend to get nervous and ramble, practice your answers beforehand and time yourself. Keep your responses in the 60 to 90 second range: long enough to show substance, but short enough to keep the director engaged.

Unprofessional Demeanor

Finally, avoid unprofessional behaviors that sometimes creep into online interviews. I've seen candidates chew gum, slump in their chairs, use casual slang, or speak as though they're chatting with a friend. Remember: this is an interview for a professional teaching role, and Korean directors expect respect, poise, and maturity. Sit up straight, speak clearly, and treat the conversation as if you were already a member of their teaching staff.

Pro Tip

The directors who hire most often tell me they're looking for someone who is both reliable and fun. That means your answers should be thoughtful and detailed, but your tone should remain warm, positive, and approachable. Think of it as a balance: serious enough to reassure them you'll show up every day, but friendly enough that they can picture you winning over a class of five-year-olds.

Questions You Should Ask the School

One of the easiest ways to stand out in an interview is by asking thoughtful questions. Many candidates mistakenly think that keeping quiet shows professionalism, but in Korea, it often has the opposite effect; it can make you appear disinterested or passive. Korean directors want to hire teachers who are engaged, curious, and proactive, not people who are simply looking for a paycheck. Asking the right questions shows that you are serious about the role and that you are already imagining yourself in their classrooms and school community.

It's essential to ask about what kind of training and onboarding you'll receive. For example, you might ask, "What kind of training do you provide for new teachers, and how long does it usually last?" or "How do you support teachers during their first few weeks?" Directors appreciate this because it shows humility and a willingness to learn. It also gives you insight into how smoothly your transition will go. A school that offers structured orientation and mentoring will likely be a better fit than one that expects you to figure things out on your own.

Another strong line of questioning involves curriculum. Instead of assuming you'll have free rein in the classroom, ask, "Is the curriculum fully prepared, or will I be expected to design lessons from scratch?" and "How much flexibility do teachers have to add their own activities to lessons?" Some schools have a very rigid set of books and scripts, while others expect teachers to prepare everything from scratch. The answer here can drastically affect your workload and your teaching style, so asking upfront helps you avoid surprises.

Schools also like it when candidates are interested in their teaching environment. Asking questions such as, "What is the typical class size and age range of the students?" or "What role does the Korean co-teacher play during lessons?" shows that you are thinking about how you will adapt your teaching methods to fit their specific needs. Korean classrooms run differently from Western ones, so directors value candidates who want to understand the structure before arriving.

Culture is just as important as curriculum. Asking, "How would you describe the relationship between foreign teachers and Korean staff?" or "What qualities make a teacher successful at your school?" often sparks helpful answers that reveal how supportive or strict the work environment may be. These questions also communicate that you care about being a good fit for the school community and not just about collecting a paycheck.

Finally, a broad but practical question is, "What does a typical day look like for a foreign teacher at your school?" This often leads directors, or current teachers, if you speak with them, to reveal details you won't find in the contract, like grading expectations, desk time, or extra non-teaching duties. It gives you a realistic preview of what life will actually look like once you start.

Pro Tip

Avoid yes-or-no questions like "Do you like working here?" Instead, try "What do you enjoy most about working at this school, and what do you find most challenging?" Open-ended questions encourage honest answers and allow you to hear both the positives and the drawbacks. Remember, you're not just trying to impress them; you're gathering the information you need to make an informed decision about your future.

Final Thoughts

When it comes to the interview process in Korea, most schools ultimately prioritize three qualities in foreign teachers: reliability, adaptability, and likeability. Credentials and certifications certainly matter, but personality fit often tips the scales. Schools want teachers who will represent them well to students and parents, collaborate respectfully with Korean staff, and remain committed to the full twelve-month contract. Appearance and presentation are also important. While you don't need to look overly formal, directors tend to dislike excessive makeup, edgy hairstyles, or multiple piercings. A polished, approachable look, casual business attire, neat grooming, and a friendly smile make the best impression.

Beyond appearance, how you conduct yourself in the interview can make or break your chances. If you show up late, respond with one-word answers, or appear distracted, you may be passed over, even with strong credentials. On the other hand, arriving on time, speaking clearly, and demonstrating genuine enthusiasm for Korean education and your future students' success will set you apart. Recruiters are also paying close attention. If they ask you to send an introduction video or a specific document, and you delay or forget, it raises concerns about whether you'll manage the many administrative responsibilities required as a teacher in Korea. Schools need more than friendly personalities; they need teachers who are organized, dependable, and responsive.

Approach every interview as a two-way conversation. Be prepared, professional, and personable. Share who you are honestly but also show that you've done your homework about Korean schools and are eager to contribute to their community. If you strike that balance, you will dramatically increase your chances of receiving job offers and thriving once you arrive. An interview in Korea is not just a test of your teaching skills; it is a personality and cultural fit assessment. Directors want to see teamwork, adaptability, energy, and genuine care for children. By blending professionalism with approachability and by demonstrating that you are both reliable and enthusiastic, you can stand out as exactly the kind of teacher Korean schools are hoping to hire.

Chapter 8: Understanding Your Job Offer & Contract

Chapter Summary

This chapter teaches you how to carefully read and interpret Korean ESL teaching contracts so you don't miss important details. You will learn how to compare salary, benefits, and allowances in the context of the cost of living, how to spot hidden clauses and vague or problematic contract language before you sign, how to recognize signs of disorganized or exploitative schools, and how to negotiate realistically and tactfully in the Korean context.

Why This Chapter Matters

Getting a job offer to teach in Korea is an exciting milestone. You've polished your application, gone through interviews, and finally landed an opportunity. But this is also the point where many teachers make mistakes. A teaching contract in Korea is not just a formality; it's a legally binding agreement that will shape nearly every aspect of your daily life for the following year. It determines your salary, housing, working hours, vacation, and even how disputes or terminations are handled.

Unlike in some Western contexts, where contracts can feel flexible or negotiable after signing, Korean schools usually treat the signed agreement as final. If you overlook a vague clause or assume a benefit will be "figured out later," you may find yourself stuck in a difficult situation with little recourse. For example, what looks like a small detail, such as whether "30 hours" refers only to classroom teaching or includes mandatory desk time, can drastically affect your workload and work-life balance.

The good news is that with a careful approach, you can avoid most pitfalls. This chapter will show you how to evaluate a job offer thoroughly, identify which contract terms matter most, recognize common red flags, and negotiate respectfully and effectively so you can enter your new role confident that both you and your school have a clear, shared understanding of expectations.

Pro Tip

Think of the contract as your safety net. A clear, fair contract not only protects you if issues arise but also sets the tone for a respectful working relationship with your school.

Reviewing the Job Offer

When you first receive a job offer from a school or recruiter, it often arrives as a simple outline: salary, location, housing, and working hours. A formal contract usually follows. At this stage, the most common mistake teachers make is rushing to accept because they're excited to finally have an offer. Instead, this is the moment to slow down. You're about to commit to a legally binding year in another country; take the time to review it carefully.

Balance Enthusiasm with Caution

It's normal to feel a rush of relief when an offer comes through, especially if you've been anxiously waiting. But don't let that excitement overshadow the need for scrutiny. Ask for at least a day or two to review the offer. Most reputable schools and recruiters will happily allow this; if they pressure you to decide immediately, that in itself can be a red flag.

Look Beyond Salary

When evaluating a job offer, it's easy to fixate on the salary figure, but pay is only one piece of the larger puzzle. A position offering 2.5 million KRW in Seoul may seem attractive at first glance, yet once you factor in the higher cost of living, transportation, and daily expenses, your disposable income may be less than if you accepted a 2.4 million KRW role in a smaller city. Living in a middle to large-sized city like

Daejeon (1.6 million population in 2025) or a suburban town in Gyeonggi-do (500,000 to 1 million population) often means lower living costs, less competition for housing, and a more relaxed lifestyle, even if the salary itself is slightly lower. However, you can typically find higher-paying jobs near Seoul in Gyeonggi-do than inside Seoul itself.

It's also essential to look closely at the student demographic and teaching context. Teaching kindergarteners requires high energy, lots of games, and a bubbly personality, while working with middle or high school students often calls for structured lessons, classroom management, and the ability to motivate teenagers. The daily rhythm of your job, and whether you leave work feeling energized or drained, will depend more on the age group and school culture than on a few hundred thousand won in salary difference.

Another overlooked factor is the schedule and how hours are defined. Some contracts say "30 hours," but this could mean 30 teaching hours (a hefty load), or it could mean 30 total working hours, which includes preparation, grading, and meetings. A hagwon may list classes as 40 to 50-minute blocks but count them as "one teaching hour," meaning you could be teaching back-to-back without breaks or with only 5 to 10 minutes between classes. A public school might require fewer teaching hours but include desk-warming time, where you're expected to sit in the office even when you're not teaching. Clarifying these differences before you sign is just as important as confirming the salary.

Housing is another area where wording matters. If the offer says "free housing," confirm whether the school will actually provide the apartment or whether you're expected to find your own and use a stipend. If a stipend is mentioned, ask for the exact amount (usually 400,000 to 600,000 KRW) and whether it's realistic for the area. Photos of housing, even if they are from current or past teachers, can be very helpful in setting expectations.

Finally, think about your personal lifestyle and goals. Do you want to live in a bustling city with endless nightlife and social opportunities, or would you prefer a quieter area where you can immerse yourself more deeply in Korean culture and perhaps save money faster? Some teachers value proximity to hiking trails or the beach, while others prioritize easy access to an expat community. Aligning your contract details with your personal priorities will make your year far more rewarding than choosing based on salary alone.

Ask for Clarity Without Over-Questioning

You should absolutely ask about anything unclear, such as whether housing is provided or it's a stipend, whether prep time counts as working hours, or if vacation days are fixed or flexible. But avoid sending a long list of dozens of hyper-detailed questions; Korean schools may see this as being "picky" or difficult to work with. Focus on the essentials: salary, hours, housing, vacation, and benefits. Approach your questions with balance. Clarifying unclear points is smart, but itemizing every paragraph of the contract with dozens of nitpicky questions will make you come across as difficult or overly demanding. Schools in Korea want teachers who are adaptable and easygoing, because the first few months in Korea involve information overload: new job, new culture, new language, and new routines. If you constantly compare Korea to your home country or seem unwilling to adapt, schools will see that as a potential problem and may rescind the offer.

Communication as a Predictor

Pay close attention not only to what the school says but also to how they communicate. If responses are prompt, clear, and professional, that's a good sign. If they're slow, evasive, or inconsistent, that may foreshadow problems once you're actually working there. The quality of communication during this stage often mirrors the relationship you'll have later.

Teacher Story: Olivia and the Location Dilemma

Olivia had all the makings of a strong candidate; her resume stood out above average, her interview was excellent, and she already had a connection to Korea from studying at Yonsei University as an exchange student. Because of that experience, she became fixated on living in one of three neighborhoods she knew well: Mokdong, Sinchon, or Hongdae. To Olivia, being in the "right" location mattered more than anything else.

The challenge was that this kind of rigidity often backfires. Olivia turned down three or four excellent offers, schools that matched her desired pay, schedule, and teaching age group, simply because they were several subway stops away from her target neighborhoods. Recruiters began to see her as overly picky, and as the peak hiring season wound down, opportunities in Seoul became scarce. In the end, Olivia had to accept a position in Gimpo, a satellite city in Gyeonggi-do, because the jobs she truly wanted in central Seoul had already been filled.

Her story highlights a common pitfall for teachers who enter the process with a "must-have" checklist that centers too much on one factor, whether that's location, salary, or type of school. Many teachers have a friend, a partner, or a social circle in a particular part of Seoul, but the more inflexible you are, the smaller your chances of landing a good position. Korea's job market rewards teachers who are adaptable, patient, and open-minded. The irony is that Olivia could have secured a great position in Seoul early on if she had been willing to accept a placement just a few stops from her ideal neighborhood.

Takeaway: Be open. You might prefer a particular neighborhood, salary level, or age group, but if you focus too narrowly, you risk missing out on excellent opportunities. A great director, stable contract, and happy students will matter far more to your day-to-day life than being a subway stop closer to your favorite café.

Teacher Story: When Too Many Questions Raise Red Flags

Sean, an Australian-Chinese teacher, stood out immediately because of his determination and strong credentials. He held a solid TEFL, had tutoring experience, and genuinely wanted to teach in Korea. On paper, he looked like a great fit, but placing him was not easy because he had a medium-to-strong accent, which already limited the number of schools willing to interview him. After some effort, I was able to secure him a good job offer in Daegu, Korea's third-largest city, with a population of over 2.5 million. The school was professional, paid on time, and had a strong track record with other foreign teachers I had placed there over the past five-plus years.

When Sean received the contract, however, he sent me two to three pages of itemized questions. He had literally gone through each paragraph of the contract and written "what if" scenarios: What if I quit early? What if the school fires me? What if I get sick for two weeks? What if I need to return home for an emergency? While it's normal and smart to ask for clarification on key points, the sheer length and tone of Sean's list raised red flags. Schools expect a few thoughtful questions, but they don't want a teacher who appears distrustful or overly focused on exit strategies before even stepping into the classroom.

I asked Sean to hold a follow-up call with me instead of sending the list directly to the school. I explained that if he submitted his three-page list, the school would almost certainly rescind the offer. To help him build confidence, I arranged for him to speak with another current foreign teacher I had placed at the school the year before and the American head teacher whom I had placed there three years prior, both of whom reassured him that it was a fair, supportive place to work. After those conversations, Sean calmed down, and he accepted the job.

Unfortunately, a few weeks later, while waiting for his visa documents to arrive, Sean began applying to other jobs, even some that my team had posted, despite having already committed to Daegu. When I confronted him, he admitted he was "keeping his options open." At that point, I suggested to the school that they rescind the offer because his behavior showed a lack of commitment, and I worried he wouldn't finish the contract, which would be bad for the school, but also reflect poorly on me. Sean brushed it off, saying he had other interviews lined up, but I couldn't place him again because schools value reliability above almost anything else.

Takeaway: Sean's experience shows how schools can interpret excessive contract questions as distrust or inflexibility. Even when you're well-qualified, appearing skeptical of every detail can hurt your chances. Sometimes it's less about what you ask and more about how you present yourself.

Pro Tip

When you get a contract, limit your questions to the essentials: salary, housing, hours, benefits, and vacation. If you're unsure about other details, request to speak with a current or former teacher instead of interrogating the school directly. This demonstrates professionalism, avoids making you look overly picky, and still gets you the clarity you need.

Signs of Communication Quality

When reviewing a job offer, don't just look at the numbers on paper; pay attention to how the school or recruiter communicates with you. Communication during the hiring process is often a preview of how you'll be treated once you arrive in Korea.

If a recruiter or school is slow to respond, consistently vague, or avoids answering specific questions, those are red flags. For example, if you ask about vacation days and they reply only with, "We'll discuss it later," that's a sign they may be deliberately avoiding transparency. Likewise, if responses take a week or more with no explanation, consider how frustrating that could be when you need urgent help with immigration paperwork or a housing issue.

On the other hand, professional recruiters and schools respond promptly, even if the answer is "We're still checking on this and will get back to you tomorrow." That kind of communication builds trust. Responsiveness and honesty, even when the answer isn't what you wanted to hear, signal that you're dealing with a school that values its teachers and understands the importance of clear expectations.

Good communication also shows up in tone. If staff are polite, respectful, and seem genuinely interested in your questions, that's a positive sign. If they're pushy, dismissive, or constantly pressuring you to make a quick decision, take it as a warning. At the same time, remember that communication is a two-way street. Be mindful of time zones and cultural work patterns. I've had teachers email me at 1:00 a.m. my time, then again at 9:00 a.m. the same day, frustrated that I hadn't responded "yesterday." While it's natural to be eager, giving less than a full business day for a reply can come across as pushy or even rude. A good rule of thumb is to allow at least 24 hours for a response, unless it's an urgent, time-sensitive matter. Also note that many recruiters and schools won't send an update unless there's actually new information to share. No news does not necessarily mean they've forgotten you; it usually just means they are still waiting on a school or a director's response themselves.

In short, a school that communicates clearly, consistently, and respectfully during the hiring process is much more likely to support you once you're on the ground in Korea. If communication feels evasive or dismissive now, expect it to be worse later when you're already committed.

Pro Tip

When waiting for replies from schools or recruiters, always factor in the Korean work week. Most schools operate Monday through Friday, 9 a.m. to 6 p.m. KST, and they typically don't respond on weekends or Korean public holidays. For example, one teacher once emailed a school late Thursday night U.S. time, which was Friday evening in Korea. When they didn't hear back until Monday afternoon KST, they felt ignored, even though in reality only a few actual business hours had passed. Give at least one full Korean business day before following up, and extend that window if it overlaps with a weekend or holiday.

Key Contract Terms to Watch For

Once you've accepted a job offer in principle, the school will usually send you a contract, often 10 to 12 pages long, detailing all the terms of your employment. Most of these contracts follow a similar structure, but the exact language and conditions can vary. This is where careful reading becomes critical. Don't skim. Read line by line, and make sure you fully understand the following areas before signing.

Salary

The first thing most teachers look at is salary. As of 2025, entry-level positions usually start between 2.4 and 2.6 million KRW per month, with some schools offering up to 2.8 million KRW for candidates with education degrees, teaching licenses, or strong TEFL backgrounds. A few high-end hagwons or corporate training centers may offer over 3.0 million, but these roles are more competitive and often demand longer hours. Always confirm whether the salary listed is gross or net. If it's gross, you'll need to account for deductions such as taxes, health insurance, and pension contributions. If you're not sure, ask directly: "Is this the amount I take home after deductions, or before?"

Housing

Housing is one of the most significant benefits of teaching in Korea, but it's also one of the most misunderstood. Most schools will either provide a furnished studio apartment or offer a housing allowance (typically 400,000 to 600,000 KRW per month). If the school is providing the housing, ask for photos and the location before you sign. Apartments can vary widely in quality; some are modern officetels with built-in appliances, while others are older units that may feel cramped or outdated. If a housing allowance is offered, be aware that renting your own apartment in Korea often requires a hefty deposit (known as "key money"), sometimes several thousand dollars. For first-time teachers, it's usually best to accept the provided housing unless you have trusted friends or family in Korea who can help you navigate the rental process. Utilities are another factor; expect to pay about $50 to $100 per month, depending on the season, with winter heating and summer air conditioning being the main drivers of higher bills.

Working Hours

Contracts almost always list "teaching hours," usually around 30 per week, but this doesn't always tell the whole story. Some schools expect additional unpaid duties like preparing lessons, attending meetings, grading, or running school events. Look for specific language in the contract. Does it say "teaching hours" or "working hours"? If it says "teaching hours," clarify what's expected beyond class time. Also note that classes in Korea are rarely a full 60 minutes; most hagwon classes are 40 to 50 minutes, meaning you'll likely teach multiple sessions per day. Ask for a sample schedule if possible; it's the best way to understand your real workload.

Vacation

Vacation time is one of the starkest differences between public schools and hagwons. Public school teachers (through EPIK or TaLK) usually receive 18 to 21 paid vacation days per year, split between summer and winter breaks. Hagwon contracts, however, typically offer only 11 days: one week in summer, one week in winter, and one "floating" day used to create a long weekend when a holiday falls mid-week (commonly called a "sandwich day"). Be very cautious of vague wording such as "vacation upon mutual agreement," which often means the director decides when (or if) you take your vacation. Ideally, specific dates should be listed or at least explained clearly by the school.

Sick Leave

This is an area that catches many teachers off guard. Most schools do not list sick leave in the contract, partly because there are no substitute teachers to cover classes. In practice, this means your classes are either taken over by other staff (like Vice Directors or Head Teachers) or canceled entirely, which schools want to avoid. Some contracts will state you have three paid sick days, but they may require a doctor's note for even one day off. Be aware that a "sick day" may still involve going to the doctor with your director and then coming back to school. In my first hagwon job, I caught the flu and asked for a day off. Instead, my director took me to the doctor, I was given medicine and an injection and then sent back to my classroom to "rest" while the students worked on worksheets. The next day, the director praised me as the "best teacher" because I didn't abandon my students. This may sound extreme, but it's common in hagwons where coverage is tight. Larger schools with multiple foreign teachers tend to be more flexible.

Pro Tip

Be proactive about your health. With kids coughing and sneezing around you daily, it's easy to catch a cold or the flu. Make sure you're sleeping well, eating correctly, and taking vitamins. National Health Insurance covers most doctor visits and prescriptions at very low costs, so don't hesitate to see a doctor if you're feeling unwell.

Airfare and Severance Pay

Most contracts include airfare, but the terms vary. Public schools typically reimburse round-trip airfare, while hagwons often provide a one-way ticket or reimburse you after you arrive. Clarify whether the airfare is prepaid or reimbursed and when you'll receive it. Also check for a completion bonus, known as "severance pay." By Korean labor law, any full-time employee who completes a one-year contract is entitled to severance equivalent to one month's salary. This is non-negotiable and should always be included.

Pension and Health Insurance

If you're a full-time teacher, both pension and national health insurance are mandatory by law. Employer and employee each contribute about 50%. Be cautious of contracts that omit these or try to substitute with a private plan; this is a red flag that the school may be cutting corners. American, Canadian, and Australian teachers are eligible to claim back both their contributions and the school's contributions (plus interest) when they leave Korea. British, Irish, and South African teachers, unfortunately, do not receive this refund due to differences in bilateral agreements. These policies can change, so double-check current regulations.

Termination Clauses

Finally, read the termination section carefully. A fair contract will allow either side to end the contract with 30 days' notice. Avoid contracts that would enable the school to dismiss you without notice or reason, as this leaves you vulnerable. If you're ever terminated unfairly, you do have the right to appeal through the local labor board, though this can be a lengthy process. Always remember: what's in writing is what counts. Verbal promises like "Don't worry, we'll figure it out later" are meaningless unless they're written into the contract.

Red Flags in Contracts

Not all contracts are created equal. While many Korean schools provide fair, supportive environments, others cut corners or exploit the fact that many teachers are signing their very first international contract. Being able to recognize warning signs early can save you from a frustrating year abroad.

A major red flag is a contract that glosses over important details. If your contract doesn't clearly state your salary, weekly teaching hours, vacation days, or benefits, you should immediately ask why. A professional school has nothing to hide and will be transparent. While some Korean contracts may be worded differently from what you're used to back home, a complete lack of clarity is a significant warning sign. For instance, vague lines like "Vacation upon mutual agreement" usually mean the director chooses your vacation dates, not you. Always request clarification before signing.

Full-time teachers in Korea are legally entitled to enrollment in both the national health insurance system and the national pension program. If a contract skips these entirely or tries to substitute them with a "private health plan" or a monthly cash bonus, treat this as a red flag. Schools that avoid these obligations often cut legal and financial corners. This not only shortchanges you during your time in Korea but also leaves you vulnerable if you need medical care or want to claim your pension refund when leaving the country.

Another warning sign is a termination section that favors the school but not the teacher. A fair contract will require both parties to give around 30 days' notice to end the agreement. Contracts that allow the school to dismiss you without cause or without any notice put you at risk of losing your job suddenly with no safety net. In some cases, these clauses are used by unstable schools to cycle through teachers without paying severance or airfare.

Some contracts, particularly with adult hagwons or corporate training academies, include "split shifts." This means teaching early in the morning, then returning late at night with a long unpaid break in the middle of the day. On paper, the hours might not look extreme, but in practice, your entire day is consumed. Unless you specifically want this kind of schedule, avoid schools that offer it. Similarly, watch for contracts that promise a higher-than-average salary but bury unpaid duties like riding school buses, weekend marketing events, or mandatory "volunteer" hours in the fine print.

Finally, beware of schools or recruiters who pressure you to sign immediately. Phrases like "You must sign today or the job will be gone" are a red flag. High-quality schools respect that teachers need time to review their contracts carefully. If an employer insists on rushing your decision, it may signal deeper issues with transparency or workplace culture.

Negotiating Your Contract

Many first-time teachers hesitate to negotiate, but it's worth remembering that polite, professional negotiation is not only acceptable in Korea, but it's also often expected. The key is balance: you want to show confidence without seeming overly demanding.

When negotiating, focus on one or two points that matter most to you. For example, if your offer is slightly lower than others you've seen, you might say: "Given my TEFL certification and tutoring background, is there any flexibility in the salary?" Similarly, if you're offered a one-way airfare but you'd prefer a round-trip, ask if it can be adjusted. Keep the tone conversational, not confrontational. Most schools nowadays do not offer round-trip airfare, but for smaller cities, they may consider it.

Be strategic about what you choose to negotiate. Trying to rewrite the entire contract will raise red flags. Instead, identify one or two practical areas, such as salary, airfare timing, or an extra vacation day, and, if granted, accept graciously. Korean directors tend to appreciate teachers who are flexible and easy to work with, and they are more likely to accommodate reasonable requests if you present yourself as cooperative.

One nuance worth noting is that housing is usually not negotiable. If a school owns its apartments, it won't substitute a housing allowance. For couples, some schools may allow you to upgrade from two studios to a one-bedroom, but often at an additional monthly cost. These are the exceptions, not the rule.

Above all, once changes are agreed upon, get everything in writing. A contract revision with signatures is the only legally binding document. Verbal promises or even friendly emails carry little weight if disputes arise later.

Pro Tip

Negotiate with respect and restraint. Schools assess not only your qualifications but also your personality fit. Teachers who are polite, adaptable, and selective about what they ask for often receive more favorable outcomes than those who come across as rigid or demanding.

When Things Go Wrong

I want to be honest with you about something that most guidebooks avoid. The majority of teaching experiences in Korea are positive. Most schools are professional, most directors are fair, and most teachers complete their contracts without serious problems. But not all of them. Over twenty years of recruiting and mentoring, I have seen enough contract disputes, withheld pay, and workplace breakdowns to know that you need a plan for what to do if your situation turns genuinely bad.

The most common problems I see are schools not paying salaries on time, withholding severance or pension contributions, requiring significantly more teaching hours than the contract states, refusing to provide the housing described in the agreement, or creating a hostile working environment that makes the job unbearable. These situations are not the norm, but they happen, and when they do, teachers who know their options handle them far better than teachers who panic.

Your first step should always be documentation. The moment something feels wrong, start keeping a written record. Save every text message, KakaoTalk conversation, and email between you and your director or school administrator. Take screenshots with timestamps. If you are asked to do something that violates your contract, note the date, time, and what was said. If your pay is late, record the date it was due and the date it arrived. This kind of evidence is essential if you later need to file a formal complaint, and it is almost impossible to reconstruct after the fact. Keep everything backed up in cloud storage so it cannot be lost or deleted.

Your second step is to contact your recruiter. If you were placed through a recruitment agency, they should be your first call when a problem arises. A good recruiter has a relationship with both you and the school and can often mediate disputes before they escalate. They know the director, they know the contract, and they can communicate in Korean in ways that are direct without being confrontational. Many of the problems I have helped resolve over the years were settled with a single phone call or meeting between the school director and me. That said, not all recruiters are equally responsive or effective. If yours is not helping, do not wait. Move to the next step.

If informal resolution fails, you have the right to file a complaint with the Ministry of Employment and Labor. Every city in Korea has a regional labor office, and they handle complaints from foreign workers regularly. You can file in person, and many offices have English-speaking staff or interpreters available. Bring your contract, your ARC card, and all of the documentation you have been collecting. The labor board can investigate claims of unpaid wages, withheld severance, illegal working conditions, and other contract violations. The process can take several weeks, but schools take labor complaints seriously because the penalties are real.

For immigration-related issues, such as a school threatening to cancel your visa or refusing to process a letter of release so you can transfer to another employer, contact the Korea Immigration Service directly. Under Korean immigration rules, an E-2 visa holder whose employer is found to have violated labor laws may be eligible for a visa transfer without a letter of release. This is not automatic and requires documentation, but it exists as a protection against schools that try to trap teachers by holding their visa hostage.

There are also community resources that can help. The Seoul Global Center and similar international centers in other cities offer free legal consultations for foreign workers. The Korean Legal Aid Corporation provides free or low-cost legal advice, and organizations like the Migrants' Rights Network can connect you with advocates who specialize in labor disputes involving foreign employees. Your embassy or consulate can also provide a list of English-speaking attorneys, though legal action should generally be a last resort.

Also, check out the LOFT (Legal Office for Foreign Teachers) Facebook group, where a real Korean civil lawyer who specializes in contract law answers questions directly. This group can be a lifesaver when you need fast, reliable legal guidance

Finally, I want to address something that comes up in almost every difficult situation: the temptation to do a "midnight run," where you simply pack your bags, leave the school without notice, and fly home. I understand the impulse. When a school is treating you badly, walking away feels like the only power you have. But a midnight run has real consequences. It burns your bridge with your recruiter, who cannot place you again. It may result in your school reporting you to immigration, which can complicate future visa applications to Korea or other countries. You forfeit your severance pay and potentially your pension refund. And it leaves your students, who did nothing wrong, without a teacher.

If your situation is truly untenable, the better path is to negotiate an early release, give proper notice, and leave through the front door with your documentation, your dignity, and your legal entitlements intact. In my experience, even the most difficult schools will agree to an early termination if you approach it calmly, put the request in writing, and frame it as mutually beneficial. They do not want an unhappy teacher in their classroom any more than you want to be there.

I am not sharing this to scare you. The vast majority of teachers never need any of this information. But the ones who do need it are always glad they had it. Think of this section as an insurance policy: you hope you never use it, but you want to know exactly where it is if the situation calls for it.

Final Thoughts

Your offer and contract will shape your entire year; treat them like mission-critical documents. Don't chase salary alone; weigh the whole package, including schedule, housing, benefits, location, and culture. Read every clause, ask concise clarifying questions, and assume that only what's in writing counts. Watch for red flags like vague terms, no pension or health insurance, unfair termination clauses, split shifts, and pressure to sign fast. Negotiate one or two priorities politely, knowing housing is often fixed. Finally, sanity-check with a current teacher and sleep on it before you sign. A clear, transparent contract is the foundation of a smooth, rewarding year in Korea.

Part Three

The Visa and Immigration Process

Chapter 9: Visa Types for English Teachers

Chapter Summary

This chapter covers the visa types that legally allow you to teach English in Korea. You will learn the eligibility requirements for each visa type and subcategory, compare the flexibility, restrictions, and renewal processes of the most common visas, and understand transition options for long-term teaching, permanent residency, or business opportunities. You will also learn how to avoid common mistakes that delay or prevent approval by planning ahead and staying organized.

Why This Chapter Matters

Before you pack your bags or sign a contract, you need the correct visa. South Korea takes immigration compliance seriously, and the visa you hold determines not only whether you can legally teach English but also what kinds of work you can do, how long you can stay, and how much flexibility you'll have if your circumstances change. Too many first-time teachers assume that the E-2 visa is just a rubber-stamp formality, but in reality, it is a binding legal status that shapes every part of your teaching life in Korea.

For example, if you start on an E-2 teaching visa, your right to live and work in Korea is tied to a single employer. If things go well, that's fine. But if your school closes, if you dislike the environment, or if you want to tutor privately on the side, the E-2 offers little flexibility. By contrast, teachers on F-series visas (spousal, long-term residency, or Overseas Korean) have full freedom to work for multiple employers, start their own businesses, or even switch jobs without restarting the visa process. Your visa, in other words, is not just paperwork; it is the foundation of your career, income, and stability in Korea.

Another reason this chapter matters is the sheer number of teachers who encounter delays or complications because they didn't fully understand the visa process. Immigration requirements change frequently, and even small mistakes, like submitting a background check that expired last week or misunderstanding whether your apostille must be from a federal or state authority, can delay your visa by weeks or months. I've had teachers lose out on their dream jobs simply because they didn't prepare their paperwork correctly.

Finally, your visa choice should align with your long-term goals. Are you planning a one-year adventure before grad school? Then the E-2 is the most straightforward path and is the visa for 99% of teachers. Are you thinking of settling in Korea long-term, marrying, or eventually opening a business? Then you should already be thinking about F-series visas or transition pathways. A little foresight now can save you years of frustration later.

In this chapter, we'll break down the main visa categories: E-series teaching visas, F-series long-term visas, the H-1 Working Holiday visa, and specialty business or professional visas. You'll learn not only the technical requirements but also the real-world implications of each, supported by recruiter insights, teacher stories, and practical tips. By the end, you'll know which visa is right for your current situation and how to position yourself for the future you want in Korea.

The E-2 Visa (Teaching English)

The E-2 visa is the most common entry point for foreign English teachers in Korea. It was created specifically for conversational English instruction at approved institutions, primarily hagwons, public schools, after-school programs, and occasionally universities. To qualify, applicants must hold a passport from one of seven designated English-speaking countries: the United States, Canada, the United Kingdom, Ireland, Australia, New Zealand, or South Africa. In addition, you must have earned at least a bachelor's degree from an accredited university in one of those countries.

The standard E-2-1 visa covers most teachers working at hagwons or public schools, while the E-2-2 is issued in niche contexts such as public broadcasters or cultural centers. In some cases, foreign professors teaching university-level courses receive the E-1 visa, which is slightly different but still part of the E-series. Regardless of the subcategory, most visas are valid for one year, renewable annually, and tied directly to your sponsoring employer.

This employer-sponsorship is both the strength and weakness of the E-2. On the one hand, it makes the visa process relatively straightforward: you secure a job, gather your documents, and the school handles much of the submission. On the other hand, it locks you into that single employer. If you quit or are dismissed, your visa is effectively void unless you obtain a Letter of Release (LOR) from your school and transfer sponsorship to a new employer, a process that can be stressful if relations with the school have soured.

The Application Process

Applying for an E-2 requires several key documents, each with strict requirements. You will need a national-level criminal background check (FBI for Americans, RCMP for Canadians, etc.) authenticated with an apostille, a notarized and apostilled diploma copy, a completed health statement, passport photos that meet Korean specifications, and a signed contract from your sponsoring school.

Your recruiter or school will apply for a Visa Issuance Number (VIN) through the Korean Immigration Office. Once approved, you'll take this VIN, along with your documents and contract, to the nearest Korean consulate in your home country to receive the E-2 visa in your passport.

This process seems simple, but minor mistakes, like an apostille from the wrong authority or a background check that is a week past its validity window, can delay your visa by weeks. Recruiters spend much of their time walking teachers through this step, since even minor errors can cause lost opportunities. Please work closely with your recruiter and school. I usually create a three-way Teams chat between the school, the teacher, and me to keep information in one place and to minimize breakdowns in communication. If your recruiter hasn't set up a three-way chat, ask them to do so. I would also download the KakaoTalk application to your mobile device and use it, since everyone in Korea uses KakaoTalk.

The Limitations of the E-2

While the E-2 is an accessible starting point, it is also restrictive. Teachers are legally bound to one employer, and private tutoring or "moonlighting" is prohibited unless explicitly approved by immigration. Many teachers try to freelance on the side, but if caught, they risk losing their visa and being deported. I will spend some time specifically on teaching private classes in the next section. The E-2 also does not automatically provide a pathway to permanent residency or long-term settlement. Teachers who envision staying in Korea long-term usually transition later to an F-series visa, which offers far more flexibility in employment and lifestyle.

Teacher Story: Michael's Expired Background Check

One teacher I worked with, Michael, was excited to start teaching at a Seoul hagwon but ran into problems with his paperwork. He had submitted an FBI background check that was more than six months old, not realizing it would be rejected. By the time he redid the process, new fingerprints, another FBI check, and another apostille, the school had filled the position. He eventually started in Korea a few months later, but he lost his preferred placement and had to accept a job in a smaller city because of the delay.

Takeaway: Start early. Your background check has a limited validity window, and redoing the entire process can cost you weeks and your preferred placement.

Teacher Story: Sarah's Apostille Mistake

Another one of my teachers, Sarah, sent her documents to the school via FedEx without scanning them first, so we couldn't check the scans before they shipped. When the school received the package, they realized that her FBI criminal record check had a state-level apostille from Washington, D.C., which is no longer accepted. The FBI criminal record check must have the Department of State apostille, which generally takes four to six weeks to process. You can get it done through an expedited apostille service in seven to ten days. Sarah had to send her PDF to obtain the expedited apostille, which took almost two weeks, plus another week to FedEx the document to the school, costing her both time and money.

Takeaway: Always scan your documents before you ship them to your school. This simple step allows your recruiter to catch errors before they become costly delays.

Pro Tip

Start gathering your documents as soon as you decide to apply for jobs in Korea, even before you've secured a contract. Being "document-ready" can mean the difference between landing a prime position in Seoul versus missing out because your paperwork isn't ready when schools are hiring. For detailed, country-specific guides on the E-2 visa process, visit teachenglishinkorea.org/blog/categories/e2-teaching-visa-process-for-korea.

Teaching Private Lessons in Korea

While the E-2 visa is the most common for first-time English teachers, it comes with one stringent limitation: you are only legally allowed to teach for your sponsoring school. This means you cannot legally give private English lessons, whether one-on-one tutoring, small group classes, or side work at another hagwon. Korean immigration treats unauthorized private lessons as illegal employment, and if caught, you can face fines, deportation, or cancellation of your visa.

That said, the practice is widespread, with most teachers teaching private classes at some point during their time in Korea. The extra money is excellent and the opportunities are plentiful. Many parents want extra tutoring for their children, and teachers are often offered cash to provide lessons outside of school hours. Some teachers take the risk, reasoning that it's "common" and unlikely to be enforced. Others decline outright, preferring not to jeopardize their visa or their relationship with their school.

Why It's Risky on an E-2

While it may seem tempting to pick up private tutoring on the side, doing so while on an E-2 visa comes with real risks. Immigration officials do conduct occasional stings, particularly in Seoul, where they monitor Craigslist, Facebook, Kakao communities, and other platforms where teachers sometimes advertise their services. In many cases, complaints are triggered not by random chance but by parents, rival teachers, or even competing schools who report foreigners they suspect of tutoring illegally.

If immigration investigates and catches you teaching outside your sponsoring school, both you and the school can face serious consequences. Teachers may be fined or deported, and schools can be penalized heavily for employing or sponsoring someone who breaks visa conditions. That said, enforcement is not simple. To take action, immigration typically needs evidence of money being exchanged or proof of an actual lesson taking place outside your contracted school. For example, meeting a student in a café like Starbucks isn't automatically an issue, unless you are visibly conducting a lesson and accepting payment. I see teachers having private classes at coffee shops all the time, but they don't exchange money there. Still, the risk exists, and even one complaint can cause unnecessary stress and scrutiny.

Beyond the legal side, there is also the issue of burnout. Most hagwon positions already demand 30 hours of teaching per week, plus preparation, grading, and school events. Adding another 5 to 10 hours of tutoring on evenings or weekends can quickly push teachers past their limits. While the extra income may look attractive, exhaustion may outweigh the benefits. Many teachers who take on too much too soon end up struggling to maintain the energy and enthusiasm needed for their primary job, the one that sponsors their visa and pays for their housing. Each teacher should weigh the gains and possible negative consequences before taking on private classes.

When It's Legal

Teachers on F-series visas (F-2, F-4, F-5, F-6) are free to teach privately, register a tutoring business, or even open their own hagwon. In fact, many long-term teachers transition to an F-visa specifically to escape the restrictions of the E-2. On an F-visa, tutoring can be an excellent source of extra income and flexibility.

My Experience and Advice on Teaching Private Classes

In my experience, the best advice I can give is to wait at least two to three months before taking on private classes. Those first few months are an adjustment period: you're adapting to Korean work culture, learning classroom routines, and managing the information overload that comes with starting a new life abroad. If you add extra teaching hours too quickly, you risk burning out before you even get comfortable. The good news is that after the first three months, your teaching job becomes significantly easier. Most hagwon schedules run on three-month cycles. Students "move up" into the next level, and you'll find yourself teaching the same classes with new students. Each cycle, your prep time shrinks dramatically, since you're essentially re-teaching material you've already mastered, just tweaking it for a different group. This natural rhythm frees up energy and time to consider additional private work.

There are a few primary ways teachers pick up private classes in Korea. The riskiest method is working part-time at another school. This is the fastest way to get caught, because immigration officials, or even your own director, can easily confirm you're teaching outside your sponsoring institution. Far more common is the network method: teachers inherit private students from colleagues or friends who are leaving Korea, or they're introduced through word-of-mouth within expat or local networks. Another frequent situation is that teachers who are already at their limit with private hours will "pass down" less desirable classes when they take on a better one.

My Early Experiences

When I first arrived in Korea years ago, I worked at a YBM Sisa hagwon near Bucheon City. My schedule was typical: kindergarten classes in the mornings from 10 a.m. to noon, followed by elementary classes from 1:30 p.m. to 6 p.m. Because I was the only expat at my branch, the school was fairly flexible with me. In my very first month, I happened to meet Min, another Korean-American teacher, at a local bar. He was in charge of coordinating expat teachers to cover middle school classes in the area. After a few beers, he asked if I could teach a girls' middle school three mornings a week from 8 to 9 a.m. The pay was 400,000 KRW per month, and at that time my salary was 1.6 million KRW (over $2,000 USD at the time), so this side gig boosted my income by 25%. A month later, Min asked me to take on another morning class at a boys' middle school on Tuesdays and Thursdays, which paid an additional 300,000 KRW per month. By my second month in Korea, I was earning an extra 700,000 KRW, nearly 60% more than my base salary.

Later, I had another lucky break. I met a Canadian teacher at a bar in Bucheon who was heading back home and needed someone to take over his morning kindergarten private class. It was a large kindergarten with over 200 students aged 4 to 7 years old. It ran five days a week, nearly two hours each day, for ten months of the year and paid 1 million KRW monthly. I jumped at the opportunity. Suddenly, my private lessons were earning me more than my actual hagwon salary. In fact, I was living off my tutoring income and saving 100% of my monthly paycheck. These extra classes allowed me to put down a large deposit and purchase my first apartment in Korea in my third year.

Pro Tip

If you pick up private classes, have the students pay you in cash and in advance. If they want you to teach one hour three times per week, reduce it to 1.5 hours two times per week to cut down on your travel time and expense.

Teacher Story: Amanda's Smart Use of Private Classes

Amanda arrived in Korea carrying a heavy financial burden: nearly $25,000 in student loans. Unlike many teachers who burn out chasing every possible private lesson, Amanda approached the opportunity strategically. She already had experience teaching online through VIPKid before coming to Korea, so she continued that routine by teaching two hours every weekday morning before school. It wasn't easy waking up early, but she quickly built a loyal following of students in China who booked her regularly. On weekends, she added another four-hour teaching block on Saturdays, giving her enough supplemental income to make a real dent in her loans.

A few months into her stay, Amanda's church asked if she would consider running a small English class for their congregation members. Since she already attended services there every Sunday, it was a natural fit to add a two-hour session afterward. The pay was solid, and Amanda enjoyed connecting with her church community while building her teaching skills.

By the end of her first year in Korea, Amanda had paid off more than $15,000 of her student loans. In her second year, she wiped out the remaining $10,000 and even saved a cushion of extra funds to take home with her. Along the way, she also met her future husband, another American teacher, and the two of them eventually moved back to the United States together. Because they had both built strong online teaching profiles with VIPKid, they continued teaching virtually after returning home, giving them a source of income while transitioning back into U.S. life. Amanda ultimately chose to make online teaching her full-time career, enjoying the freedom to work from home and create her own schedule.

Takeaway: Amanda's story shows that private teaching, done wisely and with balance, can be transformative. By sticking to sustainable hours and choosing opportunities that fit into her life naturally, she was able to achieve her financial goals without burning out.

Pro Tip

Use private classes to serve a specific purpose, whether it's paying down debt, saving for travel, or building an online teaching profile. Avoid piling on extra work just for the sake of earning more, because exhaustion will catch up quickly.

Teacher Story: Lucas's Risk

Lucas, on the other hand, learned the hard way. He had picked up a private student, a young elementary schooler, and taught lessons at the student's home. One day, immigration officers waited outside, checked his bag after class, and found both teaching materials and an envelope of cash. They fined him 1 million KRW and fined his school 500,000 KRW. He was warned that a second offense would mean deportation. Lucas finished his contract, but his time in Korea was cut short. In this case, the immigration officials knew exactly who he was teaching, when he was teaching, and that he got paid every class, so they caught him red-handed. This shows that loose lips sink ships; someone he knew well must have reported him to immigration.

Takeaway: Cutting corners with private lessons might seem profitable in the short term, but the risks, including fines, school penalties, and possible deportation, are very real.

Pro Tip

If you're on an E-2 visa, remember that all private tutoring is technically illegal unless registered with immigration. Never take on risky classes at students' homes or other schools. If you're committed to teaching privately, work toward an F-series visa for the legal flexibility.

Teacher Story: The Extreme Saver

On the opposite end of the spectrum, I knew a British teacher who never taught a single private class but still left Korea with more savings than almost anyone else I knew. His strategy was extreme frugality. He lived off baguettes from Paris Baguette with peanut butter for two meals a day, relied on his school's free lunch, and filled reused bottles with purified water from the school. When he left Korea, he had saved over 80% of his salary. He admitted his lifestyle wasn't for everyone, but he was proud of the nest egg he was going home with.

Takeaway: Even without private lessons, disciplined saving can yield impressive results. Teaching in Korea can either be a paycheck-to-paycheck lifestyle or an incredible savings opportunity; your daily choices make the difference.

F-Series Visas

For teachers who decide to make Korea more than a one-year adventure, the F-series visas become especially attractive. Unlike the E-2 visa, which ties you to a single employer and restricts outside work, F-type visa offers an extraordinary degree of freedom. Holders of these visas can legally change jobs without reapplying for sponsorship, tutor privately, freelance, or even start their own business. They are, in many ways, the visas that transform you from simply "working in Korea" to truly living in Korea. While they require more commitment, either through marriage, ancestry, or long-term residence, they are often the key to building a stable and flexible life here.

The F-6 (Spouse of a Korean National)

Perhaps the most common long-term visa path for teachers is the F-6 spouse visa. This visa is granted to foreign nationals legally married to Korean citizens and comes with almost no employment restrictions. Teachers on the F-6 can take full-time jobs at schools, build a private tutoring base, or even run a business. The flexibility is unparalleled compared to the rigid E-2 system.

I've worked with several teachers who began their Korean journeys on E-2 visas, only to switch to F-6 after marrying Korean partners. For instance, one teacher told me that before marriage, she had to turn down a lucrative tutoring offer because her E-2 prohibited it. After obtaining the F-6, she not only continued her hagwon work but also started tutoring corporate clients privately, essentially doubling her income. Beyond income, the F-6 also makes day-to-day life smoother: there are fewer immigration appointments, fewer restrictions on housing contracts, and multi-year visa validity. Importantly, an F-6 holder can later apply for the F-5 Permanent Residency visa, making it a long-term stepping stone.

The F-2 (Long-Term Residency)

The F-2 visa offers another pathway to stability. There are two routes: the standard F-2 residency visa, available after five years of continuous legal residence, and the F-2-7 points-based visa. The latter is increasingly popular because it allows qualified applicants to apply sooner if they accumulate enough points. Points are awarded for age (younger applicants score higher), education level, salary, Korean language proficiency (measured by TOPIK (토픽) scores), and even volunteer work in Korea.

For example, a Canadian teacher I knew had been in Seoul for five years, completed a master's degree in TESOL, and achieved TOPIK Level 4. With these qualifications, he successfully obtained the F-2-7, which allowed him to break free from the E-2 system. He later transitioned into curriculum development work at a bilingual school, a role he couldn't have accepted while tied to his original employer. The F-2 can be life-changing for teachers who want to diversify their careers in Korea without constantly reapplying for visas through their schools.

The F-4 (Overseas Koreans)

The F-4 visa is designed for individuals of Korean descent, often second- or third-generation overseas Koreans whose parents or grandparents once held Korean citizenship. For teachers, the F-4 is an incredibly valuable option because it provides nearly all of the benefits of permanent residency while still requiring periodic renewal (usually every two years). Holders are not tied to a single employer, meaning they can freely switch schools, take on private tutoring legally, and pursue work in nearly any field.

However, many new teachers misunderstand the requirements. While an F-4 does not require the extensive paperwork that an E-2 visa does for entry, teachers on F-4 visas must still provide specific documents if they intend to work in schools. To be registered with the local education office, F-4 holders need to submit an apostilled, notarized copy of their bachelor's degree as well as a national-level criminal record check. These are the same key documents required for an E-2, and schools cannot legally employ F-4 holders without them. This distinction often surprises teachers who thought the F-4 would completely bypass documentation requirements.

Another significant difference between the E-2 and the F-4 is the application process. The E-2 visa can only be completed outside of Korea, meaning that applicants must typically visit a Korean consulate in their home country to finalize the process before arriving. The F-4, on the other hand, can be obtained inside Korea. This means that individuals of Korean descent who are visiting on another status (like a tourist visa or student visa) can apply for and receive an F-4 without leaving the country. It's a major convenience that makes the F-4 especially appealing for heritage Koreans already spending time in Korea.

The flexibility of the F-4 also extends beyond teaching. For non-teaching jobs, such as working in business, hospitality, or other professional sectors, applicants are not required to provide apostilled degrees or background checks. This difference highlights just how much broader the F-4's scope is compared to the narrowly defined E-2.

For many overseas Koreans, the F-4 is the visa that allows them to reconnect with their heritage while enjoying maximum flexibility in Korea's job market. Unlike the E-2, which locks teachers into a rigid one-year commitment with a single employer, the F-4 is a pathway to freedom, mobility, and greater control over one's career.

Teacher Story: Minjun's Path to the F-4 Visa

Minjun grew up in the U.S. after immigrating with his family at the age of four. Like many overseas Koreans, he assumed that his immigration to the States meant he had fully transitioned to American citizenship. When he began exploring opportunities to teach in Korea, he checked with the Korean Consulate in Los Angeles and was surprised to learn that his parents had never formally renounced his Korean citizenship. On paper, he was still recognized as a Korean citizen and could even apply for a Korean passport.

At first, this seemed like an incredible opportunity. Having Korean citizenship would eliminate the need for an E-2 visa, and he could live and work freely in Korea. But his excitement quickly turned into anxiety when he discovered the implications of Korea's mandatory military service law. As a male citizen under the age of 38, Minjun was technically subject to conscription. The idea of being forced into the Korean army, even though he had lived most of his life in the U.S., was a shock. After careful thought, he decided the best route was to formally give up his Korean citizenship and apply instead for the F-4 visa, which would still give him nearly the same freedom as a citizen but without the military obligations.

The process, however, wasn't simple. To apply for the F-4, he needed to gather detailed documents proving his family lineage, such as the Korean family registry or 호적등본 (hojeok deungbon) showing his parents' and grandparents' citizenship history. While he had immigration documents, copies of his parents' old Korean passports, and proof of their U.S. naturalization, obtaining the family registry itself from Korea was a challenge. Facing delays, Minjun decided to pivot. He accepted a position under an E-2 visa first, which allowed him to come to Korea and begin teaching. Once he was in-country, he had more time and resources to collect the missing documents needed for the F-4 application. Later, he successfully transitioned from the E-2 to the F-4 without leaving Korea, a path that gave him long-term stability and flexibility.

Takeaway: Minjun's experience shows that heritage connections can complicate the visa process in unexpected ways. What seemed at first like an advantage, retaining Korean citizenship, came with serious obligations he wasn't prepared for. By staying flexible, starting on an E-2, and then shifting to an F-4, he created a smoother long-term path. For overseas Koreans, it's essential to research your citizenship status early and be prepared for both bureaucratic hurdles and cultural expectations.

Pro Tip

If you have Korean ancestry, don't wait until you've already lined up a teaching job to figure out your visa options. Contact your nearest Korean consulate early and ask whether you qualify for the F-4 visa. The rules and required documents can vary depending on your family history, so clarify precisely what you'll need before you begin the E-2 process. In some cases, you may be able to apply for the F-4 directly, saving you time and avoiding duplicate paperwork.

The F-5 (Permanent Residency)

The F-5 visa represents the pinnacle of long-term residency for foreigners in Korea. It eliminates the need for visa renewals, allowing holders to live and work in Korea indefinitely with almost the same rights as Korean citizens (minus voting). The requirements are high, usually five or more years of continuous residency, stable income, proof of assets, and proficiency in Korean (typically TOPIK Level 4 or higher). However, once granted, it provides unparalleled stability.

For teachers, the F-5 is often the culmination of a career in Korea. It opens doors to everything from teaching at universities without sponsorship to opening a hagwon or starting a business completely independently. While difficult to obtain, the F-5 is the clearest signal that you have fully committed to building your life in Korea. Having an F-5 visa makes you a permanent resident, which is like being a green card holder in the USA with permanent residency instead of conditional residency.

Why F-Series Visas Matter

Ultimately, the F-series visas provide freedom that the E-2 cannot match. They allow you to shape your career rather than having your career dictated by your visa status. Whether you want to build a base of private students, try different schools, start a small business, or avoid the stress of annual renewals, these visas give you control. The trade-off, of course, is that they require years of commitment, legal marriage, or family lineage. But for teachers who see Korea as more than just a one- or two-year adventure, the F-series pathways often define whether they are visitors or residents in Korea.

The H-1 Visa (Working Holiday)

The H-1 Working Holiday visa is designed for young people, usually between the ages of 18 and 30 (sometimes 25 depending on the country), who want to experience life in Korea for up to one year. It's offered through reciprocal agreements with several countries, including the United States, Canada, Australia, New Zealand, and the United Kingdom, as well as a number of European nations. The spirit of the program is cultural exchange, allowing young adults to travel, explore, and earn some money through short-term work to support themselves during their stay.

For teachers, however, the H-1 visa comes with significant limitations. Holders are not legally allowed to work at hagwons or public schools, and they cannot be hired full-time as English teachers. Some people still find ways to use this visa to gain informal teaching experience, for example, working at a language café, offering conversation practice, or tutoring privately, but these arrangements operate in a legal gray area. Immigration rules technically forbid teaching English as a primary job under this visa, so teachers who attempt to do so risk fines or deportation if caught.

That said, the H-1 can still be useful for specific individuals. Some use it as a "trial year" in Korea, a chance to immerse themselves in the culture, take Korean language classes, and test whether they enjoy living in Korea before committing to a longer-term E-2 or F-series visa. For instance, I once knew a Canadian traveler who used his H-1 to spend six months in Seoul studying Korean at a language institute while working part-time at a guesthouse. On weekends, he offered informal English conversation meetups at cafés, which gave him some teaching exposure and a bit of pocket money. After returning home, he later applied for an E-2 visa through a hagwon and came back to Korea as a full-time teacher with a clearer idea of what to expect.

It's important to understand that the H-1 visa is usually non-renewable and is limited to one year. It's not a pathway to a teaching career in itself, but for those who want to explore Korea on a gap year or gain cultural immersion before committing, it can be a stepping stone. However, if your primary goal is teaching, you'll be much better off pursuing the E-2 or F-series visas, since they provide the stability, legal protections, and benefits (housing, health insurance, pension) that come with formal employment. Going from an H-1 visa to an E-2 visa is not common, and it will still require you to go outside of

Korea to change your visa. You will also probably have to go back home to get your national criminal record check and apostille.

Other Working Visas

While the majority of foreign English teachers in Korea work under the E-2 or F-series visas, several alternative visa types may be relevant to professionals with advanced qualifications, technical skills, or entrepreneurial ambitions. These visas are far less common in the ESL community but can open unique opportunities for those seeking long-term or specialized careers in Korea.

The E-7 visa (Specialty Occupation) is issued to foreigners employed in specialized professional fields such as engineering, IT, finance, education, and design. Within education, some highly qualified English teachers and curriculum developers have successfully transitioned to the E-7 visa when working for international schools, publishing companies, or corporate training programs. For example, a U.S. teacher with a master's degree in TESOL and years of experience moved from an E-2 visa to an E-7 after being hired by a Korean publishing house to design ESL textbooks and digital learning content. The E-7 visa offers greater flexibility than the E-2, since it isn't restricted to conversational English teaching at hagwons, but the application process is more rigorous and requires proof of specialized skills. It is not common to obtain an E-7, since it is difficult to do so.

The E-4 visa (Technology and Research) is granted to foreigners who provide technological guidance or research in areas requiring advanced expertise. While it is rare for ESL teachers to qualify, this visa sometimes overlaps with education when foreign instructors are hired to develop or evaluate advanced training programs in universities or corporate R&D environments. For example, an American linguist specializing in speech recognition technology was granted an E-4 while collaborating with a Korean AI startup on English-language processing tools. This visa underscores Korea's demand for foreign experts in highly technical fields.

The D-8 visa (Business Investor) is particularly relevant for entrepreneurial teachers who wish to establish their own businesses in Korea. This visa requires a foreigner to invest a minimum amount (generally around 100 million KRW, roughly $75,000 to $80,000) into a Korean business. For teachers, this pathway often involves founding a private language academy, consulting company, or specialized educational center. One British teacher I knew transitioned from teaching into entrepreneurship by opening a children's English storytelling academy in Daegu. With the D-8 visa, she not only taught but also hired staff, managed the business, and eventually expanded her academy to multiple branches. The D-8 is challenging to obtain due to strict financial and regulatory requirements, but it offers independence and the ability to shape one's own educational vision.

In addition to these, there are other less common visa types, such as the D-10 (Job-Seeking Visa), which allows foreigners already in Korea to search for employment for up to six months after finishing a contract, and the E-1 visa, typically reserved for university professors and lecturers. These are highly situational but can provide temporary or transitional solutions for teachers exploring long-term options.

Choosing the Right Visa for Your Situation

With so many visa options available, it can feel overwhelming to decide which path is best. The good news is that for most new English teachers, the choice is relatively straightforward; the E-2 visa remains the most accessible and widely used. It offers a straightforward process, a predictable one-year structure, and is supported by nearly every recruiter and hagwon in Korea. However, as your career and personal circumstances evolve, other visas may become more attractive.

The F-series visas are ideal for those who see themselves living in Korea for the long haul. These visas provide freedom to work in a variety of roles, including private tutoring, freelance teaching, or even opening a business. If you have Korean ancestry, are in a long-term relationship, or meet residency requirements, transitioning to one of these visas can give you stability and flexibility beyond what the E-2 allows.

For teachers on a gap year or those who want to experience Korea temporarily, the H-1 Working Holiday visa can be a good short-term option. It's not meant for full-time English teaching, but it offers cultural immersion and part-time work opportunities. Just remember that it cannot be renewed, so it should be treated as a stepping stone rather than a long-term solution.

Specialized professionals, entrepreneurs, or those with advanced degrees might find the E-7 or D-8 visas worth exploring. While less common, they allow teachers to move into niche roles, like corporate training, curriculum design, or starting their own academy. These visas are harder to qualify for, but they open doors that the E-2 simply cannot.

Ultimately, the "right" visa depends on your personal goals. If you want to come for one or two years, the E-2 is your fastest and simplest entry point. If you fall in love with Korea and want to stay, it's smart to start thinking early about transitioning to an F-series visa or another long-term pathway. Your visa not only determines your legal status but also your freedom, flexibility, and opportunities in Korea.

Final Thoughts

Your visa isn't just a stamp in your passport; it determines your work options, mobility, and long-term stability in Korea. Plan ahead, since visa processing can take longer than many teachers expect and begin gathering your documents at least three to four months before your intended start date. Stay organized by creating both a digital and physical file for your visa documents, keeping scanned copies of your degree, apostille, criminal record check, passport, health statement, and job contract. Many experienced teachers also carry a USB drive with backups.

Stay up to date, since Korean immigration rules change frequently, sometimes with little notice. Always double-check requirements with your nearest Korean consulate before sending documents, and don't rely solely on teacher forums or Facebook groups; immigration officials are the only authoritative source. Even Korean officials at different consulates may give varying responses, so you may want to check with a Korean immigration lawyer if you cannot get a clear answer.

If you're coming to Korea for just a year, the E-2 visa is likely your best option. But if you envision staying beyond one or two years, start planning early and research whether you qualify for an F-series visa through ancestry, marriage, or the points-based system. Think of your first year as a stepping stone, not your final stop. And don't try to navigate this process entirely on your own. Recruiters can clarify which documents are needed and when, immigration lawyers can provide guidance for complex cases, and veteran teachers are an invaluable resource with candid, practical advice. Approach the process with patience and foresight, and making informed choices now will help you transition smoothly to more flexible options in the future.

Chapter 10: Step-by-Step Visa Application Guide

Chapter Summary

This chapter walks you through the exact steps required to secure your E-2 teaching visa for Korea, from document preparation to consulate approval. You will gain clarity on required documents, including the notarization and apostille procedures that often trip teachers up, along with tailored guidance for U.S., Canadian, UK, Australian, and New Zealand applicants. You will also learn how to plan around timelines and costs, budget realistically for hidden expenses, and avoid the most common mistakes that cause delays so you can handle setbacks proactively without jeopardizing your job offer.

Why This Chapter Matters

After weeks of applications, interviews, and preparation, receiving a job offer to teach in Korea is an exciting milestone. But before you can step on a plane and start your new role, you must secure the proper visa, most often the E-2 visa, which is specifically designed for foreign nationals hired to teach conversational English.

The E-2 visa process is not particularly difficult, but it can be detail-heavy and time-sensitive. Missing a single document, submitting the wrong kind of apostille, or sending forms to the wrong office can delay your departure by weeks. For teachers who are eager to begin, or schools that have fixed starting dates for terms, even a slight delay can cause significant stress. That's why approaching this process with organization, patience, and accuracy is critical.

Think of the E-2 application as a project with multiple phases: gathering the correct documents, getting them notarized and apostilled, sending them to your school so they can apply for your Visa Issuance Number (VIN), and finally completing the visa application at your nearest Korean consulate. Each phase has its own rules, costs, and timelines, which vary by country.

The good news is that tens of thousands of teachers complete this process successfully every year, and once you understand the steps, it becomes manageable. Teachers who prepare early and stay organized often get through the process smoothly; those who wait until the last minute or cut corners with documentation frequently face delays.

This chapter will serve as your step-by-step roadmap to the E-2 visa, complete with insider tips, pro advice, and country-specific shortcuts to help you avoid the mistakes I've seen over the years. By the end, you'll know exactly what to do, how long it will take, and how to troubleshoot if something goes wrong, so you can arrive in Korea ready to start your new life with confidence.

Documents required for an E-2 visa

To begin your E-2 visa application, you'll need to gather several essential documents that verify your identity, education, and legal standing. These documents will be submitted to your employer or recruiter in Korea, who will then apply for your Visa Issuance Number (VIN) through Korean Immigration. Once the number is issued, you can apply for the visa at the Korean consulate in your home country. Each document must be prepared exactly as required, or your application may be delayed or rejected.

Here's a detailed look at each document, with updated instructions for U.S. and Canadian applicants in particular.

Valid Passport

Your passport must be valid for at least six months beyond your expected date of entry into Korea and have at least two blank visa pages. You can easily renew your passport in Korea if it expires while you are there. If you apply for a visa but change your passport during this process, that may cause issues, so it is better to avoid this possible problem by renewing your passport three months in advance of applying for an E-2 visa.

Signed Employment Contract

Your employer will provide this. Review it carefully, sign and date it, and make a copy for your records. Many schools will give you a school-signed contract after arriving in Korea. However, it is recommended to request the school to sign a contract before coming to Korea. Some Korean consulates require a signed agreement by both the employer and employee as part of the documents necessary to apply for the E-2 visa. The reason you send three signed contracts to Korea to apply for the VIN is that one will go to immigration, one for the employer, and one for the employee.

Copy of Your University Diploma

A public notary must notarize a copy of your bachelor's degree, which must then be apostilled at the state level (in the U.S.) or authenticated according to your country's process. Korean Immigration no longer requires the original diploma and, as of 2025, accepts a scanned PDF of the certificate with an apostille. Your degree doesn't need to be apostilled or notarized in the state where your university is located.

Apostille and Notarization for Diplomas

For U.S. applicants, make a photocopy of your diploma, have it notarized by a licensed notary public in your state, then submit the notarized copy to your state's Secretary of State office to get the apostille. For a faster option, many services can handle the notarization and apostille process in one to two business days. For a detailed walkthrough of this process, including a recommended expedited service for both diplomas and FBI apostilles, visit teachenglishinkorea.org/post/how-to-obtain-an-apostille-notarization-in-1-2-business-days-in-the-usa-for-an-fbi-crc-or-a-diploma.

National-Level Criminal Background Check (with Apostille)

This is one of the most critical and time-sensitive documents, and where many new teachers make mistakes. Korean immigration requires a national-level criminal background check that is both federally issued and federally apostilled. They no longer accept state-level or expedited apostilles on federal documents unless the apostille is issued by the U.S. Department of State.

For U.S. applicants, you'll need an FBI Identity History Summary (FBI CRC). The recommended route is to use an FBI-approved channeler (like Accurate Biometrics) for expedited results in 2 to 48 hours. Once you have the PDF version, you must have it apostilled by the U.S. Department of State, which you can do quickly through a service like USAuthentication.com. For a step-by-step guide on obtaining your FBI CRC through Accurate Biometrics, follow the instructions at teachenglishinkorea.org/post/how-to-apply-for-an-fbi-crc-electronically-using-www-accuratebiometrics-com-from-any-state-in-the-us. A separate guide on obtaining the FBI CRC in one to two days is available at teachenglishinkorea.org/post/how-americans-can-obtain-an-fbi-criminal-record-check-through-an-fbi-approved-channeler-in-1-2-days.

Pro Tip

Never attempt to submit a non-apostilled or state-apostilled FBI CRC. Korean Immigration now strictly enforces this requirement and will reject improperly authenticated background checks.

For Canadian applicants, you must obtain a Certified Criminal Record Check from the RCMP. The document must be authenticated by Global Affairs Canada (GAC) and then legalized by the Korean Consulate in Canada. You can apply for your RCMP CRC at rcmp.ca/en/criminal-records/criminal-record-checks. Use a fingerprinting agency that offers end-to-end apostille/authentication and mailing services to avoid delays. Many Canadian teachers have recommended the expedited online service at commissionaires.ca.

For UK, Australian, and New Zealand applicants, you must obtain a national police certificate (Disclosure and Barring Service for the UK, AFP for Australia, etc.). These documents must be apostilled by your home country's Ministry of Foreign Affairs or an equivalent authority. UK applicants can order a new DBS CRC in 5 to 10 business days at gov.uk/request-copy-criminal-record. Many UK teachers get their DBS CRC apostilled quickly using the expedited service at hagueapostille.co.uk/order/teik-jobs-apostille-and-solicitor-certification; be sure to mail them your original DBS CRC, original degree, and a photocopy of your degree.

Teacher Story: Abby's Apostille Ordeal

Abby, a teacher from Northern Ireland, found herself in one of the more complex visa situations I've ever seen. Although she was born and raised in Northern Ireland, she held an Irish passport. On paper, that didn't seem like a problem. She had already obtained a clean criminal background check from the UK and had it apostilled, as well as her degree documents. But when she submitted her paperwork to Korean immigration, the officer insisted that because Abby was entering Korea with an Irish passport, she also needed a criminal background check from Ireland, even though she had never lived there a single day in her life.

Things became even more complicated when immigration also questioned her university transcripts because she had studied in Wales. The officer asked for notarized university transcripts, which typically aren't required at all. It quickly became clear that immigration officers have significant discretion in what documents they ask for, and their requests can vary from case to case.

Abby attempted to comply. She applied through the official Irish Garda website, but because she had never resided in Ireland, they could not issue her a CRC. Instead, they simply told her she had "no record," which didn't meet Korean Immigration's documentation requirements. The officer then requested a notarized and apostilled letter from the Garda stating why they couldn't issue her a CRC. Unfortunately, the Garda would not issue that kind of letter either.

After multiple trips by her school director to immigration, the officer finally agreed to accept a simpler solution: a letter from any Irish police station, with an apostille, stating that Abby had never resided in Ireland and therefore could not obtain an Irish CRC. Determined to make it work, Abby flew to Dublin. After visiting several police stations, she finally persuaded one officer to write the necessary letter. She then paid an expedited service to apostille the document, along with notarized copies of her transcripts.

The entire ordeal cost her more than a month of delays and over £500 in unexpected fees. Eventually, she was able to process her visa, but it was one of the most stressful and expensive onboarding experiences I've witnessed.

Later, another Northern Irish teacher I worked with, Beth, faced a similar situation. Learning from Abby's ordeal, Beth decided to apply for a British passport instead of using her Irish passport. The process took about a month, but it saved her from potentially running into the same immigration nightmare.

Takeaway: Even when you think your documents are in perfect order, Korean immigration can ask for additional paperwork that seems arbitrary or redundant. Abby's case taught her that flexibility, persistence, and support from her school director were critical in navigating unexpected obstacles.

Pro Tip

If you hold dual nationality, contact the Korean consulate before applying for an E-2 visa to confirm which passport and documents are required. Immigration officers may apply different standards depending on the passport you use, so clarifying early can save weeks of delays and hundreds of extra costs.

Health Statement

This is a basic questionnaire that asks about your medical history, drug use, and mental health. You will later complete a full health check in Korea, but for now, complete the self-declaration form truthfully and accurately. Be warned: if you test positive for any illegal drugs (even if they are legal in your home country), it will result in deportation. If you have any concerns about this, you need to rigorously exercise and drink vast amounts of water for four to eight weeks before your test, depending on your body fat.

Passport Photos

Photo requirements for Korean visas are precise. While many countries accept standard 2x2-inch photos, Korea now requires a 35mm x 45mm format. Using the wrong size or format may lead to rejection. In the USA, most immigration officers accept the standard American passport size of 2 by 2 inches, but a few have rejected them over the past year. Use a professional visa photo service and specify "Korean visa photo, 35x45mm." Avoid cropping old photos or using home-printed images. Keep several extra copies with you in Korea for ARC registration and future job applications. Always ask the studio for the high-resolution image file so you can print out more photos for $0.50 to $1.00 in Korea if you need them; the studio should give you this digital file for free.

Sample Passport Photo (35x45mm)

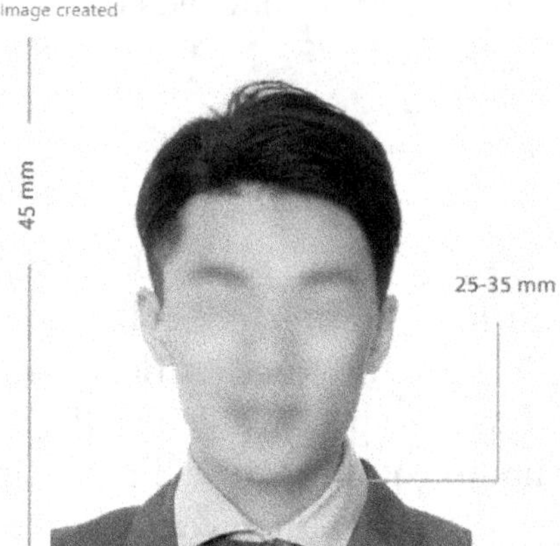

Visa Application Form (Apply for a VIN)

You'll complete this form at two different stages. Initially, you'll fill it out for your school to apply for your Visa Issuance Number (VIN). After receiving the VIN from your school or recruiter, you will fill out a new form to submit to the Korean consulate nearest you in your home country for your final visa stamp. You must be sure to only apply at the Korean consulate in whose territory you reside. Many Korean consulates in the USA ask for a copy of your driver's license or a bill stating your address.

When filling out the E-2-1 visa application form, there are several fields that commonly confuse applicants. Leave field 1.2 blank, as non-Latin characters are not needed. For field 1.7, U.S. citizens should use their SSN while others should use their national ID. For field 2.1, select "Regular." For field 6.1, state your current job status ("Unemployed" is fine). Leave fields 7.2 through 7.5 blank, select "No" for field 8.1, and leave Section 9 blank since your employer will complete it.

For a detailed, printable E-2 visa required document list, along with links to each Korean consulate's specific forms, visit teachenglishinkorea.org/post/required-visa-documents-for-the-e2-1-visa. For a detailed guide on how to complete the E-2-1 visa form with links to each Korean consulate website, visit teachenglishinkorea.org/post/how-to-complete-an-e2-1-visa-links-to-the-korean-consulate-website.

Pro Tip

For UK residents, you do not finish your visa at the Korean Consulate in London. You must send your visa application to KVAC to complete the visa process. KVAC takes 5 to 10 business days to process the visa (usually 10 days), and the fee is almost five times more than in other countries, thanks to Brexit. For a detailed walkthrough of the KVAC process, visit teachenglishinkorea.org/post/how-uk-teachers-finish-an-e2-teaching-visa-after-receiving-a-vin-visa-issuance-number.

Apostille and Notarization Process

Navigating the apostille and notarization process is one of the most technical and often confusing parts of the E-2 visa application. Korean immigration requires all foreign documents to be both legally notarized and internationally authenticated through an apostille. Understanding how this process works in your home country is crucial to avoiding delays. The information in this book may change, so always recheck the information from the Korean consulate's website to make sure the data is correct and up to date.

For U.S. applicants, your diploma requires a state-level apostille, while your FBI criminal background check (a federal document) requires a federal apostille from the U.S. Department of State. It's a common mistake to use the wrong level of apostille.

For Canadian applicants, since Canada is not a member of the Hague Apostille Convention, you will need to authenticate and then legalize your documents. This involves sending your documents to Global Affairs Canada for authentication and then to the Korean Consulate for final legalization.

For UK, Australian, and New Zealand applicants, you will use your country's national legalization office for an apostille. The UK uses the Legalisation Office (FCDO), Australia uses the Department of Foreign Affairs and Trade (DFAT), and New Zealand uses the Department of Internal Affairs (DIA).

Best Practices

When handling notarization and apostille requirements, one of the most important things to remember is that your notary and apostille must come from the same jurisdiction. For example, if your document is notarized in California, you cannot send it to New York for the apostille; it must go through California's Secretary of State. Mismatched jurisdictions are one of the most common reasons teachers experience delays.

If you're short on time or nervous about making mistakes, consider using a professional service that specializes in apostilles. These agencies can handle the entire process from notarization to mailing, often in just a few business days, which gives you peace of mind and saves time.

It's also best practice to create digital backups of everything. Scan and save every page of your notarized and apostilled documents to a secure cloud folder like Google Drive or Dropbox. Having copies on hand makes it easier to resend documents if something gets lost or to provide quick proof to your school or consulate. I suggest sending an email to your recruiter or school with the document checklist and attaching scans of every document on the checklist for them to review before you spend loads of money on overnighting your documents to Korea.

Finally, treat your original documents with care. Always use a reliable courier service such as FedEx, DHL, or UPS when mailing sensitive items. Make sure tracking numbers are included and save them so you can follow your package's progress. Lost or delayed documents can derail your visa timeline, so professional courier services are worth every penny. I've had several teachers try to skimp by using USPS International Priority, which doesn't have a tracking number. This takes over three weeks and can't be tracked, so don't do it, even though it is much cheaper.

I've had teachers lose their documents or face delays so long that they lost their job placement, since the schools grew irritated about not following directions about using an expedited shipper. You are spending a lot of money and time to produce your documents, so don't throw that away by trying to save a little by sending them via regular mail.

Pro Tip

Use express courier services when mailing documents between agencies, especially if you're facing tight deadlines or a fixed school start date.

Processing Timeline and Costs

Understanding the timeline and financial costs involved in securing an E-2 visa is essential. The process can take anywhere from a few weeks to over two months, depending on how quickly you gather documents and the efficiency of various government offices.

Here is a general estimate of the typical processing timeline:

Step	Expedited Timeline	Standard Timeline
Document Preparation	7–14 business days	4–6+ weeks
Visa Issuance Number	7–10 business days	Up to 3 weeks
Korean Consulate Processing	5–10 business days	1–4 weeks
Total Time	4–5 weeks	5–10+ weeks

Pro Tip

If you want to come to Korea sooner, try getting a job outside of Seoul, Incheon, and the Gyeonggi-do region, since those three areas have the busiest immigration offices for processing visas for foreign workers.

While visa processing is relatively affordable, the document preparation phase can involve multiple small expenses that add up. For U.S. applicants, costs for fingerprinting, apostilles, notarization, passport photos, and courier shipping can range from $150 to $250 USD for standard speed and $250 to $400 or more for expedited services.

Your school in Korea will pay for the visa application fee when they apply for your VIN. However, it's the teacher's responsibility to pay for all visa costs in their home country. Always save and scan receipts, as some schools offer reimbursement when agreed upon in advance.

A crucial point about your visa: your initial E-2 visa is typically a single-entry visa. This means if you leave Korea, your visa will be canceled. If you plan to travel outside of Korea during your contract, you must purchase a single or multiple re-entry visa from your local immigration office in Korea before you depart.

What to Do If Your Visa Application Is Delayed

Even with the best preparation, delays sometimes happen during the visa process. The key is not to panic, but to act quickly and methodically the moment you sense something isn't moving as expected. By breaking the problem down into steps, you can usually get things back on track without jeopardizing your start date.

First, pinpoint where the delay is occurring. If your FBI Criminal Record Check or apostille is taking longer than expected, contact the agency directly and ask about expedited services; many offer faster turnaround for an additional fee if you request it early. If the delay is with your VIN and more than 10 to 14 business days have passed, ask your recruiter or school to call the immigration office on your behalf. For consulate delays, confirm that your application was received and complete; sometimes the holdup is simply due to a missing passport photo or form. If the issue is with a courier service, track the package immediately, and if necessary, consider resending critical documents digitally while originals are in transit.

Second, communicate clearly with your school or recruiter. If you expect a delay, notify them right away. Be proactive and explain what has happened, what you've already done, and what you are doing next to fix it. This shows that you are organized, reliable, and committed, qualities that schools value in teachers. Silence, on the other hand, makes schools nervous, since they may assume you've changed your mind about the job.

Third, ask for help and stay organized. If you're struggling, don't be afraid to ask for guidance. Recruiters, online teaching forums, or other expat teachers who've been through the process can often point you to solutions you might not have considered. Staying organized is also key: keep scanned copies of every document in a dedicated cloud folder, maintain a simple checklist of steps completed, and set calendar reminders for deadlines. This prevents confusion if you need to resend a document or answer a school's question quickly.

One important word of caution: do not try to bypass the process by entering Korea on a tourist visa and attempting to convert it to an E-2 once you arrive. Korean immigration does not allow this, and you will be required to leave the country and reapply from your home country's consulate. Attempting shortcuts usually leads to more time being lost and added expenses.

Pro Tip

Before sending your documents to your recruiter or school, scan every single page, front and back, of your notarized diploma, apostille, and criminal record check. Store these scans in a secure cloud folder so you always have a backup in case something gets lost or rejected. Double-check that you obtained the correct type of background check (FBI CRC for Americans, RCMP CRC for Canadians, DBS for UK applicants) and that the apostille is issued at the proper level (federal for federal documents, state for state documents). Many delays happen because teachers mistakenly submit the wrong version, and fixing it can take weeks. Taking 15 minutes to review and scan now can save you from months of frustration later.

Final Thoughts

Delays in the visa process are stressful, but they don't have to derail your plans if you stay calm, proactive, and organized. The key is to approach every setback as something solvable rather than catastrophic. Most delays, whether it's a background check taking longer, an apostille service missing a step, or a consulate backlog, are relatively minor and can be fixed with a few phone calls, emails, or by paying for an expedited service.

What matters most is how you respond. Teachers who get flustered and wait passively often end up missing start dates or even losing their offers. Teachers who take the initiative, contacting agencies directly, keeping their recruiters informed, and tracking every step of their application, almost always find a solution before things spiral out of control. Clear communication also reassures schools that you're responsible and committed, even if circumstances slow you down.

If you follow the guidance in this chapter, you'll not only know exactly which documents are required and how to prepare them, but you'll also be prepared for the inevitable bumps along the way. Treat your visa process like a project: make a checklist, keep everything scanned and backed up, and set reminders for each step. That way, if something goes wrong, you'll already know your options and won't lose valuable time scrambling for answers.

The bottom line: delays are manageable, but only if you remain solution-oriented and persistent. Think of this process as your first test of adaptability in Korea; it's excellent preparation for life as an ESL teacher.

Chapter 11: Preparing for the Move

Chapter Summary

This chapter covers everything you need to know about the transition from home to Korea. You will learn what to pack and what not to pack for life and work in Korea, what to expect during arrival, immigration, and your first few days, how to complete essential first-week tasks like your ARC and mandatory health check, what standard housing setups look like and how to make them feel like home, and how to adjust smoothly to your new environment while avoiding common rookie mistakes.

Why This Chapter Matters

By the time you reach this stage, you've already done the hard work of securing your contract, gathering visa documents, and preparing yourself mentally for teaching abroad. Now comes the part that feels the most real: packing your life into suitcases, boarding a plane, and moving halfway across the world. For many teachers, this is when the excitement peaks, but so does the stress.

Moving to Korea isn't just about having the proper paperwork. It's about knowing what to expect on the ground: what to bring from home and what you can easily buy once you're here, how to navigate the airport and immigration process, and how to handle the first week when you're jetlagged, overwhelmed, and still trying to remember how to say "hello" in Korean. The teachers who transition most smoothly are the ones who arrive prepared, not just with their documents in order, but with realistic expectations for housing, transportation, and daily life.

This chapter is designed to give you that preparation. We'll cover everything from packing essentials and pro tips about clothing, shoes, and electronics, to what really happens at the airport, what your first week will look like, and how to handle the health check and Alien

Registration Card (ARC) registration. By the end, you'll feel confident that you know exactly what to do from the moment you step off the plane until you're fully settled into your new apartment and ready to teach.

Packing Essentials for Korea

One of the most common concerns new teachers have before boarding their flight is: What should I bring with me to Korea? It's easy to overpack, but it's equally frustrating to realize you left behind something expensive or difficult to buy in Korea. While everyone's packing list will be a little different based on personal needs, there are some essentials that nearly every teacher will want to bring.

Clothing

Korea has four sharply defined seasons, so packing a balanced wardrobe is essential. Winters are long and bitterly cold, with snow and wind, so you'll need a thick, insulated coat, gloves, scarves, and thermal layers. Summers, on the other hand, are hot, humid, and rainy; lightweight, breathable clothing is a must, along with a compact umbrella and shoes that can handle heavy downpours. Spring and fall are short but very pleasant, so layering pieces such as light jackets and sweaters will serve you well during the transitional months. Remember that Costco is your friend in Korea. They have Western-size and Asian-size clothing, and it is clearly marked. I'm 6'2" and 195 pounds and I can't wear Asian-size clothes because the arms are too short, the shoulders are too narrow for tops, and the pants are too tight with slightly shorter legs than back home.

School Attire

Work attire deserves special attention. Schools expect teachers to dress modestly and professionally, with business casual being the standard. For men, collared shirts and slacks are ideal, usually without the need for ties. Women should bring blouses, modest skirts, or slacks. Sleeveless tops, short skirts, and sandals are often discouraged in classrooms. Another point to consider is sizing:

clothing in Korea is cut smaller than in the West. Teachers who are tall or broad-shouldered may struggle to find professional clothing in local shops. Shoes are even more challenging; men who wear US size 11 or higher and women above size 9.5 should pack enough pairs from home to last the year.

Pro Tip

Most Western women find shopping for undergarments, especially bras, challenging, as most sizes are 32–34 A through C cup. Be sure to bring what you like from home and enough to last you for the year.

Shoes

Shoes deserve their own category because of Korea's indoor culture. Since most apartments and even schools use heated floors (ondol), shoes are removed indoors. This means teachers need multiple types of footwear. Comfortable slip-on shoes make it easier to take shoes off and put them on quickly throughout the day. Clean "indoor teaching shoes," such as sneakers or loafers reserved only for classroom use, are also a must. At work, appearance still matters, so professional yet comfortable shoes are ideal.

Large sizes are notoriously tricky to find, so pack accordingly. As a rule of thumb, men's shoes larger than size 280mm (US 11) and women's shoes larger than 260mm (US 9) are rare in local shops. To save luggage space, don't bother bringing sandals or shower shoes; these can be bought cheaply at local stores such as Daiso or Emart for just a few dollars.

Toiletries and Personal Items

Korea has an impressive beauty industry and many high-quality skincare products, but certain items are limited or much more expensive. Deodorant, for example, is difficult to find and comes in limited brands and weak formulas. Teachers who rely on deodorant should bring enough for the year. Women who prefer tampons should also stock up before leaving, since pads are far more common locally.

Prescription medications are another priority. Teachers should bring at least a two- to three-month supply of any essential medications, along with a copy of their prescription and doctor's note. This helps when transferring prescriptions to local doctors. Contact lens wearers should bring spare lenses and solutions, and eyeglass wearers should pack an extra pair along with their prescription. While Korea has pharmacies everywhere, brands and dosages may differ from what you're used to.

It's also wise to bring a small first-aid kit stocked with pain relievers, allergy medicine, and cold remedies you prefer. Many Western cold medicines (especially those containing pseudoephedrine) are banned in Korea, so double-check before packing whether your preferred brands are legal in Korea.

Electronics

Korea uses 220V, 60Hz outlets with two round prongs. While most laptops, smartphones, and tablets are dual voltage and only require plug adapters, appliances like hair dryers or curling irons may burn out if you use them with voltage converters. In these cases, it's often better to buy the appliance in Korea rather than risk damaging it.

Essential items to pack include plug adapters, a portable power bank for long commutes or weekend trips, and a VPN subscription if you want access to streaming services from home. While Korea is home to tech giants like Samsung and LG, electronics are surprisingly more expensive than in North America or Europe. If you need a new laptop, phone, or tablet, it's better to buy it before you arrive.

Pro Tip

Access to pornographic websites and some other types of websites is banned in Korea. However, many expats pay for a VPN service to access their favorite websites that non-VPN users can't access.

Teaching Materials

While most Korean schools provide textbooks, workbooks, and some classroom supplies, having your own set of teaching tools can make a tremendous difference in how smoothly you start. The first few weeks are usually the most stressful as teachers are adjusting to new students, new methods, and a new environment. Having ready-to-go, familiar materials can help you feel more confident and impress your school by showing initiative.

A good starting point is a personal "teacher toolkit" that includes lightweight, portable items. Small English-language storybooks are excellent for younger learners, as many hagwons do not stock enough supplementary reading material. Flashcards, whether store-bought or homemade, are another versatile tool. They can be used for vocabulary drills, games like "memory," or quick warm-ups. Laminated flashcards last longer, and you can even bring blank laminated cards with dry-erase markers to make your own on the fly.

Games are always a hit in Korea. Card games like Uno or board games like Boggle and Scrabble (junior edition for younger students) are engaging and educational. Puzzle books, such as crosswords and word searches, are also inexpensive to buy at home and can be used as fun fillers for days when you or the students are low on energy. Stickers and small stationery items also go a long way with kids; they are inexpensive, lightweight, and can be used as simple rewards that motivate students to participate.

Bringing some cultural items from your home country can also enrich your lessons. Postcards, coins, miniature flags, or photos of your hometown can make great props when introducing yourself or teaching lessons on geography, culture, and holidays. Students love to see "real" items from abroad, and these can spark curiosity and conversation.

Don't overlook digital teaching materials. Having a few PowerPoint templates, pre-made worksheets, or videos saved on a USB stick or your laptop can save time if your school's resources are limited. Some schools may not provide much beyond a textbook, so being able to supplement with your own content makes you more adaptable. Just keep in mind that certain Western websites or platforms may not work in Korea without a VPN, so download or prepare resources in advance.

Finally, consider bringing a few personal comfort teaching items, for example, a portable whiteboard and markers if you like writing while walking around the classroom, or even small puppets for kindergarten students. While these aren't required, they can help you stand out as an energetic and engaging teacher.

Pro Tip

Many of these materials, like Uno cards, stickers, or puzzle books, are cheap and easy to find back home but harder or more expensive in Korea. Stock up before leaving, and you'll have a ready-made toolkit to lean on when you need it most.

Teacher Story: A Care Package Surprise

During my first year teaching in Korea, I was Skyping with my dad back home and mentioned how hard it was to find affordable English-language magazines. I told him about Kyobo (교보) Bookstore in Gwanghwamun, Seoul, the largest bookstore in Korea, where there was a limited selection of English magazines. Still, even then, most of the titles I enjoyed weren't available. I didn't think much of it at the time, but a few weeks later, a large care package arrived at my school addressed to me. My dad had sent me a box filled with English magazines and Almond Roca chocolates from Tacoma.

The box was sitting on my desk in the teacher's room when I stepped out to teach a class. At the time, three of my female Korean co-teachers and the kindergarten art teacher, Belle (whom I was dating), were in the room. Belle asked what was inside, and I told her my dad had sent me magazines and chocolates. I invited her to open the box and help herself with some Almond Roca while I was gone.

When I came back, I nearly fainted. All four women were crowded around my desk, flipping through Playboy magazine that my dad had unknowingly included in the care package, while happily munching on the Almond Roca. Belle calmly handed me one of the magazines, smiled, and said, "Korean women are different from Western women," before walking out. The other teachers giggled, folded up the magazines, and slipped them back into the box.

Mortified, I decided to skip lunch in the teacher's room that day. That evening, I called my dad to thank him for the package and to let him know it had been a "big hit" with my coworkers. When I told him what had happened, he burst out laughing so hard he could barely breathe. I might have been embarrassed in that moment, but years later, it remains one of my funniest and most memorable experiences from teaching in Korea. I can laugh at that story now, but at the time, I thought I was going to die from embarrassment.

Takeaway: I learned the hard way to check what's in a package before letting coworkers open it. A harmless surprise from back home can land you in an awkward situation if you're not careful. Those types of magazines also violate Korean law, so always screen care packages from home before sharing them at work.

Documents

When preparing to move to Korea, it's crucial to organize your essential documents carefully. Always keep both printed and digital copies of your employment contract, diploma, passport, visa, ARC application, and health check paperwork. Having backup copies stored securely in a cloud folder (such as Google Drive or Dropbox) ensures you'll have access even if your physical documents are lost or delayed.

You should also bring multiple passport-sized photos that meet Korean specifications (35mm x 45mm). These photos are required not only for your initial ARC application, but also for other processes during your stay, such as renewing your ARC, joining gyms, setting up memberships, or applying for new jobs. Many teachers underestimate how often they're needed and end up scrambling to find a photo studio in their first week. Pack at least two to four extra copies of properly sized photos before you leave home, and ask the photo studio to give you the high-resolution digital file as well, so you can easily print additional photos in Korea at convenience store kiosks or photo shops for a very low cost.

What to Expect at the Airport and Immigration

For most teachers, your journey to Korea begins at Incheon International Airport (ICN), which is located just outside of Seoul in Incheon. It's one of the busiest and most modern airports in the world, consistently ranked among the top for efficiency and cleanliness. The arrival process is generally smooth, but it helps to know what to expect to avoid confusion when you're tired after a long flight.

After deplaning, you'll follow the clearly marked signs for Immigration. Make sure you have your passport with your E-2 visa already stamped inside, your completed arrival card (fill it out on the plane or while waiting in line), and a copy of your school's address and contact information printed out or saved on your phone. Immigration officers may ask you why you are entering Korea. Keep your answer simple, professional, and clear: "Hi. I'm an English teacher working at [school name] in [city name]." This is usually enough, and in most cases, you'll be stamped in without issue. However, some officers may ask for additional details such as the address of your school, a phone number, or even to see your employment contract. That's why having these documents handy is important.

After immigration, you'll proceed to baggage claim and then through customs. Customs declarations are typically straightforward. Unless you are carrying more than the duty-free allowance of alcohol, cigarettes, or large sums of cash, you can usually pass through the "Nothing to Declare" line. That said, Korean customs officials can be strict, so avoid bringing restricted medicines, illegal substances, or large amounts of undeclared electronics.

Once you exit customs, you'll enter the Arrivals Hall. Since the COVID-19 era, it has become less common for schools to meet teachers at Incheon Airport. While this can feel intimidating, navigating from Incheon to your new school or housing is very straightforward. If you are headed to Seoul, Gyeonggi-do, or Incheon, the simplest option is to take a taxi directly to your apartment from the designated taxi queue outside the Arrivals exit. These taxis are licensed, run on a meter, and accept credit cards. Be wary of drivers who approach you inside the airport offering rides; these are often unlicensed, charge inflated rates, and sometimes intentionally take longer routes. After a long flight and with heavy luggage, a metered taxi is often worth the cost, especially if it's your first time in Korea and you're already managing jet lag.

If you're traveling to a city farther away, such as Busan, Daegu, or Gwangju, it is easiest to take a Limousine bus from the airport to a central bus terminal in your destination city. The Airport Railroad (AREX) express to Seoul Station takes about 50 minutes and costs 10,000 KRW, and the KTX train at Seoul Station connects to most major cities in Korea. Be sure to coordinate with your school to know which station to get off at and who will meet you there. Take a photo of your bus ticket and share it in your group chat with your school and recruiter, since the buses have GPS and they can track your progress.

Stay Connected from the Start

Before you even board your flight, set up a three-way KakaoTalk or WhatsApp chat with your recruiter and your school. This chat becomes your lifeline during travel and arrival. Use it to provide updates as you go: when you clear immigration, when you leave the airport, and even when you get into a taxi or bus. Snap a photo of your bus ticket or your taxi's license plate and share it in the chat. This not only reassures your school that you're on track but also creates a record in case of any mix-ups during the journey.

Having a working phone immediately upon arrival is a game-changer. You can pre-purchase a temporary SIM with unlimited data (3 to 30 days) through Trazy.com or buy one at a telecom provider kiosk near the Arrivals exit. With this, you'll be able to access maps, contact your recruiter or school, and update your group chat right away. If you plan to set up a permanent phone plan later, this short-term SIM will bridge the gap.

Pro Tip

Keep your school or recruiter's contact number and Korean address handy, either printed out or saved on your phone, in case you need to share it at immigration or with your taxi driver. Always obtain a working SIM card or eSIM after arrival and at least one universal adapter. Even if you think you'll use Wi-Fi, delays, dead batteries, and late-night arrivals can leave you disconnected when you need help the most. You can also buy local phone chargers (iPhone and Android) at convenience stores inside Incheon Airport or use recharge stations there before leaving the terminal.

Teacher Story: Joey's Arrival Struggles

One of the most memorable cases I came across was Joey, a teacher from the U.S. who ran into a chain of problems upon arrival. His flight was delayed due to a transfer issue in Japan, so he arrived at Incheon Airport much later than scheduled. Because he hadn't unlocked his phone before traveling, he decided against purchasing a SIM card and figured he would rely on Korea's plentiful Wi-Fi.

That decision worked against him. Since he missed the last bus to Gwangju, he thought it would be fine to crash at a cheap motel near the airport and head back to ICN in the morning. Unfortunately, he hadn't packed a power adapter or converter, and both his phone and laptop died overnight. Without Wi-Fi or a working telephone, Joey couldn't contact his school or recruiter. By the next morning, he managed to take the bus to Gwangju, but when he got to his housing, he had no way to access the door key code since it had been shared via KakaoTalk. He ended up stranded outside his new apartment until he borrowed a phone from a kind bus station employee. His director was eventually able to meet him in person, open the door, and even brought him a new charger from a convenience store.

It all worked out in the end, but Joey's school had spent almost 24 hours anxiously wondering what had happened to him.

Takeaway: Joey learned the hard way that relying only on Wi-Fi and skipping basic travel prep, like having an unlocked phone and a power adapter, can create serious problems during those critical first hours in Korea.

Your First 48 Hours

Most teachers depart their home countries on a Friday and arrive in Korea on Saturday, which gives them Sunday to rest and recover before beginning school orientation or training on Monday. This buffer day is essential; use it to sleep, unpack, and explore your neighborhood a little.

Most teachers' first stop after dropping their luggage is the local convenience store, a staple of Korean life. Stores like GS25, CU, or 7-Eleven are open 24/7 and offer everything from bottled water and snacks to basic toiletries and even hot meals. It's a comforting first step that helps you feel grounded.

Before you even leave the airport, however, it's wise to exchange about $200 USD into Korean won (KRW). While nearly every shop and restaurant in Korea accepts credit cards, it's still smart to carry some cash for taxis, smaller restaurants, or emergencies. You can always exchange larger amounts later at better rates in the city, but that first bit of cash will make your arrival much smoother.

One of the most important things you can do on your first day is manage jet lag. Resist the temptation to nap in the afternoon; instead, try to stay awake until at least 10 PM Korean time. Doing so will help reset your internal clock and keep you from waking up at 3 or 4 in the morning for the next several days.

When training starts, your first day at school usually includes a meet-and-greet with the director, staff, and co-teachers. Some schools may ask you to observe a few classes or introduce yourself to students, but generally, the first day is light. If your accommodation is not within walking distance, your school staff will typically show you how to commute to school by bus, subway, or taxi. This hands-on introduction will make your daily routine much less intimidating.

Your Housing

Most first-time teachers in Korea are provided with a small one-room studio apartment, often referred to locally as an officetel or one-room. Don't be surprised if it feels compact compared to what you're used to back home. These apartments typically include a washing machine, stove or hot plate, refrigerator, small table, and bed. Closet space is often limited, so it may be worth investing in organizers or storage bins once you settle in.

While your school will furnish the basics, the quality and condition of apartments can vary greatly. Some will feel brand-new and comfortable, while others may look more worn. Be prepared to purchase or replace smaller essentials such as bedding, towels, cookware, or cleaning supplies. Stores like Daiso, E-Mart, Lotte Mart, and Homeplus are lifesavers for affordable home goods. A simple toolkit and a few kitchen basics packed from home can also make your first week much smoother.

It's fairly common for new arrivals to overlap with departing teachers. In these cases, your school may place you in temporary housing (like a guesthouse or short-term stay) for a few days until the apartment is ready. Another common situation is not receiving your housing address and door code until just before your arrival. While this can feel stressful, it's a standard practice in Korea and doesn't mean anything is wrong. Flexibility during your first week will go a long way toward making your transition smoother.

Your First Week in Korea

Your first week in Korea will be busy, but it's designed to help you settle into your new environment quickly and begin adjusting to both your professional and daily life. Schools typically assist foreign teachers with several key tasks during this time, which makes the transition smoother. One of the first responsibilities is registering your address with the local education district office, an essential step for legal and administrative purposes. Schools will also help you open a bank account, though it's wise to wait until after you receive your ARC, as this ensures you can open a fully functional account rather than a limited one. Your ARC also allows the school to enroll you in Korea's national health insurance system, which is mandatory for full-time teachers. In addition, you'll usually be introduced to your co-teachers or Korean staff members on your first day, giving you an early opportunity to start building rapport and understanding your new workplace culture.

During this initial week, don't hesitate to ask questions about procedures, the classroom environment, or even how to navigate the local bus system. It's far better to clarify uncertainties early than to remain unsure and make avoidable mistakes later. Bring your passport and any official school documents to all appointments, as they may be required at banks, district offices, or immigration visits. While your school will provide guidance, it's ultimately your responsibility to keep track of your paperwork, deadlines, and important documents. Being proactive and organized shows professionalism and makes the adjustment easier for everyone involved.

Jet lag will likely hit you hard during these first few days. Many new teachers find themselves falling asleep early in the evening, around 7 or 8 PM, and waking up before dawn. To combat this, it's a good idea to establish a gentle routine that helps your body adjust to the time difference. For example, when I first arrived in Korea, I would wake up around 3:00 or 4:00 AM and take walks around my neighborhood for a few hours. At first, I walked in small circles close to my apartment, but each day I expanded my route a little further. This habit gave me exercise, sunlight, and the chance to map out my surroundings. Within a week, I not only felt better adjusted to the new time zone but also knew where all the essential shops, restaurants, parks, and landmarks were located.

It's also a good idea to explore different restaurants in your neighborhood during your first week. Korea's local eateries are affordable, welcoming, and often family-run. By trying out a handful of small restaurants, you'll soon find a "regular spot" you can rely on for cheap and delicious meals. Using a few simple Korean phrases, like greeting the staff or thanking them, goes a long way in establishing goodwill. In my case, I became a regular at a local restaurant, where the staff would excitedly call out, "The foreigner is back again!" whenever I walked in. I once took a Korean co-worker with me, and she noticed they gave me five side dishes instead of the usual three, laughing about how I'd earned "special treatment" simply by showing appreciation and enjoying their food. These early connections help you feel more at home and can even lead to some fun and heartwarming experiences.

Pro Tip

When you're ready to order food, a simple and universally understood phrase is "(Item) juseyo" (주세요), which means "Please give me (item)." For example, "Bibimbap juseyo" (비빔밥 주세요) will get you a bowl of bibimbap. Even if you don't know the Korean word for something, you can simply point to the menu and say "juseyo." It's an easy, respectful, and effective way to order in Korea, and it's a great confidence boost for beginners learning the language.

The Mandatory Health Check

Within your first week in Korea (usually between 2 and 7 days after arrival), you'll need to complete a government-required health check at a designated hospital or public health center. This step is not optional; it's a legal prerequisite for obtaining your ARC, which functions as your official ID during your time in Korea. Without this health check, you cannot finalize your visa registration, open a full-function bank account, or be enrolled in the national health insurance system.

The exam is routine but thorough. It typically includes measuring your height, weight, blood pressure, and vision, as well as taking a chest X-ray to screen for tuberculosis. You'll also provide blood and urine samples for testing, which check for communicable diseases (like HIV) and for the use of illegal substances. The appointment ends with a brief consultation with a doctor who reviews your results. The entire process usually takes between one and two hours, depending on how busy the clinic is.

Zero Tolerance for Drugs

It's critical to understand that Korea has strict zero-tolerance laws when it comes to drug use, even for substances that may be legal in your home country. Cannabis, for instance, is legal or decriminalized in parts of the U.S. and Canada, but in Korea, any trace of THC in your system can result in immediate termination, deportation, and a permanent ban from re-entry. This is non-negotiable.

THC can remain in the body for weeks or even months, depending on body composition, usage habits, and metabolism. Teachers who casually used cannabis before leaving home have sometimes been caught off guard by positive test results. To avoid this nightmare scenario, it's safest to abstain entirely in the months leading up to your departure. Some teachers also prepare by exercising regularly, drinking plenty of water, and maintaining a clean diet to help their system process more efficiently. However, time and abstention are ultimately the only reliable safeguards for passing the drug test.

Why the Health Check Matters

The health check isn't just bureaucracy; it's directly tied to your ability to live and work legally in Korea. Your results are sent to the immigration office, and only after they're approved can your ARC application be processed. If you test positive for illegal substances, your job offer will be rescinded, your visa invalidated, and you will be deported. This can happen even if you've already started teaching.

Schools are equally strict because they can be fined or penalized for sponsoring a teacher who fails the exam. For this reason, most employers schedule the health check within the first week to ensure there are no surprises later.

You don't need to fast before the exam, but avoid alcohol for at least 24 hours, since it may skew liver enzyme results. Wear comfortable clothing and bring your passport and a couple of passport photos (sometimes required for hospital paperwork). The exam usually costs between 60,000 and 120,000 KRW (roughly $50 to $100 USD); usually, schools do not cover the medical exam cost, since it is your responsibility. Some schools do cover this cost, so be sure to ask your school how the fee is paid and by whom.

After the exam, results are typically ready within 7 to 10 days, though some hospitals provide them sooner. Keep a copy of your results for your personal records, as you may need to show them again when applying for an additional job, university course, or visa renewal in the future.

Teacher Story: Lucy's Money Misunderstanding

Lucy, a Canadian teacher, arrived in Korea full of enthusiasm, but she quickly ran into trouble with her new school over money. During her first week, she was frustrated that the school did not reimburse her for the cost of the mandatory medical exam or for the fees she had paid to prepare her visa documents back in Canada. Even though it is standard practice for teachers to cover these costs themselves, Lucy insisted that she had read online that "schools often reimburse" such expenses. Because she pushed the issue so strongly, her school felt she was being combative and unreasonable, even though they had never promised reimbursement.

A few weeks later, the issue resurfaced. Lucy argued that since her contract promised "free housing," she shouldn't have to pay utility bills like water, electricity, or internet. Once again, the school, then I, had to explain to her that in Korea, "free housing" means the rent and apartment itself are covered, but utilities are always the teacher's responsibility. By this point, the school had grown wary of her constant complaints about money, and their relationship with her was strained.

Fortunately, Lucy was a talented teacher in the classroom, and she eventually built a strong rapport with her students. Over time, she also connected with other foreign teachers, who helped her realize that her school was treating her fairly and that she had misunderstood what standard practice was. With this new perspective, she calmed down and adjusted, but those first impressions had already left a mark on how the school viewed her.

Takeaway: Lucy learned that starting a job by arguing over money, especially when the school was following standard practice, created unnecessary tension. Even though she recovered later, her early insistence made it harder to build trust with her school. Do your research on what schools typically cover versus what you're responsible for, and budget for utilities each month, even if housing is "free."

Alien Registration Card (ARC)

Once you've completed your medical exam, your school will help you schedule an appointment at the immigration office to apply for your ARC. This card is essentially your Korean ID, and it will become the most essential piece of identification you carry during your stay. The ARC links you to your visa status and is required for nearly every aspect of daily life, from setting up a bank account to enrolling in health insurance, registering for a phone plan, and even picking up parcels at the post office.

For the appointment, you'll need to bring your valid passport, your completed ARC application form, one photo of an official passport (35mm x 45mm), your health check results, and your housing contract or another proof of residence document. You'll also need to pay a fee of about 30,000 KRW, usually in the form of a revenue stamp purchased at the immigration office or nearby convenience stores. Most schools will accompany new teachers to immigration during the first few weeks to make the process smoother.

Immigration typically issues the ARC within three to six weeks of your appointment, but the timeline varies depending on how busy your regional office is. Schools located in large cities like Seoul or Busan sometimes face longer processing times due to the higher volume of applicants. During this waiting period, keep your passport and a copy of your visa with you whenever you travel locally in Korea, as these serve as your identification until the ARC is issued.

Once issued, your ARC should always be carried with you. Korean law requires foreign residents to have it on hand for identification if asked by authorities. Your passport should stay safely stored at home, used only for international travel or official consular business. You will need your passport along with your ARC to open a bank account or set up a mobile phone contract.

It's also crucial to keep your ARC updated. If you change housing, immigration requires you to update your address within 14 days. Missing this deadline can result in fines of 100,000 KRW or more. Many teachers forget this small detail, but immigration does check, especially during renewals or if you are pulled into administrative processes for another reason.

Pro Tip

Make multiple photocopies of your ARC once you receive it and store them in different safe places: one at home, one in your wallet, and one in digital form as a scanned copy in a secure cloud folder. You'll often need to provide your ARC number on forms, and having a copy handy save you from carrying the original everywhere. If you lose your ARC, reporting and reissuing it can be a stressful process, so treating the card as carefully as your passport is essential.

Traveling Internationally Before or After Receiving Your ARC

If you plan to travel outside Korea before your ARC is delivered, or at any point during your contract, it is essential to check whether your E-2 visa was issued as a single-entry or multiple-entry visa. A single-entry visa will be canceled once you leave the country, and you'll need to obtain a re-entry permit from immigration before your departure to avoid major complications upon return.

Teacher Story: Roger's Weekend in Osaka

Roger, a British teacher, learned the hard way about the importance of understanding visa rules. Halfway through his first contract in Korea, he decided to take advantage of a three-day holiday and booked a short trip to Osaka, Japan. The problem was that he made two crucial mistakes: first, he forgot to bring his ARC card to the airport, and second, he didn't realize that his E-2 visa was stamped as a single-entry visa, not multiple-entry.

When he returned to Korea, immigration stamped his passport with a 90-day tourist visa instead of reinstating his E-2. This meant his work visa was effectively voided. Without realizing the seriousness of this, Roger returned to his school and continued teaching. For the next four months, he was technically working illegally on a tourist visa. Fortunately for him, he didn't get caught during that period, and because he only had a few months left on his contract, he managed to finish without issue. As the 90 days on his tourist visa ran out, Roger booked another weekend trip to Japan to reset his visa and secure another 90 days.

A year later, when I interviewed him for a new position in Korea, he openly told me about this experience. He admitted that it was a "rude awakening" and something he never thought could happen simply by forgetting a card and not reading the fine print on his visa. He was nervous that this mistake might jeopardize his chances of receiving another E-2 visa, but luckily, immigration approved his new application without holding the past issue against him.

Takeaway: Roger's story shows how small oversights, like forgetting an ARC card or misunderstanding single-entry versus multiple-entry visas, can snowball into big immigration issues. While he got lucky, he realized afterward that he had taken a serious risk that could have cost him his job and future opportunities in Korea.

Pro Tip

Always check your visa type before traveling outside Korea. If your E-2 is a single-entry visa, you must purchase a re-entry permit from immigration before leaving the country. Always carry your ARC card, especially when traveling internationally. A five-minute check before you book flights can save you months of stress and potential trouble with immigration.

Final Thoughts

Arriving in Korea is a whirlwind. New teachers face so much at once: jet lag, unfamiliar signs, different food, and a completely new work culture. It's easy to feel overwhelmed. Yet the truth is that everyone goes through this stage, and your outlook will largely determine whether you thrive or struggle.

I once knew two teachers who arrived at the same school at the same time. Both faced identical challenges: confusing commutes, miscommunications with co-teachers, and the occasional cultural faux pas. The first teacher saw these hiccups as part of the adventure. Every mistake became a funny story to share with friends and family back home, and every new experience, whether awkward or confusing, was embraced as part of the journey. The second teacher, however, viewed each minor setback as a personal failure or embarrassment. Instead of laughing at their mistakes, they dwelt on them, which made adjusting much harder.

What struck me was that both teachers had the same experiences, but one left after a year feeling energized, adventurous, and proud of all they had overcome, while the other left drained and discouraged. The difference wasn't the school, the students, or even the workload; it was the mindset. Teaching abroad comes with inevitable challenges. If you approach them with curiosity and resilience, they'll become some of the most rewarding and memorable moments of your life. If the idea of uncertainty, constant learning, and occasional discomfort excites you, then Korea is a fantastic fit. But if you expect everything to feel familiar or easy, you may struggle. Living abroad isn't about recreating your home life in a new place; it's about embracing a different rhythm, culture, and way of being.

Give yourself grace in this adjustment period. It takes time to settle into your role, your home, and your new cultural environment. Lean on your support system: your school staff, fellow expat teachers who have been through the same challenges, and online TEFL or expat communities that offer guidance and reassurance. Korea is one of the most modern, safe, and efficient countries in the world, and while paperwork and bureaucracy may seem daunting at first, most processes are manageable with clear instructions and a bit of patience. The key is to approach your first weeks with flexibility and curiosity. Every small challenge, figuring out the subway system, ordering a meal in Korean, or setting up your utilities, is part of the adventure. Go into your year abroad expecting challenges, awkward moments, and mistakes; they're unavoidable. If you can laugh at yourself and stay curious, you'll thrive no matter what comes your way.

Part Four

Arriving and Settling In

Chapter 12: Getting Situated in Korea

Chapter Summary

This chapter covers the practical foundations of daily life in Korea. You will learn what to expect from school-provided apartments and the pros and cons of renting independently, how to set up essential services like phone, internet, banking, and utilities, and how to navigate Korea's world-class public transportation system.

Why This Chapter Matters

Settling into a new life abroad isn't just about showing up for your first day of teaching; it's about creating a stable and comfortable foundation for your year in Korea. Housing, utilities, banking, and transportation may not sound as exciting as cultural exploration or weekend trips, but they are the backbone of your daily routine. The sooner you feel confident in these practical areas, the sooner you can focus on enjoying your teaching, building friendships, and immersing yourself in Korean culture.

For most new teachers, the first month in Korea is the steepest learning curve. You'll not only be adjusting to your school's expectations but also figuring out how to navigate an entirely new system of living, from how to pay your bills, to where to buy bedding, to which subway line will get you across the city. Getting these essentials sorted out early helps reduce stress and prevents minor issues from snowballing into big frustrations.

Housing is vital. Most schools provide it, which is a huge relief, but the reality of Korean apartments, compact one-rooms, wet bathrooms, and utility bills can be surprising to first-timers. Knowing what to expect ahead of time prevents disappointment and helps you make the most of your new space. On the other hand, some teachers receive a housing stipend and need to navigate Korea's unique real estate market. Understanding the differences between jeonse (전세),

which is a lump-sum lease, and wolse (월세), which is a deposit plus monthly rent system, is critical if you ever go this route.

Equally important is setting up the tools that will make daily life manageable: a reliable phone plan, high-speed internet, and a functional bank account. Without these, even simple things like paying bills, contacting your school, or ordering food delivery become unnecessary obstacles. Korea has a reputation for being fast and efficient in these areas, but only if you know what documents and steps are required.

Finally, transportation is the lifeline of living in Korea. Whether you're commuting to school, taking weekend trips, or just exploring your neighborhood, Korea's public transport system is one of the best in the world. Learning how to use subways, buses, and apps like Kakao T or Naver (네이버) Map will make you feel at home faster and give you the freedom to explore confidently.

This chapter matters because it bridges the gap between "arriving" and "living." By understanding housing, utilities, banking, and transportation, you'll transition from being a newcomer overwhelmed by details to an expat who feels grounded, independent, and ready to thrive in Korea.

Understanding School-Provided Housing

For most first-time English teachers in Korea, housing is one of the most significant reliefs. Unlike many countries where teachers must secure their own accommodations, Korea's standard practice is for schools to either provide an apartment directly or offer a monthly housing stipend. This arrangement removes a lot of stress from your transition, but it's essential to know exactly what to expect so you're not caught off guard.

The Standard Setup

Most E-2 visa holders are given what is called a "one-room" (원룸) apartment. This is a compact studio unit with a small kitchenette, bathroom, and sleeping area all in one space. Sizes can vary depending on whether you are in a major city like Seoul (where space is more expensive) or in a smaller city or rural town (where apartments tend to be more spacious). Some schools provide modern units with updated appliances, while others may offer older buildings with fewer amenities.

Typical furnishings include a bed (often a single), a wardrobe or clothing rack, a small refrigerator and basic cooking setup such as a two-burner gas stove or hot plate, a washing machine (but rarely a dryer), a desk or small table, an air conditioner (wall unit) and heating (ondol, floor-based heating), and a TV.

Many one-room apartments also come with a "wet bathroom," where the shower is not separated from the sink and toilet. This can be surprising at first, but it is quite common in Korea. Over time, most teachers adapt by keeping bathroom essentials in covered storage to avoid them getting wet. This means that there is no shower door or shower stall. The faucet is usually detachable from the wall, and you use the whole bathroom as the shower. Most Korean showers also have a small stool to sit on while you shower, which is very comfortable and convenient.

Minimalist but Functional

It's worth noting that teacher housing is often minimalist. You'll usually find pots, pans, bedding, and small appliances left behind by the previous teacher, but their condition varies widely. Some schools clean and refresh the apartment before you move in, while others expect you to do the initial cleaning yourself. Most teachers supplement the basics with affordable items from stores like Daiso, Homeplus, or IKEA (in larger cities).

While you may not get to preview your exact apartment before arrival, it's always reasonable to ask for sample housing photos. Many schools are willing to provide them or connect you with the current teacher so you can get a realistic sense of what to expect. As a rule of thumb, I always provide sample housing photos because I know how important housing is. My first two accommodations (20+ years ago) went from not good to, oh hell no. If I had seen the photos before taking the job, I would have turned down the job. I am not joking when I say I lived above a Buddhist temple for a few months until I was able to negotiate different housing. Luckily, nowadays in Korea, most schools know how important decent accommodation is to teachers. Any reputable school will be happy to share sample housing photos, and if they won't, do not accept a job with them.

The Hidden Costs

Although schools cover the rent, "free housing" does not mean entirely cost-free. You will be responsible for utilities, which usually include electricity, water, gas (for heating and cooking), and internet. These average around 80,000 to 120,000 KRW per month but can rise in the winter (for heating) and summer (for air conditioning). Internet costs are relatively low, averaging 25,000 to 35,000 KRW per month, and connections are among the fastest in the world.

A key advantage of taking school-provided housing is that the school typically arranges the deposit and rental agreement, and you are not required to pay anything regarding the deposit or the monthly rent. In Korea, housing deposits, known as "key money," can range from several thousand to tens of thousands of dollars. Most foreign teachers could not afford this upfront cost, which is why accepting the housing offered by your school is almost always the better choice, especially in your first year. It is rare for first-year teachers to take the housing stipend, and I strongly urge you in your first year to take the free housing provided, unless you have friends or family in Korea who have an extra room that you can rent from them or stay at for free.

Pros and Cons

The most significant benefit of school-provided housing is convenience. You can move in right away, skip the bureaucracy of real estate agents, and avoid navigating Korea's unique housing deposit system. On the downside, you don't get to choose the exact apartment, and sometimes the housing is older or smaller than what you might ideally want.

If you're assigned housing, approach it with flexibility. Remember that this arrangement is temporary, and most teachers quickly adapt once they add personal touches. On the other hand, if you're given a housing stipend, proceed with caution; unless you have Korean friends or family to help, finding and securing your own place can be a confusing and costly process. Many teachers who have lived in Seoul for a few years eventually take the stipend because they end up renting a two or three-bedroom house in Haebangchon (해방촌, or HBC), a neighborhood in Seoul's Yongsan District next to Itaewon, which is popular with expats living in Seoul. Itaewon is the "International District" that has a plethora of expat-owned and run bars and restaurants that cater to English-speaking people. It also has four to five great Mexican restaurants. A side note: only Itaewon has excellent Mexican food. However, Dos Tacos in Gangnam is very good, and in Songdo Incheon, Santa Barbara is also outstanding. Sorry, I love Mexican food...

When it comes to school housing, be prepared to purchase basic items like fresh bedding, towels, cookware, and cleaning supplies during your first week, since you will be short on luggage space. Stores like Daiso, Homeplus, and E-Mart are great for affordable essentials. Always ask for photos in advance, even if the school cannot show you your exact unit; most teachers live in identical units in the same building or nearby buildings. If you have any doubts, speak to a current teacher about their housing. And be prepared for some overlap with the departing teacher. Schools often place new teachers in temporary housing for two to three nights while the apartment is prepared, since departing teachers usually train their replacements. Just be sure to have all details hammered out at least a week before arriving. Budget for at least $100 USD per month in utilities, with higher costs during Korea's hot summers and cold winters.

Pro Tip

If you would like to see available job listings from all over Korea, which include sample housing photos, job descriptions, and more, visit teachenglishinkorea.org/jobs-1. You can also check out the popular Dave's ESL jobs board at eslcafe.com.

Teacher Story: Maria's Apartment in Songdo, Incheon

Maria, an American teacher placed in Songdo, Incheon, was pleasantly surprised when she first saw her apartment. Like many new teachers, she expected a cramped, bare-bones studio. Instead, her unit, while compact, was well-designed and efficiently furnished. It came with built-in appliances such as a refrigerator, washing machine, and closets, along with thoughtful touches like a shoe cabinet by the entrance, a dining table, and even a small veranda. On pleasant evenings, she could slide open the veranda window, set up a little table and two chairs, and enjoy a breeze while sipping tea or reading.

At first, Maria didn't realize just how fortunate she was. Her apartment still felt "tiny" compared to what she had back in the U.S. But when a few of her teacher friends from Seoul visited, they immediately commented on how much nicer and larger her apartment was compared to theirs. Some of her friends lived in older, more basic units in Seoul that lacked storage or natural light, and they were impressed by Maria's space-saving design and bonus features like the veranda. This was when Maria realized that she had lucked out with her placement. Not only was Songdo a modern, well-planned area, but her housing was a step above what many teachers in Seoul could expect, and just a five-minute walk to her school.

Takeaway: Maria learned that it's easy to overlook the positives in your situation until you compare experiences with others. What seemed "small" to her at first turned out to be enviable housing compared to many teacher apartments in Korea. Don't judge your apartment solely by your expectations from back home. Korean housing often uses clever design to maximize space, and even compact units can be comfortable with the right perspective.

Renting an Apartment Independently

While most first-year teachers accept school-provided housing, some choose, or are required, to rent independently, especially if their employer offers a monthly housing allowance instead of a furnished apartment. This option gives you more freedom to select where you live, but it also means navigating the complex and unfamiliar Korean rental system, which is very different from what most foreigners are used to. Unless you already have family or friends in Korea to help you, I strongly recommend new teachers take the school-provided housing, at least for their first year.

Korea's Two Rental Systems

Korea operates under two main housing systems: jeonse (전세) and wolse (월세). Jeonse is a unique arrangement where the tenant provides a massive lump-sum deposit, sometimes 50 to 80% of the apartment's market value, directly to the landlord. In return, the tenant pays little or no monthly rent, only covering utilities and maintenance fees. At the end of the lease, the deposit is refunded in full. While this can be financially attractive for locals with significant savings or for long-term residents who want stability, it's generally impractical for foreign teachers. Few new arrivals can afford deposits of $100,000 USD or more, and it's risky if you don't fully understand the market.

Wolse, on the other hand, is more similar to the rental systems in the West. You pay a smaller deposit, often between 5 to 10 million KRW (roughly $3,500 to $7,500 USD), and then pay monthly rent on top of utilities. This is by far the most common system for foreigners, but it still requires substantial upfront cash. Landlords also often prefer long-term tenants and may ask for additional guarantees.

Documentation and Requirements

Renting independently requires paperwork that most first-year teachers don't have in place right away. To sign a lease, you'll need your ARC, a Korean bank account, and in many cases, a Korean guarantor or co-signer. This can be tricky since most teachers don't yet have close local contacts willing to act as guarantors. Some real estate agents may also hesitate to work with foreigners due to the language barrier or a perception that expats are less reliable long-term tenants.

Working with a Real Estate Agent

If you pursue independent housing, your best bet is to use a real estate agent (부동산 / budongsan). Agents are everywhere in Korea; look for the red-and-blue circular 부동산 sign on small office fronts. Many agents don't speak much English, but in larger cities or foreigner-heavy areas like Itaewon (Seoul) or Haeundae (Busan), you can find some who specialize in helping foreigners. Agents will typically require one month's rent as their commission fee, which is paid up front when you sign the contract.

Things to Watch Out For

When viewing apartments, inspect carefully and ask questions, even if you need a translator or help from a Korean colleague. Common issues include poor insulation (leading to high heating bills in winter), noisy neighbors (especially if the building is above a bar, noraebang, or restaurant), and limited ventilation. Confirm whether utilities and internet are already set up, and clarify who is responsible for maintenance. Some landlords expect tenants to handle small repairs themselves, while others include it in the rental agreement.

Pro Tip

If you decide to rent independently, never sign a lease without physically inspecting the apartment first. Photos can be misleading, and you may not notice issues like mold, noise, or poor heating until you see the space. Take note of the internet speed, location of bus or subway stops, and whether the area feels safe at night. If you aren't fluent in Korean, consider bringing a Korean friend, coworker, or even a translator app to make sure you fully understand the terms before signing.

Teacher Story: Megan's Move to Itaewon

Megan loved her first teaching job in Gimpo. Her school was supportive, her students were enjoyable to teach, and by the end of her first year, she felt genuinely settled. When the school offered her a raise of 200,000 KRW per month and allowed her to switch to a housing allowance of 400,000 KRW, she was thrilled. This flexibility opened up a new possibility she hadn't considered before: living in Seoul with her two close teacher friends.

Her friends had recently rented a three-bedroom house in Haebangchon (해방촌, HBC), a lively neighborhood near Itaewon known for its large international community, quirky cafés, and Western restaurants. They invited Megan to take the third room for 400,000 KRW per month, but it came with a catch: she would also need to pay a third of the 10 million KRW deposit. After crunching the numbers, she realized her raise and housing allowance would cover her share perfectly. Excited by the chance to live in such a vibrant area and be surrounded by close friends, she accepted.

At first, it was everything she hoped for. Megan loved being just steps away from her favorite European-style bakery, the vegan shop she frequented for specialty foods, and a handful of international restaurants that reminded her of home. Life in HBC was dynamic and full of energy, and after the workday in Gimpo, she enjoyed returning to a neighborhood that felt like a global village.

But six months into their arrangement, one of the roommates decided to move back to the UK. Suddenly, Megan and her remaining housemate were left with the stress of covering rent and deposit until they found someone new. It took nearly a month to fill the vacancy, and those weeks were financially and emotionally draining. Fortunately, they eventually found another teacher to move in, and from then on, the house felt stable again.

Megan ended up living in that house for three years, extending her stay in Korea far longer than she had initially planned. The experience gave her a taste of independence, community, and real-life problem-solving. When she finally returned home to Austin, Texas, she often looked back fondly on her "HBC years," remembering both the excitement of life in Seoul's international hub and the challenges that taught her resilience.

Takeaway: Megan learned that living with friends in a prime location can be rewarding, but it comes with financial risks when one roommate leaves. If you're considering renting independently with friends, budget for unexpected situations and have a plan for covering the deposit or rent in the short term. Shared housing can be a fantastic experience, but it's best approached with both excitement and financial caution.

Setting Up Phone, Internet, and Utilities

Once you are settled into your housing, you will need to take care of practical services that allow you to live comfortably in Korea. Fortunately, most of these can be set up in your first couple of weeks, especially once you receive your ARC.

Mobile Phone Service

To get a Korean phone number, you will need your ARC and passport. You can choose a postpaid plan with a Korean carrier (KT, SK Telecom, or LG U+) or a prepaid SIM. Prepaid SIMs are great for short-term stays or while you are waiting for your ARC. Postpaid plans offer more data and stability for long-term residents and often require an ARC and a Korean bank account for setup. For immediate connectivity upon arrival, a prepaid SIM card is a convenient option you can often purchase at the airport or a convenience store, giving you a phone number right away for essential communication.

You can either sign a new two-year contract for a mobile phone and number, which is a common practice that often includes a new device, or you can take over an existing plan from a departing expat. The latter option can be a cost-effective way to get a phone and an established plan, and it's a great way to "pay it forward" by giving your phone away to another new teacher when you leave.

Pro Tip

If you want to keep your home country's mobile number active while in Korea, port it to a virtual phone service like usphoneabroad.com (USPA) or a similar provider for around $6 to $8 per month. This keeps your number active and enables you to receive important texts, such as banking or two-factor authentication (2FA) codes, via the internet. Many of these services have apps that can forward SMS messages to your Korean mobile device. This ensures you stay connected to your home-country services while in Korea and allows you to easily port your number back to a new carrier when you eventually return home.

Internet and Utilities

If your school arranges your housing, they may already have the internet and utilities set up. If you're renting on your own, you'll be responsible for setup and monthly payments. Internet installation is a one-time fee, and monthly costs typically range from 25,000 to 35,000 KRW. Utility bills will vary by season, but you should budget 80,000 to 150,000 KRW per month total. The internet is on average two to three times faster in Korea due to its dense population and a history of being early adopters of high-speed fiber optic infrastructure.

This advanced network means that even in smaller cities, you can expect reliable and lightning-fast internet service. It's a significant advantage that makes it easier to stay in touch with family and friends or stream your favorite shows without interruption.

Pro Tip

Take a photo of your utility meters when you move in to avoid being charged for prior usage.

Bank Accounts

Opening a bank account is one of the first things you will do after receiving your ARC. Major banks like Kookmin Bank (KB), Shinhan, Woori, and Hana all have English-speaking staff in larger branches or dedicated foreign customer service centers. You will need both your passport and your ARC to open a fully functional account. When it comes to international transfers, you can wire money to your home bank from a designated Korean bank but be aware that you can only transfer up to $10,000 per year without requiring additional documentation.

Navigating Korean Transportation

Korea's public transportation is one of the best in the world. Clean, punctual, and affordable, it connects even rural areas to major cities with surprising efficiency.

Subways and Buses

If you are living in a city like Seoul, Busan, or Daegu, the subway will be your primary mode of transport. All subway systems are color-coded, bilingual, and operate from 5:30 a.m. to midnight. Use a T-Money (티머니) or Cashbee card to pay for both buses and subways. These cards are essential for seamless travel and offer a small discount compared to paying with cash. You can purchase and reload them at any convenience store or subway station. Be sure to tap your card when you get on and off, as this ensures you receive a free transfer discount when switching between buses and subways.

Pro Tip

Download apps like Kakao Metro, Kakao Bus, and Naver Map (with English settings) to get accurate transit schedules and real-time route information.

Taxis and Ride Apps

Taxis are plentiful and affordable in Korea. You can hail one on the street or, more conveniently, use the Kakao T app. This app works similarly to Uber, connecting you with nearby drivers and allowing you to set your destination digitally, which helps overcome potential language barriers.

In Korea, you'll encounter two main types of taxis: regular and black cabs. Regular taxis are typically orange, white, or silver and are the most common and affordable option. Black cabs, also known as "Deluxe" or "Mobeom" (모범) taxis, are a premium service. They are black with a yellow stripe and offer a higher level of service, featuring more spacious and luxurious vehicles driven by experienced drivers. The fare for black cabs is significantly more expensive than that of regular taxis, but they are often a good option if you want a guaranteed high-quality ride or if a regular cab is hard to find.

Pro Tip

For female solo travelers, I always suggest using Kakao T. Not only is it convenient, but it provides an extra layer of safety, especially when traveling alone at night. The app registers both the taxi and the driver, and your account information is on file, creating a digital record of your trip. While Korea is generally considered very safe, this extra precaution offers valuable peace of mind.

Final Thoughts

Getting settled in Korea can feel overwhelming at first. Between learning how your apartment works, figuring out phone plans, navigating transportation, and handling unfamiliar systems, the first few weeks often feel like constant problem-solving. That feeling is completely normal. Almost every teacher I've worked with, regardless of experience or confidence level, has described the first month as the most mentally and emotionally demanding part of their time in Korea.

The good news is that you are rarely expected to figure everything out on your own. Most schools are well-practiced in onboarding foreign teachers and will actively assist with housing logistics, banking, phone setup, hospital visits, and transportation. Even beyond formal support, many Korean coworkers genuinely enjoy helping their foreign colleagues adjust. It's common for co-teachers, coordinators, or staff members to walk you to the bank, translate phone contracts, explain utility bills, or show you where to shop and eat near your apartment. These small acts of kindness add up quickly and make the transition far smoother than it might initially seem.

As the days pass, routines begin to form. You learn which bus to take without thinking, which convenience store is open late, how to order your favorite meal, and where to go when you need something fixed or replaced. Tasks that felt confusing in your first week, like reloading a transit card, paying a utility bill, or navigating a phone app, become automatic. With each small success, your confidence grows, and daily life starts to feel less like survival mode and more like living.

By the end of the first month, most teachers find that Korea no longer feels foreign in the same way. Your apartment starts to feel like home, familiar faces appear in your neighborhood, and the city begins to feel navigable rather than overwhelming. What once felt intimidating becomes empowering. Many teachers look back on those first chaotic weeks and realize that they were a necessary part of the adjustment process, and often the foundation for some of their most memorable experiences.

Give yourself patience during this transition. Ask questions, accept help, and don't expect perfection from yourself. Within a few weeks, the systems that once felt unfamiliar will feel second nature, and Korea will begin to feel less like a temporary destination and more like a place where you truly belong.

Chapter 13: Adjusting to Korean Culture and Work Life

Chapter Summary

This chapter covers how to build trust and strong relationships with your Korean coworkers, understand workplace hierarchy, etiquette, and communication norms, and identify ways to navigate and overcome culture shock. You will also learn how to master what I call "flex-and-flexibility" to handle last-minute changes with grace and why avoiding ethnocentrism and embracing multicultural understanding will make your experience in Korea significantly more rewarding.

Why This Chapter Matters

Moving to Korea to teach English is more than just a career move; it is a complete cultural immersion that will require adaptation, patience, and an open mind. The excitement of a new job, a new apartment, and a new environment will inevitably be accompanied by moments of disorientation or uncertainty. These feelings are entirely normal and part of the learning curve that comes with living and working in another country. To thrive as a teacher in Korea, it is essential not only to understand the classroom and job expectations but also to learn how to work within the cultural framework of Korean society. This chapter will walk you through building those relationships, navigating the workplace, managing culture shock, and developing the cultural intelligence that will make your time here more fulfilling and harmonious.

Building Relationships with your Korean Co-workers

Relationships in Korean workplaces are built on trust, respect, and harmony. Your Korean coworkers may not immediately open up to you, but that does not mean they are cold or unfriendly. Once you establish a level of mutual understanding, many will go out of their way to support you, both professionally and personally.

To foster good relationships, start with small but meaningful gestures. Greet everyone when you arrive and leave the office, as these daily interactions are key to building a positive rapport. Saying "Hello, how are you?" with a warm smile each morning, or "Annyeonghaseyo" (안녕하세요), and "Goodbye" ("Annyeonghi gyeseyo," 안녕히 가세요) when you leave, are more than just formalities; they show respect and politeness, which are foundational in Korean culture. Offering snacks or coffee occasionally is a subtle but effective way to break the ice. If a coworker helps you with a translation or explains a school procedure, a sincere "gamsahabnida" (감사합니다), or "thank you," goes a long way. Even limited Korean phrases, when spoken with good intent, demonstrate humility and a genuine effort to connect with your colleagues.

If your school organizes team lunches or dinner outings, known as "hoesik," do your best to attend. These informal gatherings are considered essential for building camaraderie and are often where deeper relationships are formed. Many teachers are surprised to find that their relationships with coworkers deepen through these shared meals rather than during the workday. At the table, titles often drop, and you may find your supervisor or co-teacher more relaxed and conversational. These moments are valuable for building rapport and learning more about Korean customs and workplace etiquette.

Teacher Story: The Silent Co-worker

When I first began teaching in Korea, one of my Korean colleagues, Belle, puzzled me. In the teacher's room, she barely spoke to me when the other three Korean English teachers were present. Yet when we were alone, she was warm, talkative, and genuinely curious. The contrast felt confusing, almost like a "hot and cold" dynamic I couldn't quite interpret.

As the weeks passed, Belle and I gradually became friends. We started spending weekends together exploring Seoul, sightseeing, hiking, and wandering through shops and cafés. During these outings, I noticed another interesting shift. In Seoul, she was relaxed and affectionate. She would hold my hand and walk closely beside me. But back in Gyeonggi-do, where we both lived and worked, her behavior changed. She often walked slightly behind me or off to the side, maintaining a visible distance.

Eventually, curiosity overcame hesitation, and I asked her about it.

Belle explained that she felt self-conscious about her English ability compared to the other Korean English teachers. She worried about making mistakes in front of them and feeling embarrassed. Speaking with me privately felt safe; speaking publicly triggered anxiety. What I had initially interpreted as aloofness was, in reality, professional insecurity.

Her explanation about our different public experiences was equally revealing. At the time, she described Seoul as far more liberal than Gyeonggi-do. In Seoul, interracial couples and foreigners were common enough to attract little attention. In suburban areas and smaller cities, however, foreign residents were still relatively rare, and social norms felt more conservative. She wasn't rejecting me; she was responding to perceived social scrutiny.

Looking back, it's striking how much Korea has evolved. The country has become dramatically more international and culturally diverse. Interracial marriages, multinational families, and cross-cultural relationships are now far more visible, not only in Seoul but increasingly throughout regional cities and rural communities. What once felt unusual has steadily become ordinary.

Takeaway: What seems like distant or inconsistent behavior may have nothing to do with you. Cultural norms, workplace dynamics, and personal insecurities often shape how people interact across languages and social contexts.

Pro Tip

I always suggest teachers bring something from their home country that is inexpensive, shareable, and delicious to share with their new Korean coworkers. It's a thoughtful gesture that can help break the ice and create a friendly first impression. I'm from Tacoma, Washington, so I brought a large bag of Almond Roca to share, and it was a massive hit with my colleagues and boss. If you can't find a local specialty from your hometown, a box of high-quality chocolates like Ferrero Rocher, or a similar well-known brand, is a safe and appreciated choice. You can easily pick these up at the duty-free store in the airport before you depart.

Understanding Workplace Hierarchy and Expectations

Korean workplaces operate with a distinct hierarchical structure, influenced by Confucian values of respect for elders and authority. Titles matter, age is acknowledged, and there are unspoken expectations about communication and conduct. Understanding these dynamics early will save you from unnecessary friction and help you earn the respect of your colleagues.

Your role as a foreign teacher is unique. While you are respected for your language skills and educational background, you are also an outsider to the system. It is essential to show deference to your supervisor and your head teacher or vice-principal, if you are in a public school. Speak respectfully, avoid public disagreement, and follow school rules, even if they are not explicitly explained. Be punctual; being even five minutes late can be viewed as disrespectful, and maintain a professional appearance at all times.

If you disagree with a decision, a simple rule is to avoid disagreeing in front of others. If something is said that you disagree with, first ask for clarification so that you understand the situation completely. Second, it is always wise to seek advice from a trusted friend or colleague who has been in Korea longer than you. If, after reflecting on the issue and having sought out advice, you still think something is wrong, then bring up the problem, but be sure to do so privately and one-on-one. If you openly disagree with your manager or a senior colleague in front of other people, even if you are 100% correct, you risk making them "lose face," which can seriously damage your professional relationship.

In meetings, wait your turn to speak and never interrupt someone more senior. You may find that decisions are not debated openly and that instructions are delivered without room for negotiation. This does not mean your input is unwelcome, but it is best to offer suggestions gently and through appropriate channels. For example, rather than saying "That lesson plan is not effective," try "May I suggest an alternative activity that the students might enjoy?" Diplomacy goes much further than directness in the Korean workplace.

There are, however, certain things you should never accept regardless of workplace norms. Nobody from your school should ever enter your housing without your permission. Nobody should ever hold your passport for safekeeping. These are examples of when you need to say no, politely but firmly. Being flexible does not mean being a pushover, and knowing where your boundaries are is just as important as knowing when to adapt.

Overcoming Culture Shock

Culture shock can sneak up on even the most adventurous teachers. During the first few weeks, everything may feel exciting and new. But as the novelty wears off, minor frustrations may begin to surface. These can include language barriers, unfamiliar food, indirect communication styles, or bureaucratic red tape.

You may also feel isolated at times, especially if you are placed in a rural area, there are not many foreign teachers at your school, or if your Korean coworkers are shy about speaking English. It is not unusual to feel misunderstood or excluded from group discussions. During this phase, it is essential to remember that cultural differences are not personal rejections. Many Korean coworkers are just as nervous about communicating in English as you are about speaking Korean.

To overcome these challenges, give yourself time and be kind to yourself. Find a balance between cultural engagement and personal comfort. It helps to join local expat communities online or in person, such as Facebook groups for teachers in Korea. Talking with other teachers who have experienced similar challenges can provide reassurance and practical advice. I, for example, joined several local tennis groups and ended up building a community of predominantly English-speaking players. Putting yourself out there and finding hobbies you enjoy is a great way to create a sense of community.

Establishing a few comforting routines, like going to the same café or having weekly phone calls with friends back home, can stabilize your emotional well-being. Learn a few Korean phrases each week, explore your neighborhood, and celebrate small victories, like ordering food on your own or navigating public transit without confusion. Learning Korean is a fantastic way to make new friends, but a word of caution: many female foreign teachers have commented that some "language exchanges" can be a euphemism for dating, as some Korean men join these groups primarily to meet foreign women. Keep that in mind, and trust your instincts if something feels off.

Pro Tip

Avoid drunk-dialing home. It's easy to get emotional after a few drinks, and calling friends or family while you're buzzed can lead to conversations that are more difficult than they need to be. Things may seem more complicated or more challenging when you're feeling tipsy. It's always best to call home when you're clear-headed to have a more positive and productive conversation. So, think before you drink and call.

Flex-and-Flexibility

A term I often use when mentoring new teachers is "flex-and-flexibility." This means having the mindset to adapt quickly, pivot calmly, and remain optimistic even when things do not go as expected. In Korea, plans can change without notice. A class might be canceled, rescheduled, or reassigned at the last minute. Your supervisor might expect you to join an event you didn't know about until that morning. While this might feel chaotic, it is not uncommon in Korean school environments.

Last-minute shifts are often a result of a highly responsive system, where priorities can change quickly based on a director's or a parent's request. Understanding that this is not a sign of poor planning but simply a different organizational style is key. Rather than reacting with frustration, learn to respond with patience and curiosity. Say, "I understand," and ask how you can help. This calm and accommodating attitude will earn you immense respect. Being flexible and having a go-with-the-flow mindset will help you overcome many awkward situations and make your experience much more enjoyable in an often fast-paced and fluid environment.

Teacher Story: The Soju Merry-Go-Round

During my first week teaching in Korea, most of the Korean staff didn't speak to me. The only people I really interacted with were the two Korean English teachers who shared my office. Our school was next to another multi-subject hagwon owned by the same director, so there was a whole building full of coworkers I had barely met.

Around 5 p.m. one evening, I was casually told, "Tonight, we're going out for dinner." I explained that I already had plans to meet a friend and was quickly informed that attendance wasn't optional. It was a hoesik (회식), a team dinner, and I was expected to be there for team building and to get to know the other teachers.

I asked the obvious Western question: "Since it's required, is it paid?"

My Korean co-teacher looked at me like her brain had briefly short-circuited. "Of course not," she said. "The director will pay for dinner, drinks, and noribang (노래방)." In Korea, a mandatory work dinner doesn't mean overtime pay; it means your boss is picking up the tab, and you show up grateful. Lesson learned. I canceled my plans and rolled with it.

At the restaurant, I was surprised by the sheer volume of soju (소주) being consumed. I had always been able to handle my alcohol, so I wasn't worried. Then, one of the male Korean teachers from the other school came over, sat beside me, introduced himself, downed his shot, and handed me his empty glass. I wasn't sure what to do. He filled it, grinned, and said, "Geonbae, (건배)!" So I downed it.

A few minutes later, another teacher did the same thing. Then another. Everyone at the table was watching and laughing. To be polite and show I was a good sport, I made my way around the entire table, exchanging shots with about ten coworkers in under an hour. When it was time to leave for the e-cha, the second round at a beer bar, I nearly fell over standing up.

At the beer bar, the director had gone home, and the atmosphere shifted completely. Suddenly, several of the female Korean teachers were smoking openly, something I had never once seen them do near the school. At work, the women never smoked in the communal smoking area on the balcony. But here, away from the boss and the school environment, they felt free to be themselves. It was my first real glimpse into the layers of Korean social behavior, how context and setting shape what people feel comfortable doing in public.

Takeaway: That night taught me two things at once. First, flexibility isn't just a nice idea when you're living abroad; it's a survival skill. Canceling my plans and showing up with a positive attitude opened doors that wouldn't have opened otherwise. Second, Korean social life has layers that take time to see. People behave differently depending on the setting, the company, and who's watching. What looks like inconsistency is actually a finely tuned social awareness that you'll come to understand and even appreciate.

Pro Tip

If a coworker hands you their empty glass and fills it, that's a traditional Korean drinking custom and a sign of friendliness and respect. You're not obligated to keep up shot for shot all night. After the first round of exchanges, it's perfectly acceptable to slow down, nurse your drink, or politely hold your glass without drinking. Nobody will be offended. The gesture matters more than the quantity. Also, always pour and receive drinks with two hands; it's a sign of respect, especially with senior colleagues.

The Power of Positivity

Positivity is a powerful tool, and in the Korean workplace, it carries more weight than you might expect. Schools appreciate teachers who are cheerful, dependable, and eager to participate. When you offer to help, smile through an awkward moment, or laugh at yourself when making a Korean pronunciation mistake, you build trust. Your coworkers are observing not just your teaching skills but your temperament. In Korean work culture, maintaining a harmonious and cooperative atmosphere is highly valued, and a positive attitude contributes significantly to this.

Your enthusiasm can be contagious, making you a great asset to both your students and your colleagues. Are you the kind of person who will uplift students and coworkers when things get tough? Your resilience will become one of your greatest strengths, not just in the classroom but also in navigating the challenges of living in a foreign country. And sometimes, the impact you're making is bigger than you realize.

Teacher Story: The Back Third

During my first year in Korea, I picked up a part-time job teaching at a public middle school three mornings a week. Every Monday, Wednesday, and Friday, I taught a class of fifty-four first-year female students from 8:00 to 8:50 a.m., right before their regular school day began, and then headed to my hagwon afterward.

The class quickly divided itself into thirds. The front third were actively engaged; they participated, answered questions, and seemed genuinely excited to be there. The middle third drifted in and out, some half-listening while others quietly worked on homework from other classes. The back third barely acknowledged I was in the room. They chatted with each other, did homework, or simply tuned out entirely.

After a few weeks, I started to get frustrated. I was waking up early, pouring energy into my lessons, and it felt like more than a third of the class couldn't care less. I began questioning whether I was making any difference at all. But instead of giving up on them, I kept showing up with the same energy and enthusiasm every class, trying different approaches to pull more students in.

About a month in, the supervisor who coordinated the foreign teachers pulled me aside after class. She told me that many of the students had been raving to their Korean teachers about my passion and how much they enjoyed my lessons. Then she asked if I'd be willing to teach Tuesdays and Thursdays at a second middle school as well. I was stunned. The whole time I thought I was failing to connect, the students had been noticing and talking.

Takeaway: You won't reach every student. That's a reality every teacher has to accept. But the effort you put in is visible even when the results aren't obvious to you. The students in the back third may not have shown it in class, but the ones I was reaching carried that enthusiasm beyond the classroom. Sometimes the recognition comes from unexpected places, and when it does, it fuels you to push even harder.

Pro Tip

Don't measure your impact by the least engaged students in the room. If you're bringing energy and genuine care to your lessons, students notice, even the quiet ones. Consistency and passion will always make more of a difference than you realize in the moment. Show up the same way every day and trust that it's landing.

Multiculturalism, Ethnocentrism, and Understanding

Living in Korea offers a front-row seat to explore multicultural dynamics from both sides. While Korea is rapidly becoming more international, many of its systems are still built for a homogeneous population. This means that some teachers may face challenges related to race, gender, nationality, or linguistic background. Non-white teachers, for example, may find they need to assert their qualifications more than others. LGBTQ teachers may find that certain social topics are less openly discussed.

It is essential to understand the difference between intentional exclusion and cultural unfamiliarity. What may seem like rudeness or insensitivity may stem from a lack of exposure to global diversity. Rather than becoming defensive, use these moments as opportunities for gentle education and bridge-building. Many questions that we consider rude back home, such as asking about your salary, religion, or political views, are common in Korea. People may also comment very directly about your appearance or weight. For instance, when I was dating my wife, a Korean businessman student of mine asked her, "Why are you dating him? You are pretty and can meet many Korean men." He was not being disrespectful; he was genuinely curious.

These moments can catch you off guard, but they are rarely meant to offend.

Avoid falling into ethnocentrism, the belief that your way of doing things is better or more correct than the Korean way. You might feel tempted to compare everything to your home country, often unfavorably. Resist this. Remind yourself that cultural differences are not cultural deficiencies. Each system has its logic, history, and advantages. Try to see the value in Korea's way of doing things, even if it doesn't immediately make sense.

Teacher Story: "In America, We..."

Early in my time as a mentor, I had a teacher come to me frustrated about how his school was being managed. At first, I listened sympathetically; everyone needs to vent occasionally. But within minutes, a pattern emerged. "In America, we would never do it this way." "In America, it's better because..." "In America, it's great because..." He must have said it four or five times in a single conversation. Everything about Korea was being measured against an American standard, and Korea kept losing.

I'd heard almost the exact same script from a Canadian teacher not long before. Different accent, same mindset.

I let him finish, then asked him a simple question: "Do you think Koreans built Korea to make foreigners comfortable?" He paused. I told him that Korea wasn't designed with us in mind. Koreans built their systems, their schools, and their culture for Koreans. That doesn't make it wrong; it makes it different. And different is not the same as deficient.

I suggested he stop measuring everything against "back home," because this isn't back home. The things he kept calling "wrong" were simply unfamiliar. Once he could see the difference between those two words, his experience would start to improve.

Over the years, I've made it a point to flag this for new teachers early. In every expat community, you'll find people I call the Debbie Downers, teachers who are deeply ethnocentric and spend most of their energy complaining about how everything was better in their home country. They think their culture, opinions, and even food are superior. They are a mental drain to be around, and their negativity is contagious if you let it in.

My advice is always the same: avoid those people when possible. Surround yourself with positive people who celebrate the differences rather than attack them. Your experience in Korea will be shaped far more by the company you keep than by any policy or cultural norm you encounter.

Takeaway: It's natural to miss things from home and to notice differences. But there's a wide gap between noticing differences and declaring everything inferior. The moment you start every sentence with "Back home, we..." you've stopped learning and started judging. Korea doesn't owe you familiarity; you chose to come here.

Pro Tip

When you catch yourself comparing Korea unfavorably to home, pause and reframe. Instead of "This is wrong," try "This is different, why do they do it this way?" Genuine curiosity will teach you more in a month than complaining will in a year. And if you find yourself surrounded by expats who only complain, it's okay to quietly distance yourself. Protect your mindset, it's one of the few things entirely within your control.

Korea is changing, and you are part of that evolution. Your presence, professionalism, and kindness can influence your students, coworkers, and community in powerful ways. Be respectful, but also be proud of your identity and perspective. When invited to share your background or traditions, do so with enthusiasm and humility. Remember that you are an ambassador of your country while in Korea, and people may judge your country better or worse by your actions.

Final Thoughts

Working in Korea is a two-way cultural exchange. By building relationships, respecting hierarchy, staying flexible, and embracing multiculturalism, you will not only thrive professionally but also grow personally. The cultural intelligence and adaptability you develop here will benefit you long after your teaching contract ends. You will leave Korea with more than a teaching credential. You will leave with a deeper understanding of yourself, a wider view of the world, and skills that no classroom back home could have taught you.

Part Five

Thriving in the Classroom

Chapter 14: Classroom Management & Teaching Styles

Chapter Summary

This chapter covers how to understand Korean students' learning styles and adapt your teaching approach accordingly, how to establish clear classroom rules and discipline strategies from day one, and how to handle common challenges such as shyness, rowdiness, and lack of motivation. You will also learn how to use cultural relevance and engagement techniques to keep your lessons dynamic, and how to collaborate effectively with co-teachers and mentors to grow as an educator.

Why This Chapter Matters

Teaching in a Korean classroom offers an enriching yet complex experience. You will work with students who are often bright, disciplined, and driven, but who also operate within a highly structured and exam-focused educational culture. As a foreign teacher, your role is to bring creativity, conversation, and cultural context to English lessons. However, doing this effectively requires understanding how Korean students learn, how to set boundaries respectfully, and how to handle classroom challenges with patience and cultural sensitivity. This chapter will walk you through managing your classroom with confidence, aligning your methods with local expectations, and drawing on mentorship opportunities that support your professional growth.

Understanding Korean Students' Learning Styles

A rigorous academic environment from a young age generally shapes Korean students. Many attend not only regular school but also private academies in the evening, known as hagwons. This results in long hours of study, test preparation, and a deeply ingrained respect for teachers and authority. As a result, many students are highly respectful, especially in the early years. Younger learners may bow when greeting you, call you "teacher," and follow your instructions without question. However, this does not mean they are always engaged, especially when English feels complicated or intimidating. The immense pressure to perform well on standardized tests can create what I call a "fear of mistakes," where students are hesitant to speak up because they are terrified of giving the wrong answer in front of their peers.

In general, Korean students are used to teacher-centered classrooms where the instructor speaks, and students listen. Rote memorization, copying from the board, and grammar translation exercises are common in public school English classes. So, when you walk in with a communicative, student-centered lesson plan that involves pair work, games, or open discussion, some students may appear confused or hesitant at first. This is a completely normal reaction to an unfamiliar teaching style and not a reflection of your ability as a teacher.

To successfully bridge this gap, your primary goal is to create a safe and low-pressure classroom environment. Students' hesitation often stems from a fear of "losing face" in front of their peers, a concept deeply rooted in Korean culture. They may worry that incorrect English will be seen as an embarrassment. Therefore, it is crucial to celebrate every attempt, no matter how small. Start with low-stakes activities like repeating phrases in unison, then transition to pair work before attempting whole-class discussions. Positive reinforcement, whether it's a high-five, verbal praise, or a simple "Good try!" can work wonders in building their confidence and helping them realize that making mistakes is a natural and necessary part of learning a language.

Adjusting Your Approach

To support their learning styles, begin by building structure into your communicative approach. Instead of simply saying, "Talk to your partner about your weekend," try modeling the dialogue first.

Provide sentence starters, vocabulary lists, and simple examples. For instance, write on the board: "On Saturday, I ____." Then act it out with a volunteer or another teacher. This explicit scaffolding reduces anxiety and makes participation easier. You can use visual aids and gestures to reinforce meaning, which aligns with their common visual learning styles. Many studies have shown that Korean students respond very well to visual and auditory learning methods, so incorporating short videos, pictures, and songs is a very effective strategy.

At the same time, reward effort, not just correctness. When students try to speak in English, even if their grammar is off, respond warmly and praise their attempt with a phrase like, "Good try!" and "That's excellent thinking!" This encouragement helps break the fear barrier that many Korean students carry into English class. Over time, they will begin to see your class as a safe place to experiment with language rather than a test of perfection. This shift in mindset is one of the most valuable things you can offer your students.

A consistent routine is another powerful tool to reduce anxiety. Korean students are accustomed to a predictable schedule, so establishing a clear class structure, perhaps starting with a warm-up, moving to new vocabulary, and ending with a game, helps them feel more secure. These games, when used correctly, are not just for fun; they are low-stakes opportunities for meaningful language practice. By making learning enjoyable and a part of a routine they can rely on, you empower students to take risks without the fear of judgment. Your ultimate goal is to transform them from passive listeners into confident communicators who are not afraid to experiment with English.

Teacher Story: The Silence After "Any Questions?"

One of the first lessons I learned in Korea, and one I keep relearning, is that asking, "Does anyone have any questions?" will almost always be met with silence. It doesn't matter if you're teaching seven-year-olds at a hagwon or university students in a lecture hall. The response is the same: quiet stares, averted eyes, and not a single raised hand.

At first, I took it personally. I thought my explanations were so clear that nobody needed clarification, or worse, so confusing that nobody knew where to begin. Then I noticed something. After class, students would line up at my desk with the exact questions they had been too afraid to ask in front of their peers. It was the Belle dynamic from Chapter 13 all over again, not a lack of curiosity, but a fear of standing out or losing face in a group setting.

Once I understood this, I stopped asking the class for questions and started anticipating them instead. A good teacher should be able to predict where confusion will arise, and rather than waiting for students to voice it, I pose those questions myself. Even better, I give them to small groups and ask the students to discuss and brainstorm answers together. While they work, I float around the room, observing, interjecting, offering praise or feedback, and shaping the discussion where needed. The energy in the room changes completely when students are talking to three classmates instead of performing for an entire class.

I also learned early on that Korean students are often reluctant to take initiative within a group because they don't want to stand out. Nobody wants to be the one who volunteers to lead. So I make them play rock, paper, and scissors to choose a team captain. Yes, even at the university level. It never fails to get a laugh, and it removes the social pressure of self-nominating. The captains get extra high-fives or participation points, and I always leave the door open for volunteers who want to step up for the bonus recognition. Over time, more and more students start volunteering on their own.

Takeaway: Silence in a Korean classroom is not a sign of disengagement or confusion. It is a cultural norm rooted in the desire to avoid standing out or making mistakes publicly. Once you stop fighting the silence and start designing around it, your classes will come alive in ways you didn't expect.

Never rely on "Any questions?" as your check for understanding. Instead, build the questions into the activity itself. Give small groups a problem to solve or a question to discuss, then circulate and listen. You'll learn far more about what your students understand, and what they don't, by listening to their conversations than by waiting for a hand that will never go up.

Setting Rules and Maintaining Discipline

Classroom management begins with clarity and consistency. Whether you teach at a public school or a hagwon, it is essential to establish rules and expectations from the very first class. Korean schools tend to emphasize group harmony over individual freedom, and many students are accustomed to strict rules from their homeroom teachers. However, foreign teachers are often perceived as more relaxed or fun, which means students may test your boundaries early on to see what they can get away with.

Start by introducing your rules visually and in simple English. Use posters or write them on the board. Go over each rule together, and instead of just stating them, demonstrate what they look like in action. For example, rather than simply saying "Be respectful," show what that means: listening when someone else is talking, raising a hand before speaking, and using polite words. Keep your rules few in number but clear in meaning. Something like "Raise your hand before speaking, use English during class, be kind to your classmates, listen when the teacher is talking, and keep your hands and feet to yourself" covers most situations without overwhelming anyone. The simpler and more visual you make them, the easier they are to enforce.

When students follow the rules, you should acknowledge it. Praise good behavior and reward participation. Many schools already have systems in place that use stickers, stamps, or points to track student progress toward a reward like a game day or a small party. A group-based reward system is especially effective in Korea because it taps into the collective mindset of the Korean school environment. When the whole class earns a reward together, it reinforces the idea that everyone's behavior matters, and students naturally start holding each other accountable.

When rules are broken, respond consistently. Start with a verbal warning, then move to a minor consequence such as losing points or moving seats. Try not to shout or display visible frustration. Korean students are often sensitive to being scolded, especially in front of others. Instead, maintain a calm authority and follow through on the consequences you have outlined. If a student continually misbehaves, speak with your co-teacher or supervisor. They may have insight into the student's background or be able to communicate with the student's parents. Avoid punishing an entire class for the actions of one or two students, as this can damage morale and erode the trust you have built.

Teacher Story: The High-Five Economy

When I first arrived in Korea, I was thrown into the classroom on day one without any training. The only other foreign teacher had finished on the Friday before I started on Monday. There was no handover, no orientation, and no transition period. I had my teacher training from back home, but the master teachers I had observed before starting my Bachelor of Education had styles that weren't necessarily suited to a Korean classroom.

So, I did what any new teacher should do: I talked to as many experienced ESL teachers in Korea as I could find and asked about their classroom management styles and techniques. Many schools used stickers, stamps, points, or candy as rewards, so on my very first day, I handed out small sweets as prizes for good behavior and correct answers. It seemed to work immediately. The problem was what I had actually done: I trained the children to expect a reward every single time they performed. Within days, hands were going up not because students wanted to participate, but because they wanted candy. I also realized I didn't want to be buying big bags of sweets every week just to keep my class motivated.

I needed a different approach, and I found it through something Koreans call "skinship," a Konglish (Korean + English) term for physical ways of conveying warmth and connection. I noticed that many of my students had very busy, hard-working parents and didn't get to see them as much as they wanted. These kids were eager to be acknowledged and to receive friendly, appropriate contact. So, I replaced candy with high-fives. I gave them high-fives when they arrived, when they left, and as prizes for good behavior and accomplishing tasks in class. Instead of sticking their hands out expecting a sweet, they started reaching out for a high-five. I even made up special handshakes for different students, the lumberjack saw, the farmer's handshake, and the kids absolutely loved having their own personalized greeting. It cost me nothing, but it built genuine personal connections that candy never could.

For discipline, I developed a simple system that tapped into something Korean students already understood group accountability. I used a three-strike policy tied to a class game. If the class made it through without three checks on the board for any infractions by anyone, we played a game at the end. On Fridays, a clean week meant ten minutes of Uno. The beauty of this system was that the students did the enforcing for me. If a student was acting up, all I had to say was, "It would be a shame if one more check meant no game today," and the entire class would turn to that student and get them back on track. They did my dirty work, and the administration loved that I rarely needed to send students to the office.

For the students who still didn't respond to positive reinforcement, I tried enlisting what I called a "white knight." I would identify the eldest or most respected student in the class, praise them, and ask them to help me out. Since they were the oldest, other students naturally listened to them. This gave the influential students a leadership role and created peer-level accountability that carried more weight than anything I could enforce from the front of the room.

Early on, I also experimented with timeouts—pulling disruptive students out of the classroom or making them stand outside. I quickly realized this was counterproductive. Some of those kids wanted any attention, positive or negative, and removing them from the group only escalated the behavior. They would sometimes act out even more just to get a reaction. Positive reinforcement, consistently applied, always worked better than punishment.

Takeaway: Reward systems shape behavior, so be intentional about what you're rewarding and how. Candy creates dependency. High-fives create connection. And when you design a system where the whole class has a stake in the outcome, students will hold each other accountable far more effectively than you ever could on your own.

Pro Tip

Don't underestimate the power of simple, personal gestures. A high-five, a personalized handshake, or a genuine "great job" carries more weight with Korean students than any sticker chart or candy jar. These kids are surrounded by academic pressure all day long. Sometimes what they need most is a teacher who makes them feel seen and valued as a person, not just as a student.

Handling Classroom Challenges

Even the best-prepared teachers will face occasional challenges. You will encounter classes that are too quiet, too noisy, unmotivated, or overly dependent on translation. The key is to approach these issues with patience, cultural understanding, and a willingness to experiment until you find what works.

If your students are too shy to speak, incorporate more group work before expecting individual responses. Allow students to practice a dialogue with a partner before performing for the class. Create low-stakes activities where they can talk to just one or two other students first. You can also include non-verbal participation like drawing, writing, or matching exercises to build confidence before asking them to speak. A simple trick is to give them a task and then walk around the room, making it clear that you're listening. This helps them get used to speaking English in a semi-private setting before moving to a public one.

If a class is too noisy or rowdy, consider your lesson pacing before assuming it's a discipline problem. Korean students are used to fast-moving classes with a precise sequence. If your instructions are unclear or the activity has too much downtime, students will fill the silence with chatter. Use visual timers, clear transitions, and structured roles to keep the pace engaging. A good transition phrase, like "Okay, eyes on me in three, two, one," or a simple hand signal, can help you regain control quickly without raising your voice.

If some students seem disinterested, the most effective thing you can do is relate the content to their world. Include popular Korean cartoon characters, songs, or themes from K-pop or K-dramas in your lessons. Use activities that involve movement, drawing, or teamwork. One of my students was obsessed with a popular cartoon character, so I created a short lesson where we described the character's appearance and personality. He was immediately motivated and participated more than he ever had before. When you meet students where their interests are, you stop competing for their attention and start earning it.

If language itself becomes a barrier, remember that you are not expected to speak Korean in the classroom. In fact, it's often frowned upon for foreign teachers to use Korean in class. Instead, be strategic about simplifying your English. Use gestures, repetition, and visuals. Write key vocabulary on the board. Practice what experienced teachers call "teacher talk," which is a slower, more precise, and more intentional way of speaking that is easier for language learners to follow. You will get better at this with time, and your students will appreciate the effort.

Teacher Story: The PC Bang and the K-Pop Report

I had two middle school classes at my hagwon that could not have been more different. On Mondays, Wednesdays, and Fridays, I taught four seventh-grade boys who were the top students in the school, one of them was the owner's son. They were sharp, talkative, and full of energy, which was great for conversation practice but a constant challenge when it came to staying on topic. They would veer off into side conversations within minutes, and I spent half my energy reining them back in.

Then I found out what they did after my class every day. They went straight to a PC bang, a Korean computer gaming room, and played Seal Team 6, a first-person shooter game, together. They either played as a team or against each other, and it was clearly the highlight of their day.

So, I made them a deal. If they stayed on task and performed well for the entire month, I would take them to the PC bang after class on the last Friday and play with them, three versus three. They lit up. For the rest of the month, all I had to say when they drifted off topic was, "Do you still want that PC bang trip?" and they snapped right back. When the day finally came, we played for an hour, and I will never forget the moment one of my students screamed, "Teacher, head-shot me! Bad teacher!" The whole group died laughing. So did I. That was years ago, and it still makes me smile.

On Tuesdays and Thursdays, I had the opposite challenge: a class of middle school girls who were painfully quiet. Getting them to speak in English felt like pulling teeth. I tried games, structured dialogues, and group activities, but the energy stayed flat. Then I discovered their passion. They were all obsessed with K-pop, the music, the gossip, who was dating who, which group had a comeback coming. Once I knew that, I started every class by asking what was happening with a particular singer or group. The room would erupt. They would talk over each other, correct each other, and debate in English without even realizing they were practicing. That five-minute warm-up set the tone, energy, and mood for the entire class.

Takeaway: The key to unlocking a quiet class or focusing a rowdy one is the same: find out what your students care about. Whether it's a first-person shooter game or the latest K-pop comeback, connecting your teaching to their world shows that you are interested in what they are interested in. That builds trust and closeness faster than any textbook activity ever will. The content of the conversation matters less than the fact that they want to have it.

Pro Tip

Make it a habit early on to learn what your students are into. Ask about their favorite games, music, TV shows, sports teams, or hobbies. The current Korean soccer player in Europe, the Korean baseball player in the MLB, and the latest drama are all goldmines for engagement. You don't need to be an expert on any of it. Just show genuine curiosity, and your students will do the rest. Once they see that you care about their world, they'll be far more willing to step into yours.

Master Teachers and Mentoring

In many schools, especially public ones, you will work alongside a Korean co-teacher who serves as a bridge between you and the school system. This teacher can be a valuable source of guidance, feedback, and support. However, the dynamics vary greatly depending on the school's structure and the personalities involved.

In some cases, your co-teacher will be actively involved in lesson planning, classroom management, and translation. In others, you may be expected to lead the lesson entirely, with the co-teacher stepping in only when needed. The key is to establish open and respectful communication early. Ask your co-teacher what they expect and how they would like to collaborate. Share your ideas and invite feedback. A simple question like, "Would you prefer I lead this activity, or would you like to do it together?" can go a long way in establishing a good working relationship. The more you treat your co-teacher as a genuine partner rather than a passive observer, the better your classroom will function.

If your school provides a master teacher or mentor, take full advantage of their experience. This person has been teaching for several years and can offer valuable advice about school policies, student behavior, and lesson planning. Ask them how they handle mixed-level classes, what has worked well for discipline with a particular group of students, whether there are upcoming school events or holidays you should prepare for, how they balance keeping classes fun while following a packed teaching schedule, and how they deal with students who are constantly disruptive. These are the kinds of practical questions that textbooks don't answer but experienced teachers can.

Even informal mentors can be invaluable. Other foreign teachers at nearby schools, teachers you meet through expat groups, or veteran teachers you connect with online can all offer perspectives that help you navigate the day-to-day realities of teaching in Korea. Don't be afraid to reach out. Most experienced teachers remember exactly how overwhelming the first few months felt, and they are usually happy to help.

Keep a notebook or folder of teaching strategies, successful activities, and reflections. Over time, this will become your personal teaching playbook. You will discover which activities energize your students, which techniques help shy learners open up, and how to adjust your tone and delivery for different age groups. Teaching in Korea is not just about grammar drills or vocabulary lists. It is about connecting with students, understanding their world, and building a classroom environment where learning feels exciting, safe, and meaningful. By mastering classroom management, adapting your teaching style, and drawing on the experience of those who came before you, you will become not just a good teacher but a memorable one.

Teacher Story: "You Need to Teach Harder"

A teacher I was mentoring came to me one day, visibly frustrated. His Korean manager had pulled him aside and told him, "You need to teach harder." He messaged me for advice and said, "What the hell does that mean?"

It's a fair question. In a Western context, "teach harder" doesn't really make sense. You either teach well, or you don't. But in Korea, I had learned that this kind of feedback is rarely about the literal words. It's about perception. What his manager was really saying was, "I need to see that you're putting in more effort." It wasn't necessarily that his teaching was poor; it was that his attitude wasn't visibly demonstrating the level of dedication the school expected.

I suggested a simple approach. Come in a little earlier. Stay a little longer. Not forever, just long enough to show that you heard the feedback and you're trying. More importantly, I told him to start actively sharing his work with his manager. Show her new lesson plans. Talk about the ideas he was trying in class. Ask for her input. Kill her with kindness and overwhelm her with enthusiasm. Don't just work harder, make sure she can see it.

Sure enough, after a few weeks, his manager told him, "That's wonderful, but you really don't need to share everything with me." The problem was solved. He hadn't dramatically changed his teaching; he had changed how his effort was perceived. In Korea, a positive attitude and visible eagerness to improve go a long way toward building trust and respect from your coworkers and managers.

This is an important mindset shift for foreign teachers. A "team player" attitude and the ability to take constructive criticism are not optional; they are essential. Korean schools invest significant time, energy, and resources into getting their foreign teachers up and running. When they offer feedback, they are not trying to hurt your feelings. They are trying to help you succeed because your success is their success.

It also helps to keep some perspective on your own qualifications. The vast majority of ESL teachers in Korea are not licensed teachers in the traditional sense. Most hold a four-year degree in any subject, and very few, perhaps five percent or less, have a Bachelor of Education or formal teaching certification. That doesn't mean you can't be an excellent teacher, but it does mean you should stay open to guidance from people who have been in the Korean education system far longer than you have. Take the criticism as an opportunity to improve and grow, not as a personal attack.

Takeaway: When a Korean manager gives you vague or blunt feedback, resist the urge to get defensive. Step back and ask yourself what they're really saying. More often than not, it's about perception and attitude, not performance. Show that you heard them, make your effort visible, and the issue will usually resolve itself quickly.

Pro Tip

In Korean work culture, being seen matters almost as much as the work itself. This doesn't mean you need to perform or put on an act. It means that arriving a few minutes early, staying a few minutes late, and proactively sharing your ideas with your manager signal respect and dedication. These small, visible gestures communicate more than any lesson plan ever could. And when feedback comes, even if it stings, receive it graciously. A simple "Thank you, I'll work on that" will earn you far more respect than pushing back or asking for specifics in the moment.

Final Thoughts

Effective classroom management in Korea is about more than rules and lesson plans. It is about connecting with students and creating an environment where learning is both fun and safe. By understanding how Korean students learn, maintaining structure while staying flexible, and leaning on the experience of your co-teachers and mentors, you will transform your classroom into a space where confidence and communication thrive. The students you teach will remember how you made them feel long after they forget the vocabulary words. Be the teacher who made English feel exciting, not intimidating, and you will leave a lasting impression on every student who walks through your door.

Chapter 15: Lesson Planning & Teaching Materials

Chapter Summary

This chapter covers how to structure engaging, culturally appropriate lessons for Korean classrooms, where to find high-quality ESL resources and materials for all levels, how to adapt lesson plans and activities for different age groups, and how to use games, teaching aids, and technology to boost engagement and retention.

Why This Chapter Matters

Lesson planning is one of the most essential skills for success in a Korean classroom. A well-structured lesson not only ensures that students are learning effectively but also creates a smooth and rewarding teaching experience for you. Whether you are working at a private academy or a public school, your ability to organize engaging, level-appropriate, and culturally sensitive lessons will directly impact student motivation and your own job satisfaction. This chapter will walk you through the fundamentals of building an effective lesson plan, introduce high-quality resources, share sample activities, and offer guidance on using games, teaching aids, and classroom technology. If lesson planning feels overwhelming right now, don't worry. It gets easier fast, and once you find a rhythm that works, you'll be able to build lessons quickly and confidently.

Structuring an Engaging Lesson

An engaging English lesson in Korea usually lasts between forty and fifty minutes and should follow a clear and consistent structure. This predictability is especially important for students who may be less familiar with a communicative teaching style, as it helps them stay on task, builds their confidence, and allows for better time management. A reliable format includes five key components: a warm-up to get students focused, an introduction of the target language with new vocabulary or grammar, guided practice with the new material, an independent activity to check for understanding, and a quick wrap-up to review what was learned. This framework provides a rhythm that benefits both you and your students, and once you've used it a few times, it will become second nature.

Warm-Up (5-7 minutes)

Begin with a warm-up activity that reviews prior learning or sets the tone for the day. This step helps students mentally transition from their more traditional Korean classes into a dynamic English-speaking environment. A well-structured warm-up activates prior knowledge and lowers anxiety, especially for shy students who are just arriving from their previous class. It creates a comfortable, low-pressure atmosphere from the very start, which is essential for building confidence and participation throughout the rest of the lesson. Aim for about five to seven minutes.

A good warm-up should be high-energy and easy to understand. This could be a quick game, a simple question-and-answer session, or a short video clip related to the day's topic. For example, if the lesson is about emotions, you might begin with a simple "How are you feeling today?" circle where each student answers with a gesture or facial expression. Another effective activity is "I Spy," where you describe something in the classroom using vocabulary from a previous lesson. The goal is to get students speaking and engaged early, building momentum for the rest of the class. If your warm-up falls flat, the whole lesson tends to drag, so invest time in making this part of your class energetic and fun.

Presentation (10-12 minutes)

Next, introduce the target language. This is the core of your lesson where you present new vocabulary or grammar points, and it should take about ten to twelve minutes. Keep your language clear and straightforward, avoiding complex sentences or idioms. Always use age-appropriate and level-appropriate English. This applies not only to your students but also when speaking with your Korean colleagues — save the academic English for your journal, not your classroom. Use visuals and real-world objects whenever possible to demonstrate meaning. For example, if you are teaching vocabulary related to food, bring in plastic fruit or print out clear, colorful images of various dishes commonly found in both Korea and your home country. These concrete connections help bridge language gaps far more effectively than definitions alone.

Repetition is absolutely key at this stage. Say the word or phrase, have students repeat it multiple times as a class, and then in smaller groups, spell it out on the board, and use it in a simple, contextual sentence. For instance, after introducing the word "apple," you might say, "This is an apple. Everyone says 'apple.' A-P-P-L-E. I like to eat apples." This multi-sensory approach — seeing, hearing, and speaking — reinforces the new information and helps with retention. During this phase, you are the primary model, providing all the necessary information and demonstrating correct pronunciation and usage.

Guided Practice (10-15 minutes)

Guided practice follows the presentation and serves as the bridge between teacher-led instruction and students working on their own. This phase should take about ten to fifteen minutes. Students work in pairs or small groups with structured support to apply the new language. You might have them fill in the blanks on a worksheet, match vocabulary with images, or complete short dialogues using the target expressions. The goal is to give students a safe environment to try out the new language with the security of your support nearby.

During this phase, your role shifts from presenter to facilitator. Circulate the room, listen in on conversations, and provide timely, gentle corrections. Focus on pronunciation and key grammar points without interrupting the flow of their practice. For example, if a student is struggling with a dialogue about ordering food, don't stop them mid-sentence. Instead, offer a quick tip or model the correct phrase and have them repeat it before continuing. This keeps the energy and confidence high. The structured nature of these activities, such as using a provided dialogue template for a restaurant role-play, ensures that students stay on task while gaining the confidence to use English in a practical context.

Independent Activity (8-10 minutes)

Independent activity time allows students to apply what they have learned more freely and solidify their understanding on their own. This phase should take about eight to ten minutes and is a crucial step for building confidence and autonomy, as it gives students a chance to work without the immediate support of a partner or the entire class. Activities can include writing short sentences or a brief paragraph using the new vocabulary, creating a simple dialogue to present later, completing a worksheet individually, making a mini-story with new verbs, or even drawing a comic strip to tell a short narrative. Variety keeps things interesting and caters to different learning styles.

During this time, your role is to act as a roving support system. Rotate around the room, observe students' work, and offer help discreetly where needed. This is an excellent opportunity for formative assessment — you can quickly gauge who is grasping the material and who is struggling. Use this information to determine which students need extra support in the next class, whether through targeted review or a simplified activity. This phase is essential for helping students become more self-reliant and provides you with invaluable feedback on the effectiveness of your lesson.

Wrap-Up (3-5 minutes)

The wrap-up brings a sense of closure to your lesson and should take about three to five minutes. This is your final opportunity to quickly review the main points and ensure students have grasped the key takeaways. You can call on a few students to demonstrate what they have learned or ask a short reflection question, such as "What new word did you learn today?" This type of active recall is highly effective for reinforcing retention and helps you quickly check for understanding before the students leave. A quick quiz or a rapid-fire question-and-answer session can also serve as an effective final check.

Ending the lesson on a positive note is just as important as starting one. You can conclude with a fun, quick game or song related to the lesson's topic. This leaves students feeling successful and engaged. Before you finish, briefly mention what's coming next. Telling students that the next lesson will feature a fun game or a new story creates anticipation and gives them a reason to be excited for your class. A well-executed wrap-up reinforces learning and boosts morale.

The wrap-up is also a perfect time to play a short game that reinforces the day's material. This is a powerful "carrot" approach to classroom management. My students would often self-police and encourage their classmates to behave because they were motivated by the prospect of a fun three-to-five-minute game at the end of class. The prizes were always positive reinforcement — specific praise and high-fives for each point earned. For example, if one student won five points, another won three, and another won two, I would give each of them a high-five for every point they scored. It cost nothing but meant everything to them.

Pro Tip

Remember that most schools have excellent curricula that have been developed over several decades, so sometimes it can be difficult to get through everything you are supposed to cover in a single class. One strategy I've used throughout my career is to move through the required material a little faster than the suggested pace. This creates five to ten minutes at the end of class for a game or activity that uses the day's material in a more relaxed, competitive way. You may want to walk students through up to half of the independent activity yourself to free up time for something you want to implement, like a game or review activity that isn't explicitly in the lesson plan. Gamify everything you can. Students are far more likely to retain vocabulary and grammar structures when they're laughing and competing than when they're staring at a textbook.

Teacher Story: The Fifteen-Week Plan That Lasted Fifteen Minutes

This can happen to any teacher at any level. I had spent weeks building a full fifteen-week course on the Microsoft Office Suite after my university administration asked me to teach it. I had a detailed syllabus, weekly objectives, and a clear progression from Word to Excel to PowerPoint. I walked into my first class, a room of about fifty students, mostly Uzbek, handed out the syllabus, and began going over the semester plan.

Within fifteen minutes, I could see it in their faces. Confusion, but not the kind where they didn't understand my English. It was the kind where they were wondering why I was teaching them something they already knew. Then one of the students raised his hand and said, politely but directly, "I'm sorry, Professor, but all of us already know how to use MS Office. Can't we learn about AI applications or something more useful?"

I could have panicked. I had an entire semester mapped out, and it had just been dismantled in a single sentence. Instead, I took a breath and turned it into a conversation. I asked the class what they actually needed, what would be most useful for their futures. After about ten minutes of back and forth, the consensus was clear: they wanted to learn about entrepreneurship and technology. I happened to have a background in both, so I proposed a compromise. We would satisfy the course title by using the Office tools, but we would build the semester around a real project, each group would develop a business idea and create a website to go with it. The students were immediately engaged, and what started as a disaster became one of the best courses I've taught.

This kind of misalignment happens more often than you might expect, and not just at the university level. In hagwons and public schools, new students can be dropped into your class mid-semester, and their levels may be wildly different from the rest of the group. Schools typically place students by age rather than ability, because putting an older student in a lower-level class often leads to them dropping out within a month. So you may find yourself teaching a class where some students are ready for conversation practice, and others are still learning basic vocabulary.

The lesson I took from all of this is simple: always be ready to adjust. No matter how carefully you plan, the reality of the classroom will sometimes be different from what you were told. The teachers who thrive in Korea are the ones who can read the room and pivot without losing their composure.

Takeaway: Preparation matters, but flexibility matters more. A perfectly planned lesson means nothing if it doesn't match the students in front of you. Learn to read the room early, ask your students what they need when something feels off, and don't be afraid to throw out your plan and rebuild on the fly. Some of the best lessons I've ever taught were ones I didn't plan at all.

Pro Tip

One strategy I've used throughout my career is to move through the required material a little faster than the suggested pace. This creates five to ten minutes at the end of class for what I call "fun time," a game or activity that uses the day's material in a more relaxed, competitive way. Gamify everything you can. Students are far more likely to retain vocabulary and grammar structures when they're laughing and competing than when they're staring at a textbook. And that end-of-class game becomes a powerful motivator. Students will self-police their behavior all period long if they know a fun activity is waiting at the finish line.

Must have ESL resources and materials

There is no shortage of ESL resources available online and in print, but the key is finding materials that are appropriate for your students' levels and engaging enough to hold their attention. Most Korean schools will provide a textbook, though the quality and structure can vary significantly. Public school textbooks might be outdated, while a hagwon's curriculum might be very rigid. Either way, it is wise to supplement with your own resources that align with the provided curriculum but offer more creative and interactive ways to practice the target language.

Some physical materials are worth investing in early. A good flashcard set and a laminator are essential tools if your school doesn't provide them. Flashcards are incredibly versatile and can be used for games, storytelling, vocabulary practice, and classroom routines. Props such as puppets, hats, or basic costumes can make storytelling or role-play more exciting, especially for younger students. In terms of textbooks, the "Let's Go" series is widely used in Korea for elementary learners, while "Side by Side" and "Four Corners" are common with middle and high school students. Teachers working with kindergartners often use storybooks with simple plots and repetitive phrases. Keep an eye out for Korean-English dual-language books, which help bridge understanding and can be found in most major bookstores.

Online resources are invaluable for supplementing your curriculum. The British Council is one of the most trusted sources for free teaching materials, offering complete lesson plans, worksheets, grammar guides, and listening activities across a wide range of proficiency levels. ISLCollective is a treasure trove of user-generated content, with thousands of free worksheets, PowerPoint presentations, and video lessons created by ESL teachers around the world, searchable by topic and student level. BusyTeacher is another massive hub offering thousands of free downloadable worksheets, games, and activities. For younger learners, ESL KidStuff offers downloadable flashcards, complete lesson plans, and songs designed to be highly visual and interactive, and MES-English is excellent for phonics and foundational skills with customizable worksheets and game boards.

For more advanced or adult learners, Breaking News English provides news articles written at various difficulty levels with vocabulary practice, listening tasks, and discussion questions. BBC Learning English offers news-based lessons, grammar tutorials, and pronunciation guides using authentic content. ESL Brains focuses on video-based lesson plans using authentic videos, podcasts, and articles. Ellii, formerly ESL Library, is a subscription-based service that many teachers swear by for its professionally designed lesson plans and flashcards based on current events. Teach This is particularly useful for intermediate learners, offering conversation starters, gap-fill exercises, and communicative games.

Teacher Story: The Butcher Paper Songbook

Most new teachers arriving in Korea today will find a well-developed curriculum waiting for them. Textbooks, lesson plan outlines, flashcards, and supplementary materials are typically provided, and many schools have refined their programs over the years of working with foreign teachers. That is a luxury I did not have.

When I first came to Korea, my two-hour daily kindergarten class came with almost no teaching materials. No textbook, no flashcard sets, no pre-made lesson plans. I had a classroom full of five-year-olds and a blank slate. So I got creative.

I went to the local art supply store and bought large sheets of white butcher paper. Then I started making what I called visual songs. I would take a simple English song, "Row, Row, Row Your Boat" was the first, and draw it out line by line, one picture for every word, in pencil first, then colored in with colored pencils. Alongside the visual song, I made two flashcards for every keyword so I could teach the vocabulary before introducing the song itself.

The flashcards became the foundation for everything. I used them for speed games, where students raced to identify the word first. I laid them face down on the floor and played the concentration game, where students had to flip over two cards and find matching pairs. By the time we had played through several rounds, the students had seen and heard each word dozens of times without it ever feeling like a drill. Then I would bring out the butcher paper visual song, and suddenly it all clicked. The students could "read" the pictures and sing the entire song from start to finish. Their faces would light up every time.

I used the same approach for Christmas songs, action songs, and seasonal vocabulary throughout the year. Those hand-drawn visual songs became some of my most effective teaching tools, and they cost me almost nothing to make.

Takeaway: A lack of materials is not an excuse for a lack of creativity. Some of the best teaching tools I ever used were ones I made myself with butcher paper and colored pencils. When you build your own materials, you know exactly how they work because you designed them around your students. Don't wait for the perfect curriculum to be handed to you, sometimes the most effective resources are the ones you create from scratch.

Pro Tip

Even if your school provides a full curriculum, it's worth building a small personal collection of go-to materials that you can pull out anytime. A set of handmade flashcards, a few laminated game boards, or a folder of activities that have worked well in the past can save you when a lesson finishes early, a planned activity falls flat, or you need to fill unexpected downtime. The teachers who always seem prepared aren't lucky; they just have a deeper bench.

Sample lesson plans and activity ideas

To see how the five-phase structure comes together in practice, here is a simple example for an elementary lesson on animals and actions. The target language is "What can a [animal] do?" and "It can [verb]." The objective is for students to name common animals and describe their actions using the modal verb "can." You would need animal flashcards, small toy animals if available, worksheets, and speakers for a song.

Start the warm-up with a short animal sound quiz. Use a soundboard on your computer or phone to play animal sounds and ask students to guess which animal makes each sound. You can have them write their answers on a small whiteboard for a quick, high-energy start. For the presentation, show flashcards of animals such as a lion, monkey, fish, and bird, and teach the structure: "What can a lion do? It can run." Use strong gestures and Total Physical Response to demonstrate each verb, helping kinesthetic learners connect the action to the word. During guided practice, have students work in pairs to match flashcards with action verbs like run, swim, jump, and fly. You can turn this into a race or play action charades where one student acts out a verb and the other guesses the animal and its action. For the independent activity, each student draws their favorite animal and writes one sentence using the target structure, and volunteers present their animals and sentences to the class. Wrap up by singing an action song like "Walking in the Jungle" and reviewing the key vocabulary, ending on a fun and memorable note.

For older students, who are often more concerned with social interaction and real-world application, role-plays, debate activities, and project-based lessons work exceptionally well. These activities build communicative fluency and critical thinking skills. For example, after teaching persuasive language, have students design their own advertisements for a product, creating a poster or a short video, and then present and defend their creation in small groups. You could also assign a project where students research a topic they are interested in, such as a K-pop group or a sports team, and create a short presentation in English. This taps into their personal interests and makes the language feel relevant to their lives. The more you can connect your lessons to what students actually care about, the less you will have to fight for their attention.

Games, teaching aids, and technology

Games are not just for fun; they are critical tools for reinforcing learning in Korean classrooms. Students here often face enormous academic pressure, and English class is one of the few subjects where creativity and humor are welcomed. Use this to your advantage. A well-placed game can transform a dry lesson into a memorable experience, helping students retain information without feeling the pressure of a test.

Some games have proven themselves time and again in Korean classrooms. Hot Seat is a favorite, where one student faces away from the board while teammates give clues about a mystery word, it's excellent for vocabulary and speaking practice in a low-pressure format. Simon Says is ideal for teaching commands and body parts to younger students and gets the whole room moving. Pass the Ball uses music and a soft ball, and when the music stops, the student holding the ball must answer a question, making it a quick and energetic way to review a topic. Bingo is endlessly adaptable, customize the cards with vocabulary from the unit and include pictures for beginners. Charades is a classic that works for all ages, where students act out vocabulary words or phrases while teammates guess, and it's especially effective for kinesthetic learners. Running Dictation is one of the most dynamic activities you can do — divide students into pairs, post a text on the wall, and have one student run to read it, memorize a sentence, and run back to dictate it to their partner. It combines listening, speaking, reading, and writing in a single, high-energy activity. Memory Card Match, where students flip cards to find matching word-and-image pairs, is simple but effective for visual learners and vocabulary reinforcement.

Technology is increasingly available in Korean classrooms, and it's worth learning how to use it well. Interactive whiteboards and smart TVs are common and can be used to show videos, play online games like Baamboozle or Kahoot, or display student work. YouTube channels such as English Sing Sing and Dream English are popular among younger learners and provide songs with animated visuals. Free apps like Quizizz, Wordwall, and Padlet offer interactive and collaborative learning opportunities. If your classroom has tablets or a computer lab, you can create digital scavenger hunts or pronunciation practice activities that students find far more engaging than a worksheet.

Physical teaching aids are also invaluable and often overlooked. Simple items like magnets, dice, timers, and stickers are inexpensive yet highly effective. A class mascot, a stuffed animal that gives out praise or participates in lessons, can make younger students feel more connected to the class. A timer, in particular, is one of the best tools for managing classroom pacing and keeping students on task. These small investments add up to a more dynamic and well-managed classroom.

Teacher Story: The Uno Effect

If I could tell every new teacher in Korea to pack three things in their suitcase, they would be a deck of Uno cards, a Scrabble board game, and a few word search magazines. These are teacher gold, and they will earn their weight a hundred times over.

Uno, in particular, became the single most effective classroom management tool I ever used. My smaller classes loved it so much that the mere possibility of playing it on Friday kept behavior in check all week long. The system was simple: if the class received three strikes in any class that week, there was no Uno on Friday. That was it. No complicated reward charts, no escalating consequences. Just the promise of ten minutes of Uno and the threat of losing it.

I started bringing my Uno deck to every class and setting it on my desk at the start of the lesson. I didn't even have to say anything. The students could see it sitting there, and they knew what it meant. It was a visual reminder, for them and for me, that a fun ending was waiting if the class went well. On the rare occasion a student started acting up, I didn't need to raise my voice. The other students would handle it for me, because nobody wanted to be the reason the class lost its game.

What made this work so well wasn't really about Uno itself. It was about understanding what these kids needed. Many of my students attended multiple hagwons and studied for hours after they got home. Their days were packed with academics from morning to night. A five-to-ten-minute game at the end of your class brings more joy than you can imagine, because for many of them, it's the only unstructured fun they get all day. When you understand that, you stop seeing games as a filler and start seeing them as one of the most powerful tools in your classroom.

Takeaway: Games are not a reward for finishing early or a way to kill time. They are a strategic classroom management tool that motivates behavior, reinforces learning, and gives students something to look forward to in a day that is often relentlessly academic. Invest in a few simple, portable games before you leave home, and they will become some of the most valuable things you bring to Korea.

Pro Tip

Put the game on your desk where students can see it at the start of class. You don't need to announce it or explain the rules every time. The visual reminder does the work for you. Students will self-regulate because the stakes are clear and the reward is something they genuinely want. And when Friday comes, and the class has earned their game, play with them. Sit down, shuffle the cards, and be part of it. Those ten minutes will do more for your relationship with your students than any lesson plan ever could.

Final Thoughts

Successful lesson planning in Korea is about balancing structure with creativity and content with flexibility. Follow your school's curriculum, but remember to make space for your own personality and ideas. Prepare more than you think you'll need, adapt to your students' energy levels, and use every tool available to you, from flashcards and butcher paper to Uno cards and Kahoot. The technical side of lesson planning will become second nature with practice. What will set you apart is your willingness to read the room, meet your students where they are, and make English class the part of their day they actually look forward to. A smiling, confident, and prepared teacher is always the most powerful resource in any classroom.

Chapter 16: Teaching Different Age Groups

Chapter Summary

This chapter covers how to adapt your teaching strategies for kindergartners, elementary students, teenagers, and adults in Korea. You will learn classroom management techniques and engagement strategies tailored to each age group, understand the cultural and developmental factors that influence how different learners respond, and explore practical examples and lesson ideas that you can use immediately. You will also gain insights into maintaining motivation and building strong rapport with students at every level.

Why This Chapter Matters

As a teacher in Korea, you may find yourself working with a wide range of learners, from energetic kindergartners to ambitious corporate professionals. Each group comes with unique characteristics and needs. Kindergartners and elementary students thrive on play-based learning and visual aids, while teenagers are often motivated by peer approval and test scores. Adult learners typically have concrete professional goals and expect practical, relevant content. Understanding how to adjust your lesson planning, classroom management, and interaction style for each group is essential for both your success and your satisfaction as a teacher.

A one-size-fits-all approach will not work. The strategies that keep a seven-year-old engaged, like songs and sticker charts, will not resonate with a thirty-year-old business professional preparing for an overseas meeting. This chapter will walk you through the unique dynamics of teaching each age group in Korea, from the giggling chaos of kindergarten to the quiet ambition of a corporate English class, and give you the practical strategies you need to support, motivate, and connect with your students no matter how old they are.

Teaching Young Learners: Kindergarten

Teaching kindergarten in Korea can be one of the most rewarding and exhausting roles you will ever have. Korean kindergartners are typically between four and seven years old, depending on how age is counted locally. Many attend private English kindergartens where the emphasis is on immersion, social development, and basic academic skills. These young learners are full of energy, affection, and curiosity, but they also have short attention spans and are still learning how to function in a structured environment. If you can handle the chaos and bring genuine warmth to the classroom, kindergarten teaching will give you some of the most memorable moments of your career.

The key to teaching kindergartners is maintaining a warm, playful, and patient demeanor. Lessons should be structured but not rigid. You will need to transition between activities quickly, typically every five to ten minutes, to match their limited attention spans. Movement, visuals, music, and games are essential components of any lesson. Start each class with a familiar routine, such as a hello song, a weather and calendar review, or a simple chant. This predictability creates a sense of security for young learners, which is vital for building trust and a positive classroom atmosphere. Beyond the hello song, a daily circle time where students share something simple like "My favorite food is..." or act as the weather reporter builds confidence in a predictable, safe environment. These small routines are the scaffolding upon which their language and social skills will grow.

A typical kindergarten lesson might include singing "Old MacDonald Had a Farm" with corresponding animal flashcards, playing a game where students pretend to be different animals, practicing vocabulary with flashcards, and finishing with a simple coloring worksheet. Use exaggerated facial expressions, gestures, and props to make concepts concrete. When introducing vocabulary, say the word, show a picture, and use the word in a sentence. Have students repeat after you with enthusiasm. You can also use a puppet or class mascot to introduce new topics, which captures their attention in a way that a teacher standing at the front of the room sometimes cannot.

Positive reinforcement is critical with this age group. Stickers, stamps, high-fives, and praise phrases like "Great job!" go a long way. Classroom rules should be visual and reinforced through modeling. Hold up a sign with a picture of a raised hand and say, "Raise your hand to speak," then demonstrate what that looks like. Most kindergartners in Korea do not yet know how to read or write, so your focus should be on oral skills, listening comprehension, and pre-literacy activities. Songs with gestures, simple stories, and role-play help build confidence and understanding.

Effective classroom management with this age group is less about punishment and more about redirection. When a student misbehaves, it is often because they are tired, bored, or overstimulated. Instead of scolding, redirect their attention calmly with simple phrases like "Hands on your head!" or "Let's sit down nicely." A behavior chart with stars or stickers for good behavior can be effective, as young learners respond well to seeing their progress. Yelling is rarely effective and can cause students to feel embarrassed in front of their peers. For recurring behavioral issues, always consult your Korean co-teacher first. Their insight is invaluable, as they can communicate with parents and help find a solution that respects both cultural norms and the child's needs. Your co-teacher is your most important ally for handling tricky situations and ensuring you are aligned with the school's expectations.

A crucial part of teaching in a hagwon kindergarten is parent communication, which is typically handled through a "gongchaek, (공책)," or communication notebook. You or your co-teacher will be responsible for writing a brief summary of the day's lesson, listing new vocabulary words the students learned, and including a positive comment about the child. This daily communication builds immense trust with parents and keeps them informed about their child's progress. It also demonstrates the value of the foreign teacher's role in the school, which matters more than you might think.

You will also need to communicate closely with your Korean co-teacher or homeroom teacher, who may assist with classroom management and translation when needed. Teaching kindergarten is high-energy work, but the emotional rewards are equally high. Students will hug you, remember your name years later, and absorb English with a sponge-like capacity that can be astonishing. This is a world away from the academic pressure of older students and makes your classroom a happy, safe space for learning.

Pro Tip

Keep in mind that kindergarten classes are the financial engine of most hagwons. Parents pay between six hundred and twelve hundred dollars per month for English-only kindergarten. This is why the majority of hagwons run kindergarten in the morning and elementary classes in the afternoon. The kindergarten students may only make up twenty-five to thirty percent of the school's total enrollment, but they can account for over two-thirds of the school's revenue. Understanding this helps you understand why schools invest so heavily in their kindergarten programs and why your performance with these young learners matters so much to your employer.

Pro Tip

To give yourself a competitive edge when applying for positions in popular cities like Seoul or Busan, consider earning a Young Learners TEFL certificate. Many recruiters and schools highly value this specialized certification because it demonstrates your commitment to and preparation for teaching kindergarten-aged children. It provides practical strategies for managing high-energy classrooms, using songs and games effectively, and addressing the specific developmental needs of young students. This can set you apart from applicants who only have a general TEFL certification. For a twenty percent discount on a forty-hour Young Learners TEFL course, you can use the promo code **TEIK40** at www.GoTEFL.com.

Teacher Story: The Crying Girl in the Baby Class

My very first class in Korea did not go as planned. My recruiter had promised me a week of training before I started teaching. As it turned out, the only other foreign teacher had finished on the Friday before I arrived on Sunday night. When I showed up Monday morning expecting orientation, the vice director, the front office secretary, the head teacher, and Belle, the art teacher, were all standing behind a large window that looked into my classroom. I said, "Training?" They handed me a book and said, "Do pages one and two for forty minutes." It was an outline of an ant and an apple.

I thought, okay, I got this. I walked into the classroom full of more than twenty-four-year-olds, brought all the energy I had, and said a big "Hello!" with wide arm gestures to show my enthusiasm and positivity. What those tiny children probably saw for the very first time was a six-foot-two, two-hundred-pound, very animated white man towering over them. Naturally, one of the smallest girls in the class took one look at me and started screaming and crying.

I glanced through the window. The four Korean women were giggling and chatting to each other. Belle came in, scooped up the sobbing little girl, and carried her out. I made it through the rest of my first class, which was essentially a coloring session where I taught colors and simple commands, because what else could I do? I tried again the next day. The result was similar. For the entire first week, that little girl cried when she saw me.

Then, in the second week, something changed. The tears dried up. Instead, I got curious looks. By the end of that week, I started getting half-smiles. By the third week, the scared, crying little girl had become the one who always wanted to sit next to me. She had realized that I was just different, not scary. She became my little buddy, and I ended up teaching her for three years until I got married, moved to Bucheon, and switched schools.

That was more than twenty years ago, and I still think about her. Sometime during my first year, I realized something profound about teaching the youngest learners. Those children in the baby class had never seen a foreigner up close. They didn't know a single word of English. They were completely blank slates, and every sound, every word, every sentence that came out of their mouths was shaped by me. I had set them up with pronunciation that would stay with them for the rest of their lives. They sounded like mini-Americans, and I took enormous pride in knowing that I had played a role in giving them that foundation. Teaching kindergarten is exhausting, chaotic, and sometimes involves a crying child on day one. But the impact you can have on these young learners is unlike anything you will experience with any other age group.

Takeaway: Young children may be frightened of you at first, and that is completely normal. Many have never seen a foreigner in person before, and your size, appearance, and energy can be overwhelming. Don't take it personally, and don't try to force a connection. Give them time, show up with the same warmth and patience every day, and let them come to you. The child who cries on Monday may be sitting in your lap by Friday.

Pro Tip

The youngest learners are the most impressionable students you will ever teach. Every word you say, every sound you model, and every habit you build becomes their foundation. Take that seriously. Speak clearly, enunciate carefully, and be intentional about the English you use in class. These children will carry your pronunciation and phrasing with them for years. You may never know the full impact you've had, but it is far greater than you think.

Teaching young learners: elementary

Elementary school students in Korea, from first to sixth grade, generally have some foundational knowledge of English. Public schools tend to introduce English formally in the third grade, while private academies often begin much earlier. Your role with this age group is to build on basic language skills, increase vocabulary, develop sentence structure, and start cultivating more natural communication. While they are still eager to please and excited by games, they are also beginning to form stronger peer groups and develop greater independence. You can expect more structure in the classroom and higher expectations from both parents and school administrators, making it essential to balance academic rigor with engaging content.

A well-structured elementary lesson might begin with a short review of previous vocabulary, followed by the introduction of a new phrase or grammar point. For instance, if the focus is on daily routines, you might teach phrases such as "I wake up at seven" and "I brush my teeth." Use visual aids and repetition, then transition to a pair activity where students ask each other, "What time do you wake up?" followed by a worksheet or role-play activity. Games remain powerful at this age. You can try running dictation, where students race to copy and report sentences, or "Find Someone Who," where they ask classmates questions to fill out a worksheet. These activities promote both communication and movement, which is essential for keeping elementary students engaged. A points system where teams compete to earn rewards at the end of the lesson also works well, tapping into their growing sense of competition and teamwork.

Some students at this age may still struggle with speaking due to shyness or lack of exposure. Encourage participation by calling on students by name and praising both effort and accuracy. Integrate themes from Korean culture and students' interests. Use Korean holidays to teach vocabulary or have students create simple English descriptions of their favorite characters, sports, or hobbies. This keeps your content relevant and makes the language feel personal to them. Take advantage of technology as well. Many schools are equipped with interactive whiteboards, which you can use for online games, educational videos, and collaborative activities that can dramatically boost engagement and make your lessons memorable.

Pro Tip

A great way to boost writing skills and build a personal connection with elementary students is by incorporating a daily diary. At the end of each class, provide a simple prompt like "I went to the park on Saturday" or "My favorite food is..." and have students copy the sentence and complete it with their own answers. These journals are a fantastic way to review what has been studied and encourage students to practice writing. The next day, you can quickly review their answers to provide personalized feedback. Students love this activity because it is a creative way to use English to express themselves, and it gives you a quick way to check for understanding and get to know them a little better.

Teacher Story: Sam and Kevin

Every teacher in Korea will eventually face this problem: a class where the gap between the lowest-level student and the highest-level student is enormous. It happens frequently because schools place students by age rather than ability. They know that if they put a low-level older student into the proper level class with children two or more years younger, that student will be embarrassed and will likely drop out within a month or two. So, the levels get mixed, and the teacher has to figure it out.

The first time this happened to me, I had a class of about twelve elementary students, and two of them stood out immediately for opposite reasons. Sam was well below the level of the rest of the class. He avoided eye contact, seemed disinterested, and was sometimes visibly frustrated. He wasn't disengaged because he didn't care, he was disengaged because he couldn't follow what was happening. Kevin was the opposite problem. He was significantly above the class level, finished every activity in two or three minutes when it was designed to take ten or fifteen, and then started acting out because he was bored. He had nothing to do while the rest of the class was still working.

I quickly realized that both students were consuming a disproportionate amount of my attention. I was spending most of my activity time trying to explain things to Sam while the other eleven students, including Kevin, were left to fend for themselves. The math didn't work. One student was taking up eighty percent of my teaching time, and the other eleven were getting the remaining twenty percent.

Then I had an idea. I asked Kevin, "Can you help Sam with this?" Kevin moved his seat next to Sam and started walking him through the activity. What happened next was something I didn't expect. Kevin didn't just help Sam with one assignment; he became Sam's mentor. He started sitting next to him in every class, explaining things in simpler terms, and encouraging him when he got stuck. Sam's frustration started to fade. He became more engaged because he had someone his own age helping him in a way that felt safe and peer-level rather than teacher-directed. Kevin, meanwhile, stopped acting out entirely. He had a purpose and a responsibility that challenged him in a different way than the coursework could.

The dynamic of the entire class shifted. Instead of one student monopolizing my time, I could distribute my attention more evenly across all twelve students. It killed two birds with one stone.

Takeaway: Mixed-level classes are inevitable in Korea, and they can feel impossible to manage at first. But the gap between your strongest and weakest students doesn't have to be a problem; it can be a resource. When you empower your high-level students to mentor their classmates, you create cooperation, build friendships, and free yourself up to teach the whole room. The struggling student gets patient, peer-level support. The advanced student gets purpose and responsibility. And you get a classroom that functions.

Pro Tip

When you identify a wide level gap in your class, resist the urge to spend all your time with the struggling student. Instead, look for your strongest student who might be getting bored and give them a role. Frame it as a compliment: "You're really good at this. Can you help them out?" Most high-level students will take pride in being asked, and the student receiving help will often respond better to a peer than to the teacher. This simple pairing strategy can transform a difficult class into your smoothest one.

Teaching Middle and High School Students

Teenage students in Korea face immense academic pressure, often studying late into the evening at hagwons after a full day of school. The high school entrance exam and, later, the university entrance exam significantly shape their daily schedules and overall mood. As a result, many students may appear tired, disinterested, or overworked. However, they are often quite intelligent and capable of deep engagement if the lesson feels meaningful to them. Your role as a foreign teacher at this level is often to promote conversational fluency, pronunciation accuracy, and cultural exchange. You may also be asked to help students prepare for the speaking components of English proficiency exams such as TOEFL, TOEIC, or IELTS.

Unlike younger students, middle and high schoolers can handle more abstract topics and critical thinking tasks, making your class a valuable space to explore ideas and opinions that they may not have time for in their other subjects. Your class is often one of the few places where they can practice speaking in a relaxed environment, which is a skill frequently neglected in test-focused curricula. That makes what you do genuinely important, even if the students don't always show it.

To engage this age group, frame lessons around real-world situations, debates, or projects. You might run a mock job interview lesson where students learn expressions like "I am responsible," "I enjoy working in teams," and "My strength is time management." Have them create a simple resume in English or assume a persona like an artist or an engineer. Other effective approaches include creating English presentations on current events, organizing short debates on topics like "Should smartphones be allowed in class?" or analyzing English song lyrics for vocabulary and idiomatic expressions. For project-based learning, have students work in groups to create a travel guide for their hometown in English, encouraging them to use descriptive language and share their culture. The more autonomy you give teenagers in choosing topics and formats, the more invested they become.

Classroom management with older students requires a nuanced approach. Many teenagers are reluctant to speak due to fear of embarrassment in front of their peers. Your primary goal is to create a supportive environment where students feel comfortable taking risks. When correcting errors, model the correct form rather than pointing out the mistake. For example, if a student says "I eated pizza," respond with a warm smile and say, "You ate pizza! Great!" and move on. Another effective technique is facilitative responding, where you subtly paraphrase what a student says using the correct grammar. This provides them with the right language without interrupting their flow or discouraging them from continuing.

Set clear expectations for participation, homework, and behavior from the beginning. Avoid sarcasm or public criticism. Teenagers respond well to consistency and fairness, and they will respect a teacher who shows a genuine interest in their lives and opinions. Build that foundation of trust early, and you will find that even the most exhausted, seemingly disengaged teenagers will come alive when the right topic hits the room.

Pro Tip

To learn about your students' interests and build rapport from day one, consider using a simple online survey through Google Forms. Ask them about their favorite hobbies, music, games, or movies. This anonymous method lets you collect valuable information without putting anyone on the spot. You can then strategically weave these interests into your lessons, showing students that you care about what they care about. It is a small investment of time that pays off enormously in engagement.

Teacher Story: The Haunted House Lesson

Sometimes the best lessons are the ones you didn't plan. I was teaching a class of female middle school students who were, like many teenagers in Korea, visibly exhausted and difficult to engage. Getting more than one-word answers out of them felt like a daily battle. On this particular day, I was trying to get through a textbook assignment about different types of housing, and I could already feel the energy draining from the room.

To make it a little more interesting, I had found a short article about a haunted house in the United States and thought it might hold their attention better than floor plans and vocabulary about apartments. We read through the article together, and something shifted. The class started buzzing. One student asked a question, then another jumped in with a comment, and within minutes the entire room was alive with conversation. Students who had barely spoken all semester were suddenly telling ghost stories they knew, describing haunted places in Korea, and trying to out-scare each other in English.

I looked at my lesson plan, looked back at the class, and made a decision not go back to the intended lesson. Instead, the rest of the period turned into an impromptu horror story competition. Students took turns sharing the scariest tales they could think of, and their classmates would react, ask questions, and try to top each other. The English wasn't perfect, but it was flowing. They were communicating, listening, and genuinely enjoying themselves.

I had no idea that ghost stories would be such a massive hit, but I rolled with it because the students were more engaged than I had ever seen them. That one accidental detour taught me something I carried through the rest of my career: when you stumble onto something that lights up a room, throw the lesson plan out and ride the wave.

Takeaway: You don't always need a perfectly crafted lesson to create a great class. Sometimes the best thing you can do is pay attention to what sparks your students' interest and follow it wherever it goes. Teenagers in Korea are exhausted and overscheduled, and they can smell a boring lesson from a mile away. But when something genuinely catches their attention, they will surprise you with how much English they are willing to produce. Stay flexible and be ready to abandon your plan when something better is happening in front of you.

Pro Tip

Keep a mental list of topics that get strong reactions from your students, whether it's ghost stories, celebrity gossip, sports rivalries, or funny cultural comparisons. These become your emergency engagement tools. When a class is flat and nothing is working, you can pivot to a topic you know will wake them up. It's not going off-script; it's reading the room and giving your students a reason to speak.

Teaching adults (Business English and conversational classes)

Teaching adults in Korea is an entirely different experience from teaching children or teenagers. Adult learners may include university students, office workers, engineers, managers, and homemakers. Their goals are usually more specific, such as passing English proficiency exams, preparing for international travel, communicating in business settings, or simply improving their conversational confidence. The first step in teaching adults effectively is understanding what they actually need. Ask your students directly what their goals are. A simple placement interview or written survey can help you tailor your materials from the start. A class of marketing professionals might want to learn how to write emails, give presentations, and handle phone calls in English. A group of homemakers might prefer travel-related vocabulary and casual conversation. The more precisely you can match your content to their goals, the more invested they will be.

Classes with adults often move at a slower pace, especially if students are self-conscious about their English ability. Be encouraging and focus on building confidence. Adults usually appreciate correction, especially if delivered tactfully. For example, if a student says "He go to work every day," respond with "Ah, he goes to work every day. Great sentence." Lessons should be highly interactive and relevant. Use role-plays, case studies, or discussion-based formats. For business English, authentic materials such as sample business letters, website content, or workplace scenarios are far more effective than textbook exercises. Incorporate vocabulary lists with industry-specific terms and practice using them in realistic contexts.

Technology can be particularly useful in adult classes. Show short videos from news sites, use language-learning apps for homework, or assign presentations using slides. Adult learners also benefit from consistent feedback. Provide written corrections, progress reports, and one-on-one consultations when possible. Flexibility is essential, as many adult learners have busy schedules and may miss class or arrive late. Keep each lesson modular so that students can jump back in easily without feeling lost.

Finally, treat adult learners as partners in the classroom. Encourage them to share their experiences, ask questions, and suggest topics. This collaborative atmosphere increases motivation and deepens learning. Adults bring a wealth of life experience to the classroom, and the best adult English classes feel less like a lesson and more like a guided conversation between equals.

Teacher Story: The Indian Accent

In my second year of teaching in Korea, one of my private adult students asked if I would be interested in teaching a group class at the Hyundai Department Store as part of their cultural program. The class was about fifteen people, mostly well-off women and one businessman. During our first hour-long session, we went around the room doing introductions. Each student shared their name, their occupation, and why they wanted to improve their English. It was straightforward and pleasant until the last person, the businessman.

He opened his mouth to speak, and I immediately had a problem. His English was fluent, confident, and delivered with a perfect Indian accent, complete with the characteristic side-to-side head nod. His import-export business was based on trade with India, so he had learned English entirely from Indian colleagues and business partners. The accent was so authentic that if I had closed my eyes, I would have sworn I was listening to someone from Mumbai. But I was looking at a Korean man. I couldn't help it, I started giggling.

The poor guy looked confused. He kept speaking, and I kept trying to hold it together. I imagine it was similar to what Korean people experience when they see Robert Holley (Harley) on television. Holley is an American who did his Mormon mission in Busan for several years and picked up such a distinct Busan regional accent that hearing it come out of a tall American's face is both jarring and hilarious to Korean audiences. My businessman had the same effect on me, just in reverse.

After class, I pulled him aside and apologized. I explained why I had been laughing, and thankfully, he found it just as funny as I did. He told me that his accent was exactly the reason he wanted to take my class; he knew his English sounded Indian and wanted to work on developing a more neutral pronunciation for his international business dealings.

He became one of my most memorable students, and he also taught me something about adult learners that I hadn't expected. Many Korean businessmen would rather take you out for dinner and drinks for several hours than sit through a formal private lesson. As a fresh teacher in Korea, I was happy to oblige. We met outside of class regularly, and he treated me to meals and drinks while we practiced conversational English in a relaxed setting. It was a lesson in itself; adult students, especially professionals, often learn best when the classroom walls come down entirely.

Takeaway: Adult learners come to you with years of English exposure from wildly different sources. Some learned from American movies, some from British textbooks, some from Australian coworkers, and some, like my businessman, from Indian business partners. Don't laugh at their accents, or if you do, apologize quickly. Every adult student has a story behind how they learned English; understanding that story helps you teach them more effectively.

Pro Tip

Teaching adults, particularly business professionals, often extends beyond the classroom in ways that don't happen with younger students. Many adult students prefer informal settings like restaurants or coffee shops for practice, and some will offer to take you out rather than pay for a formal lesson. These outings are genuinely valuable; the relaxed atmosphere lowers inhibitions and produces more natural conversation. As a new teacher in Korea, these connections can also broaden your social network and give you access to perspectives on Korean culture and business that you won't get from teaching children. Just keep it professional and enjoy the perks.

Final Thoughts

Teaching across age groups in Korea requires adaptability, empathy, and a keen understanding of how learning needs shift with age. Kindergartners need warmth, structure, and a teacher who isn't afraid to be silly. Elementary students thrive on interactive routines and respond to teachers who make learning feel like play. Teenagers need real-world relevance and a classroom where they can speak without fear of judgment. Adults appreciate practical, goal-oriented instruction and a teacher who treats them as equals. By adjusting your approach and remaining sensitive to the developmental and cultural needs of each group, you will become a more effective and impactful teacher, and you will discover that each age group, in its own way, has something to teach you in return.

Chapter 17: Understanding Korean Culture and Education

Chapter Summary

This chapter covers how Confucian values shape classroom behavior, school hierarchy, and teacher expectations in Korea. You will learn how Korea's competitive education system affects student attitudes and learning styles, recognize common management styles and how to navigate them, and discover the "Golden Circle" principle, the key to keeping students engaged, parents satisfied, and directors supportive. You will also develop a career mindset built on resilience, relationship-building, and long-term growth.

Why This Chapter Matters

By now, you have a strong foundation in classroom management, lesson planning, and teaching different age groups. This chapter goes deeper into the cultural and systemic forces that shape everything you will experience as a teacher in Korea. Understanding why Korean schools operate the way they do, not just how, will help you navigate your workplace with greater confidence and fewer misunderstandings. More importantly, this chapter introduces what I consider the single most important concept for long-term success in the Korean hagwon system: the Golden Circle. Master this, and everything else, your relationship with your director, your job security, and your daily satisfaction, falls into place.

Cultural Foundations of Korean Education

We touched on Confucian values and their influence on workplace dynamics in Chapter 13, and you've seen how they play out in classroom behavior throughout the teaching chapters. But it is worth understanding these foundations at a deeper level, because they don't just affect how students behave; they shape the entire education system you are working within.

Korean culture is deeply influenced by Confucianism, which emphasizes respect for authority, loyalty, harmony in relationships, and the paramount importance of education. Teachers are highly respected in Korean society, and English teachers, though foreign, are held to similar standards of professionalism, diligence, and moral example. Your conduct, both inside and outside the classroom, is observed by students, parents, and colleagues. You are not just an instructor; you are a role model, whether you signed up for that or not.

The Korean education system is one of the most competitive in the world. From a young age, students are taught to study rigorously and perform well on exams. The university entrance exam, known as the Suneung (수능), can determine a student's social and professional trajectory for life. As a result, even young children are under immense pressure from parents, peers, and schools to excel academically. English education begins as early as kindergarten and continues through university. In public schools, English is often taught by Korean homeroom teachers in the early years, with native-speaking teachers leading or assisting from third grade onward. In hagwons, English instruction is more immersive and intensive. These academies are a key part of Korea's "shadow education" system, seen as a necessity for students to gain a competitive edge. Students may attend multiple English classes each week after regular school hours, sometimes on weekends and during vacations.

What this means for you as a teacher is significant. Your students may be tired and stressed by the time they walk into your classroom. Your class may be one of the few places where they experience a different, more relaxed style of learning. That is both a challenge and an opportunity. If you can make your classroom a place where students genuinely want to be, you will stand out in an education system that often prioritizes testing over enjoyment. And as you will see in the Golden Circle section of this chapter, that distinction is the foundation of everything.

Korean Management Styles and Expectations

Chapter 13 covered workplace hierarchy and the importance of showing deference to supervisors. Here, I want to go deeper into how Korean managers actually think and operate, because understanding their mindset will save you from mistakes that can damage your professional standing.

Korean school directors and administrators overwhelmingly manage from the top down. Decisions are made at the top and flow downward through the vice director, the academic coordinator, the head teacher, and eventually to you. Each link in the chain delivers the instruction with the same justification: "Because my boss said so." The expectation at every level is compliance, not collaboration. This is not a system that invites debate, and if you come from a Western workplace where managers routinely ask staff for input before making decisions, the adjustment can be jarring.

One of the most important things I learned about Korean management is that communication is often indirect, and the politeness of a request is frequently inversely proportional to its importance. If someone says, "Maybe next time you could try...," take it as a directive you should implement, not a casual suggestion to consider. Similarly, if a Korean manager asks for your opinion, they have usually already made their decision. They are checking for alignment, not inviting a counter-proposal. This doesn't mean your ideas are worthless; it means that how and where you share them matters enormously.

Punctuality remains a critical expectation. Arrive early, dress appropriately, and greet your supervisors and colleagues respectfully. It is also common courtesy to wait for your supervisor to leave before you do, as this shows respect for their position. Flexibility is expected even within rigid structures. You may be asked to attend a last-minute staff meeting, cover for an absent colleague, or help with after-school events. Refusing these requests outright can be perceived as lacking team spirit. Approach such situations with cooperation, and if a request genuinely conflicts with your contract terms, explain that politely and privately rather than in front of others.

Pro Tip

Observe how your Korean colleagues behave in meetings, interact with students, and respond to feedback. Mirroring their communication style can build trust and help you navigate cultural nuances effectively. If your colleagues offer you snacks or coffee, reciprocate. These small acts of mutual courtesy carry more weight than you might expect.

Teacher Story: "Because I Said So"

When I first started working in Korea, I learned very quickly that Korean managers overwhelmingly operate in one direction: top down. This was especially true with male managers. An instruction wasn't a suggestion or a starting point for discussion; it was an order, and they expected you to follow it the way a drill sergeant expects a private to obey a command. I came to understand that this management style is deeply shaped by mandatory military service. The majority of Korean men spend two years in the military, and that experience fundamentally shapes how they lead, communicate, and expect to be followed. Female managers tend to have more nuance in how they delegate and request things, but the hierarchical structure is still firmly in place regardless of who is in charge.

I saw this dynamic play out not just in hagwons but across every Korean organization I worked in. When I later worked for the Korea Tourism Organization in Seoul as a public relations manager, and again at the KTO's Chicago office as a regional marketing manager for the Midwest, the same top-down culture was present. It is not unique to schools; it is how Korean organizations function.

As an American, this was difficult for me at first. I was trained to ask questions, offer input, and help improve processes. When I received an instruction, my instinct was to ask for the reasoning behind it so I could understand. I would make suggestions when I thought I had an insight that could improve something. In a Western workplace, this would be seen as proactive and valuable. In Korea, it was met with nervous, uneasy responses, and sometimes outright agitation.

My biggest mistake was the time I offered a suggestion in front of other staff. We were in a meeting, and the director had outlined a plan. I thought I had a logical improvement, so I spoke up and explained my idea. The room went silent. I could feel the other staff members tense up. A few suddenly started typing or shuffling papers to look busy. My director's expression hardened, and he simply said, "Because I said so."

Afterward, the Korean head teacher pulled me aside and explained what had happened. She told me that my idea was actually very logical and reasonable. The problem wasn't the suggestion itself; it was the setting. By offering it in front of other staff, I had inadvertently challenged the director's authority publicly. He had to say no, even if my idea was good, because agreeing would have looked like he was being corrected by a subordinate in front of his team. He couldn't afford to lose face in that moment, regardless of the merit of my suggestion.

That conversation changed how I operated in Korean workplaces from that point forward. If I disagreed with a decision or had an idea I thought could help, I would ask to speak with the manager privately, one-on-one. In that setting, the same suggestion that would have been rejected publicly was often received openly. Without an audience, there was no face to lose, and the director could consider the idea on its merits rather than as a threat to his authority.

Takeaway: In Korean workplaces, the chain of command is not a suggestion; it is the operating system. Decisions flow from the top down, and employees are expected to execute, not negotiate. This doesn't mean your ideas don't matter, but how and where you share them matters enormously. Never challenge a directive in front of other staff, no matter how good your suggestion is or how well-intentioned you are. Ask for a private conversation instead, and you'll find that the same manager who shut you down publicly may be surprisingly receptive behind closed doors.

Pro Tip

When a Korean manager asks for your opinion in a group setting, understand that they have usually already made their decision. They are checking for alignment, not inviting debate. If you have a genuinely different perspective, save it for a private conversation after the meeting. Frame it as a question rather than a correction: "I was curious about the reasoning behind the new schedule. Would it be possible to consider adjusting the afternoon block?" This approach respects the hierarchy while still giving you a voice.

The Golden Circle

If there is one concept I want you to take away from this entire book, it is the Golden Circle. This is not an abstract philosophy; it is the most practical, measurable framework I have found for building a successful career in the Korean hagwon system. It begins in the classroom, and when it works, it creates a virtuous cycle that benefits everyone: your students, their parents, your school, and your career.

The Golden Circle works like this. You teach well, manage behavior effectively, and above all, make learning fun. If you can consistently do those three things, your students enjoy coming to class. When students enjoy class, they go home and tell their parents. When parents hear that their children love English class, they keep paying tuition month after month. When enrollment stays stable and students aren't dropping out or transferring to competing schools, your director is happy. And when your director is happy, your contract gets renewed, your reputation grows, you experience less stress, and you may even be given more autonomy, better schedules, or bonuses. Everyone wins.

For me, the classroom was always the center of everything. My success started with how much joy and engagement my students felt during my lessons. I knew that if students were bored, restless, or unmotivated, they would complain at home, and eventually their parents might pull them out and send them to one of the many competing hagwons just down the street. But if they went home and told their mothers, "I love English class!" then I was doing more than delivering lessons. I was securing another month of tuition, keeping enrollment stable, and building a reputation as a teacher that students genuinely enjoyed learning from.

To achieve this, I gamified my teaching approach. Every lesson, no matter the topic, included an element of competition, creativity, or reward. I treated my classroom like a live performance. I brought energy, humor, and unpredictability. I introduced activities like team-based vocabulary challenges, sentence-building races, or speaking games with point systems. The last five minutes of each class, and the last ten minutes on Fridays, were reserved for a game. However, students only earned that time if they behaved during the lesson. If the class misbehaved, I would place a check mark on the board. One check was a warning. Two meant no game time. This carrot-and-stick method worked exceptionally well, especially with elementary students.

What surprised me most was how quickly the students internalized the system. It created a sense of shared accountability. If a student acted out or disrupted the flow of class, other students would speak up, reminding their peer, "Stop it, we'll lose our game time." My students began to police their own behavior, not because I told them to, but because they genuinely wanted to earn that final five minutes. The structure empowered them to become responsible participants in maintaining classroom order. I did not have to shout, punish, or spend energy constantly disciplining. The incentive was simple, transparent, and effective.

But the Golden Circle is about much more than games and behavior management. It is about understanding the business reality of the hagwon system. Korean mothers often make schooling decisions based on direct feedback from their children. If a student consistently says they enjoy class, that feedback translates directly into tuition renewal. My director quickly noticed that none of my students were dropping out or transferring to other hagwons. In an industry where student turnover is a constant financial headache, that consistency made me invaluable.

The benefits come full circle. Students are happy. Parents are satisfied. Directors see results and receive fewer complaints. Your contract is renewed, your reputation grows, and your daily work becomes less stressful. You may even find that you are given freedoms and opportunities that other teachers don't receive, simply because you have earned trust through results.

Your Golden Circle may not look exactly like mine. Maybe your version is built on storytelling, music, project-based learning, or technology. The specific method matters less than the principle. The key is to identify what works for your students and create a system where engagement, good behavior, and active participation are consistently rewarded. When the classroom becomes a place of both discipline and delight, you lay the foundation for long-term success.

So, as you prepare to teach in Korea, ask yourself not just how to deliver a lesson, but how to deliver an experience. Make it your mission to ensure students walk out of your classroom smiling, even as they are learning. That is your "why." That is your Golden Circle. And once you find it, everything else, your job satisfaction, your relationship with management, your reputation in the school community, will fall into place.

Teacher Story: How I Found the Golden Circle

When I first started teaching in Korea, I handled discipline the way I saw many other teachers do it, the traditional approach of removing troublemakers from the classroom. My system was simple:

three strikes and you're out. If a student disrupted class three times, they were sent outside. It seemed logical and fair.

Then reality hit. After I kicked one particularly difficult student out of my class, his mother called the school. Her son didn't want to come back. He dropped. My director was understanding; she knew this student had been a challenge for every teacher at the school, but she made it clear that she hoped I could find a way to manage my classroom better. The subtext was unmistakable: a dropped student is lost tuition, and lost tuition is a problem, no matter how difficult the child was.

That conversation forced me to rethink everything. I realized that removing students from the classroom didn't solve behavior problems; it created new ones. It could turn a disruptive student into an enemy. It meant kids loitering outside my door with nothing to do. And worst of all, it risked losing students permanently, which hurt the school's bottom line and my standing with the director.

So I switched from individual punishment to collective accountability. Instead of kicking students out, I tied behavior to something the entire class wanted: game time. If the class made it through without three checks on the board, they earned a game at the end of the lesson. On Fridays, a clean week meant ten minutes of Uno. The transformation was almost immediate.

Students started policing each other. If someone was acting up, their classmates would step in, not because I told them to, but because they didn't want to lose their game time. The disruptions dropped dramatically. I stopped having students kicked out and loitering in the hallway. Most importantly, I stopped losing students. Nobody dropped out of my class or the school because of a discipline incident.

My director noticed. She started publicly praising me in front of other teachers for how well I was managing my classes. She seemed genuinely happy, and I realized why. My students were enjoying class and telling their parents about it. Happy students meant parents paid for another month. Consistent enrollment meant stable revenue. And a teacher who kept students enrolled and parents satisfied was a teacher the director wanted to keep.

That was when the Golden Circle clicked for me. It wasn't an abstract theory; it was a direct, visible chain of cause and effect. Engaging classes led to happy students. Happy students led to satisfied parents. Satisfied parents led to retained tuition. Retained tuition led to a happy director. And a happy director led to job security, praise, autonomy, and a career I could build on. Everyone won.

Takeaway: The Golden Circle isn't just a teaching philosophy; it's a business reality. In the hagwon system, your ability to keep students enrolled is just as important as your ability to teach them English. When you create a classroom that students genuinely enjoy, you aren't just being a good teacher; you are protecting the school's revenue, earning your director's trust, and securing your own future.

Pro Tip

If you ever lose a student because of a discipline incident, take it as a signal to rethink your approach rather than blame the student. Removing a child from class might feel like the right move in the moment, but it can have consequences you don't see: an angry parent, a lost enrollment, and a director who questions your classroom management. Find ways to keep every student in the room engaged and accountable, and you'll rarely have to deal with those consequences again.

Building a Successful Career Mindset

Thriving in Korea as an English teacher requires more than classroom skills. It demands a mindset that balances cultural awareness, professional development, and a long-term vision. The teachers who flourish are those who take ownership of their experience, build positive relationships, and approach each day as an opportunity to learn and contribute. The teachers who struggle are almost always the ones who came with the wrong expectations or the wrong attitude.

One of the most essential qualities is resilience. Korea's fast-paced and hierarchical culture can feel overwhelming at first. There will be moments when you feel isolated, misunderstood, or uncertain. Instead of retreating, engage. Seek support from fellow teachers, connect with the broader expat community, and remember that adapting takes time. Missteps are a natural part of the process, and every experienced teacher you admire went through the same adjustment period you are going through now.

Growth is equally important. Do not settle into a routine too quickly. Take advantage of professional development opportunities, whether that means enrolling in online teaching courses, earning a specialized certification like a Young Learners TEFL, joining English teacher communities, or learning the Korean language. Many teachers build impressive long-term careers in Korea by expanding their skill sets, moving into head teaching or training roles, or pursuing advanced degrees while working. The teachers who stagnate are the ones who stop learning after their first year.

Building strong relationships with your Korean colleagues is another key to long-term success. A simple act like joining a staff lunch, offering to help with a school event, or remembering a colleague's birthday can go a long way. These gestures demonstrate that you respect and value the school community beyond your teaching duties. Be genuine, be proactive, and invest in your relationships the same way you would with any friendship. Every new teacher in Korea needs to make this effort, especially in the first year, to build both their social and professional networks.

Long-term success also requires planning. Decide early whether your goal is to teach in Korea for one year, three years, or longer. If you plan to stay, start thinking about how to advance, whether by improving your teaching portfolio, pursuing F-series visas for more flexibility, or exploring leadership roles. If you plan to move on, use your time in Korea to develop transferable skills like cross-cultural communication, classroom technology proficiency, and project management. Either way, be intentional about the experience rather than letting it happen to you.

Story: The Gap Year and the Long Game

Over the years, I've watched hundreds of teachers come to Korea, and they generally fall into two camps. The first group treats Korea as a gap year. They've just graduated from college, they want to travel, party, and experience life abroad, and teaching is the thing they're required to do in order to fund the adventure. The job isn't the reason they came; it's the price of admission. The second group comes with a different mindset. They may want the same travel and cultural experiences, but they're also genuinely curious about where the Korean path might lead. They're open to staying multiple years, investing in their teaching, and building something beyond a one-year story to tell at dinner parties back home.

I want to be clear: there's nothing wrong with wanting a gap year. Living abroad as a local rather than a tourist is a fantastic experience, and Korea is one of the best places in the world to do it. You can save over half your salary, travel across Asia on weekends and holidays, and immerse yourself in a culture that most people only see through a screen. That part is genuinely wonderful, no matter which camp you fall into.

But here's what I've observed consistently over more than two decades. The teachers who treat Korea as just a gap year tend to put minimal effort into their jobs. Teaching is the part they have to get through, not the part they care about. And schools can sense it. Directors notice when a teacher is just going through the motions. Co-teachers notice when someone isn't preparing lessons or bringing energy to the classroom. Students notice when their teacher would rather be somewhere else. That attitude creates friction, and friction leads to complaints, strained relationships, and contracts that don't get renewed.

The teachers who truly excel are the ones who commit to the experience fully, not just the travel and the social life, but the teaching itself. They see the classroom as an opportunity to learn real skills, improve as educators, and make a genuine impact on their students' lives. These teachers consistently report higher job satisfaction and higher life satisfaction during their time abroad. They build stronger relationships with their colleagues, earn more trust from their directors, and open doors to opportunities that the gap-year teachers never see, things like head teacher positions, curriculum development roles, or transitions into corporate training and university teaching.

The majority of teachers I've seen with serious attitude problems at their schools fall into the gap-year mentality. They see teaching as a means to an end, and it shows. The ones who thrive are the ones who recognize that teaching in Korea is both the means and the end; an experience worth investing in fully, not just enduring.

Takeaway: You don't have to choose between enjoying Korea and taking your job seriously. The teachers who do both are the ones who get the most out of their time here. Come for the adventure, absolutely. But invest in the teaching too, and you'll find that the adventure becomes richer because of it, not in spite of it.

Pro Tip

Schools can read your attitude faster than you think. If you show up prepared, bring energy to your classes, and demonstrate that you care about your students' progress, your director will notice within the first month. That early impression shapes everything, your schedule, your autonomy, your contract renewal, and even how much slack you're given when things go wrong. First impressions in Korea carry enormous weight, so start strong and stay consistent.

Final Thoughts

Understanding Korea's cultural and educational context is not about abandoning your own values; it is about expanding them. By respecting local customs, navigating the management hierarchy with awareness, and connecting your classroom success to the broader school community through the Golden Circle, you position yourself as more than just an English teacher. You become a cultural bridge, helping students learn about your home country while you share in Korean culture. You become a trusted colleague who understands how the system works and operates within it effectively. And you become a professional with a sustainable, rewarding career built on mutual respect, genuine engagement, and the understanding that in Korea, how you teach matters just as much as what you teach.

Part Six

Life Beyond the Classroom

Chapter 18: Exploring Korea: Travel, Food, and Fun

Chapter Summary

This chapter covers Korea's top destinations from bustling Seoul to tranquil Jeju Island, hidden gems for weekend getaways and cultural immersion, Korea's world-class cuisine and essential dining etiquette, seasonal festivals, traditional guesthouses, and temple stays. You will also learn how to maximize your weekends and holidays for unforgettable adventures that will enrich your time in Korea far beyond the classroom.

Why This Chapter Matters

Living and working in Korea as an English teacher is about more than lesson planning and classroom management. One of the greatest rewards of teaching abroad is the opportunity to explore a vibrant and culturally rich country that most people only see in photos or on screens. Korea is compact yet remarkably diverse, offering everything from megacities and ancient palaces to mountain temples, volcanic islands, and coastlines on both the East and West seas. Whether you are into culinary adventures, hiking, nightlife, history, or just getting wonderfully lost in a new culture, Korea has something for you. This chapter is your starting point, a guide to the places, food, and experiences that will turn your time in Korea into something you talk about for the rest of your life.

Must-Visit Places in Korea

Seoul: The Heart of Korea

Start with the capital. Home to over ten million people, Seoul is the heart of Korea's culture, history, economy, and innovation. It is a city where ancient palaces sit beside gleaming skyscrapers and street food stalls coexist with Michelin-starred restaurants. As a teacher, you will likely visit Seoul often, whether for weekend getaways, professional development, a Korean professional sports game, or simply to explore.

Some must-see sites include Gyeongbokgung Palace, the largest of the Five Grand Palaces, where you can watch the changing of the guard ceremony in traditional Joseon (조선)-era dress. Nearby, Changdeokgung Palace features the famous Huwon, or Secret Garden, a UNESCO World Heritage site known for its exquisite design and serene beauty. After exploring history, head to Insadong, a maze of alleys filled with teahouses, antique shops, and street performers. For a more modern experience, the futuristic Dongdaemun Design Plaza, designed by Zaha Hadid, is a must-see landmark, and the massive COEX Mall in Gangnam includes a fantastic aquarium and a stunning multi-story library. The neighborhood of Hongdae is famous for its art scene, indie music, and youthful vibe, making it perfect for a night out, while Myeongdong is the go-to destination for shopping and street food. Seoul's public transportation is world-class, making it easy to hop between historical sites, trendy cafés, river parks, and cultural venues all in one weekend.

My favorite route to take new people on is to meet in front of Gwanghwamun, walk to Gyeongbokgung Palace, continue to the Blue House, and then stroll through Insadong. After Insadong, we walk to the Cheonggyecheon Stream and follow it back up toward Gwanghwamun. It is a beautiful three-to-five-hour route through the heart of the city, offering a perfect blend of ancient history and modern city life. We usually stop for lunch in Insadong at one of the traditional makgeolli (막걸리) houses that serve milky, sparkling rice wine alongside excellent side dish menus and full-course meals. If we have more time, I add Changdeokgung Palace for more sightseeing or head to Itaewon for dinner and craft beers. My favorite spot for good beers and food is Phillies Pub, which in 2025 moved from Noksapyeong Station to near Itaewon Station and now has a fabulous rooftop deck.

Busan: Coastal Charm

Busan, Korea's second-largest city, offers a completely different energy. Located in the southeastern corner of the country, Busan is famous for its beaches, fresh seafood, vibrant nightlife, and a laid-back coastal vibe that feels worlds away from Seoul. Haeundae Beach is the headline destination during summer, often hosting international sand sculpture festivals and fireworks displays. You can take a leisurely walk along the scenic trail to Dongbaekseom Island for stunning views of the coastline, or head to Gwangalli Beach for an evening stroll with the Gwangan Bridge lit up in the background.

Culture lovers should not miss Gamcheon Culture Village, a hillside neighborhood transformed into a colorful art community with murals, galleries, and panoramic views of the sea, often called the "Machu Picchu of Busan." The Jagalchi Fish Market provides an authentic local experience where you can point to a live fish and have it prepared for you on the spot. For something truly unique, visit Haedong Yonggungsa Temple, one of the few Buddhist temples built directly on the coastline. Busan is one of those cities that rewards you for wandering without a plan, and it will almost certainly become a place you return to again and again.

Teacher Story: Sunrise on Haeundae

My first real trip in Korea came about three or four months after I arrived, and it set the tone for every adventure that followed. My Korean American friend Min and I decided to head down to Busan for a weekend in late June, right before the rainy season hit. It was my first time on the KTX high-speed train, and just the ride itself was an experience, three hundred kilometers per hour, Seoul to Busan in just a few hours. I remember watching the countryside blur past the window and thinking that this country was going to show me things I hadn't imagined.

Nothing prepared me for Haeundae Beach. We stepped off the train, made our way to the coast, and I found myself standing in front of what had to be over a million people packed onto one stretch of sand. The energy was electric. For a young guy experiencing his first

Korean beach day, it was sensory overload in the best possible way. What struck me most was the scene itself: Korean women in bikinis and high-heeled shoes, makeup perfectly done, standing in the shallow water looking like they were posing for a magazine shoot. Everyone wore dark sunglasses, and it quickly became clear that people-watching was as much a part of the beach experience as the ocean itself. Everyone was there to see and be seen, and the whole atmosphere felt more like an outdoor festival than a typical day at the beach.

After a full day of sun and people-watching, we did what any young teachers in Busan would do: we found a nightclub and danced until the early hours of the morning. When we stumbled out as the sun was coming up, we grabbed a couple of beers from a convenience store, found two lounge chairs on the beach, and sat down to watch the sunrise. At some point, we fell asleep right there on the sand.

I woke up late morning to the sun blazing directly on my feet. When I brushed off the sand and looked down, my feet were the color of Red Hots candy, bright, angry red from hours of unprotected sun exposure. Min's were the same. We hobbled around Busan for the rest of the day, laughing about it, sunburned and exhausted and completely happy.

That trip was more than twenty years ago, and I still remember every detail. It was the weekend that made me realize Korea wasn't just a place I was working, it was a place I was going to fall in love with.

Takeaway: Don't wait months to start exploring. Korea is compact, the transportation is world-class, and some of your best memories will come from spontaneous trips with friends you've just made. You don't need a detailed itinerary or a perfect plan. Sometimes the best adventures start with a train ticket and a vague idea of where you're going.

Pro Tip

The KTX high-speed train is one of the best things about living in Korea. Seoul to Busan takes just over two and a half hours, and you can reach most major cities in the country in under three hours. Book tickets through the Korail app or website and try to book in advance for weekends and holidays when trains fill up fast. If you're planning multiple trips, look into the Korail Pass, which offers unlimited travel for a set number of days and can save you a significant amount of money.

Jeju Island: Korea's Natural Wonderland

Jeju Island, known as the "Hawaii of Korea," is a volcanic island filled with natural wonders that feel like they belong in another country entirely. Hallasan Mountain, Korea's highest peak, dominates the center of the island and offers a challenging but rewarding all-day hike. The island is dotted with lava tube caves like the stunning Manjanggul Cave, waterfalls, and black-sand beaches. Jeongbang Waterfall is one of the few in the world that falls directly into the ocean, and it is every bit as dramatic as it sounds. For something lighter, the quirky Loveland sculpture park and the island's many traditional thatched-roof villages offer a mix of humor and heritage. My favorite beach on Jeju is in the town of Halim — Hyeopjae Beach, an incredible stretch of white sand with turquoise water that rivals anything in Southeast Asia.

Pro Tip

If you visit Jeju, buy a fly-and-drive package. The island is much easier to explore by car, and the scenic coastal roads and off-the-beaten-path cafés are half the experience. While you're there, you must try the local specialties: grilled Jeju black pork belly, grilled hairtail fish (galchi, 갈치), and fresh seafood, abalone, shellfish, and other catches, served grilled at your table or in a spicy seafood stew called haemultang (해물탕). Jeju food alone is worth the trip.

Pro Tip

If you are a hiker, then you must visit Jeju and check out the Jeju Olle Trail system! I wrote a research paper about it, and you can check it out here: Sustaining the Modern Pilgrimage: Governance, Community Impacts, and Environmental Challenges on Korea's Jeju Olle Trail.

Gyeongju: The Museum Without Walls

For teachers who enjoy history and spirituality, Gyeongju is a treasure trove. Known as "the museum without walls," Gyeongju was the capital of the Silla Kingdom for almost a thousand years, and its rich history is visible everywhere you look. The city is filled with ancient landmarks, from magnificent palace ruins to scattered, grassy burial mounds known as tumuli. Bulguksa Temple is a masterpiece of Buddhist art and architecture, and the nearby Seokguram Grotto houses a serene Buddha statue that has been watching over the East Sea for over a millennium. Both are UNESCO World Heritage Sites. The Daereungwon Tomb Complex is particularly striking, with enormous grassy mounds where you can wander among the tombs of ancient royalty. Gyeongju offers a slower, more peaceful pace and a deep historical resonance that contrasts beautifully with the bustling energy of modern Korean cities.

Pro Tip

You should try a half-day or an overnight Templestay experience. I have participated in overnight Templestay programs at Golgulsa Temple and twice at Beomeosa Temple. I also published an academic paper about the Beomeosa Temple and sustainable tourism and wellbeing. Here is the link if you are interested in reading it: From Ritual to Renewal: Templestays as a Cross-Cultural Model of Sustainable Wellness Tourism in South Korea.

Other Gems

Smaller cities and towns also offer rich experiences that are well worth a weekend trip. Andong, the heart of Korean Confucian culture, is home to the Hahoe Folk Village, a UNESCO World Heritage Site where visitors can watch traditional mask dances. Sokcho provides access to the stunning Seoraksan National Park, famous for its rugged peaks and breathtaking fall foliage. Boseong's rolling green tea fields are beautiful and serene, Jeonju's historic Hanok village is one of the most charming neighborhoods in the country with a famous culinary scene to match, and Chuncheon's lakes and legendary chicken galbi (갈비) make it an easy and delicious day trip from Seoul.

Pro Tip

Use Korea's high-speed trains and long-distance buses to plan affordable weekend getaways. The KTX from Seoul to Busan takes just over two hours, making even the far end of the country accessible for a weekend. Booking through the Korail app or website is straightforward, and the KakaoBus app makes long-distance bus travel easy to navigate in English. If you're planning multiple trips, look into the Korail Pass for unlimited travel over a set number of days. It can save you significant money over individual tickets.

Korean cuisine and dining etiquette

One of the most enjoyable ways to immerse yourself in Korean culture is through its food. Korean cuisine is rich in flavor, history, and diversity, offering something for every palate. Whether you are grilling pork belly at your table, slurping noodles at a street stall, or sampling kimchi for the first time, every meal is a chance to explore the country's soul. And in Korea, eating is rarely a solitary activity; it is a social experience that brings people together in ways that go far beyond the food itself.

Korean BBQ and Classic Dishes

The first thing I tell every new teacher to try is samgyeopsal (삼겹살), Korean barbecue with thick slices of pork belly grilled right at your table. You wrap the meat in a lettuce leaf with garlic, chili paste, and rice, and the combination of smoky, savory, and spicy flavors is addictive from the first bite. Don't stop at pork belly; marinated beef short ribs, known as galbi, are equally incredible. Korean BBQ meals are served with a generous spread of banchan (반찬), or side dishes, which can number over a dozen and are refilled for free. These typically include various types of kimchi, pickled radish, and seasoned vegetables.

Beyond barbecue, there are classics you will come to love. Bibimbap is a visually stunning bowl of warm rice topped with sautéed vegetables, meat, and a fried egg, mixed together with spicy gochujang (고추장) chili paste for a nutritious and customizable meal. For soup lovers, dishes like doenjang jjigae (된장 찌개), a savory soybean paste stew, sundubu jjigae (순두부찌개, a soft tofu stew), and kimchi jjigae (spicy kimchi stew with pork) are perfect comfort foods, especially during Korea's cold winters. You will develop your own favorites quickly, and part of the joy of living here is the endless variety waiting to be discovered.

Teacher Story: The Octopus That Fought Back

When I arrived in Korea from Tacoma, Washington, I was about as adventurous with food as a person could be in the wrong direction. I had never tried sushi. I had never eaten anything particularly spicy. My palate was, to put it generously, sheltered. That changed in my first week.

After one of my earliest hoesik dinners with two of my Korean male colleagues, what I thought was a single dinner turned into the Korean tradition of multi-round socializing. Round one was samgyeopsal, Korean BBQ with thick slices of grilled pork belly. It was incredible, smoky, savory, and unlike anything I had eaten before. Round two was a beer bar. Round three was a noribang, where we belted out songs with more beer than talent. By round four, I was thoroughly inebriated, and my colleagues led me to an orange tent on the street called a pojangmacha, a Korean street-side drinking tent that serves fresh side dishes and soju .

They ordered something I wasn't prepared for: live nakji, baby octopus, freshly diced and served with sesame oil and salt for dipping. The pieces were still moving on the plate. Tentacles were curling and squirming in the dish as if the octopus hadn't quite accepted its situation. I stared at it and said, "I can't."

My colleagues insisted. "It's ber-ry ex-pen-siv-ba (it's very expensive)!" they said, as if the price tag should override the fact that my dinner was still trying to escape the plate. So, I bit the bullet. I downed a shot of soju for courage, picked up a piece, dipped it in the sesame oil, and put it in my mouth. It immediately stuck to my teeth. The suction cups on the tentacle grabbed on like they had one last fight left in them. I chewed as fast as I could, swallowed, then chased it with my soju shot and one of their soju shots for good measure.

Then I waited. And I thought, well, I'll be damned. It actually tasted fresh and clean, almost sweet, once I got past the part where it was moving in my mouth. That same night, they ordered maeuntang (해물탕), a spicy fish bone stew that was rich and fiery and went perfectly with the absurd amount of soju we had consumed. I went home that night sunburned from the inside out, exhausted, and completely converted.

That one evening demolished every food boundary I had walked into Korea with. Within a week, the guy who had never tried sushi was dipping live octopus in sesame oil and chasing it with soju in an orange tent at two in the morning. Korea will do that to you.

Takeaway: Korean food culture is inseparable from Korean social culture. Some of your most memorable meals won't happen in restaurants; they'll happen in pojangmacha (포장마차) tents, at hoesik (회식) dinners that stretch into four or five rounds, and in moments where a colleague insists you try something that terrifies you. Say yes whenever you can. The food that scares you the most often becomes the food you end up craving.

Pro Tip

Korean dining is social by design. Meals are shared, drinks are poured for each other, and saying no to food that someone has ordered for you can come across as rude. You don't have to eat everything, but always try at least a bite and express appreciation. A simple "mashisseoyo!" (맛있어요, "It's delicious!") goes a long way, even if your face is telling a different story. And if you're worried about adventurous dishes, remember that sesame oil and soju make almost anything palatable.

Chimek and Street Food

You haven't truly experienced Korean food culture until you've had chimek, the beloved portmanteau of "chicken" and "maekju" (beer). This combination of fried chicken and cold beer is a national obsession, enjoyed at local pubs, ordered for delivery late into the night, or shared with friends at plastic tables outside a neighborhood chicken shop. The chicken comes in endless varieties, classic fried, soy garlic, honey butter, fiery spicy glaze, cheese-dusted, and more. Every restaurant has its own signature style, and hunting for the best chimek in your neighborhood will become one of your favorite pastimes.

Street food is equally essential, especially in night markets like Gwangjang Market in Seoul or Nampo-dong in Busan. Look for hotteok (호떡, sweet pancakes filled with brown sugar and nuts), tteokbokki (떡볶이, spicy rice cakes in a thick, sweet chili sauce), odeng (fish cakes on skewers in a savory broth), and twigim (Korean tempura). Kimbap, rice and vegetables rolled in seaweed, is available at every convenience store and street corner and makes the perfect cheap, filling meal. Mandu (만두), Korean dumplings, are another staple that you will come to rely on. These affordable snacks are a core part of everyday life in Korea, and grazing your way through a night market is one of the best evenings you can have.

Teacher Story: The Chimek Revelation

Not long after I arrived in Korea, one of my Korean coworkers, an eighth-dan Hapkido instructor, no less, invited me out for chimek after work. I had no idea what chimek was, but I said sure. When a martial arts master invites you somewhere, you don't ask questions.

We met after work and walked to a nearby hole-in-the-wall chicken restaurant, the kind of place that had plastic chairs, fluorescent lighting, and zero ambiance. None of that mattered. What they had was cheap fried chicken and cold beer, and that combination turned out to be one of the greatest culinary discoveries of my life. The basic fried chicken was crispy and perfectly seasoned, but what really got me was the yangnyeom (양념) chicken; pieces coated in a gochujang-based sauce that was hot, sweet, and spicy all at once. It was the kind of flavor that made me close my eyes and wonder why nobody had told me about this sooner.

Later, as we worked our way through more beer than was probably wise, I tried something called dak-ttongjip-twigim (닭똥집튀김), which my coworker cheerfully explained translates roughly to "chicken poop house" in Korean. It is actually fried chicken gizzard, breaded and deep-fried, incredibly chewy and weirdly addictive. Paired with cold beer, it was the kind of snack I never would have ordered on my own but couldn't stop eating once I started.

From that night on, I was hooked. I became a chimek hunter, trying every chicken restaurant I could find in search of the best version. And the beautiful thing about Korea is that there are thousands of chicken places, each with their own variation or signature style, garlic soy, honey butter, cheese-dusted, fire-breathing spicy, and everything in between. You will never run out of new places to try.

Takeaway: Chimek is more than just fried chicken and beer. It is one of the most social and beloved food traditions in Korea, and it will almost certainly be one of the first things a Korean colleague or friend invites you to experience. Say yes immediately. It is affordable, delicious, and one of the fastest ways to bond with the people around you. Don't be surprised if it becomes your go-to comfort food and your default answer to "What should we eat tonight?"

Pro Tip

Chicken delivery in Korea is fast, cheap, and available late into the night. If you don't feel like going out, apps like Baedal Minjok (배달의민족) or Yogiyo let you order chimek straight to your door, often within thirty minutes. It is one of the great luxuries of living in Korea, and on a Friday night after a long week of teaching, there are few things better than cold beer and hot fried chicken delivered to your apartment.

Vegetarian and Vegan Options

While meat is central to many traditional Korean dishes, finding vegetarian options is possible with a little effort. Many stews can be made without meat, and dishes like bibimbap can be ordered without beef. Pajeon (파전), savory scallion pancakes, are naturally vegetarian and delicious. A large portion of banchan side dishes are vegetable-based, so you will usually find something to eat at any Korean restaurant. When ordering, it helps to learn the phrase "gogi-eopseo-juseyo" (고기 없이 주세요), which means "please give it to me without meat." Vegetarian and vegan restaurants are becoming more common in larger cities, particularly in Seoul, though they can be harder to find in smaller towns.

Café Culture

Korea's café culture is one of the first things that will surprise you, and it will quickly become a part of your daily life. Korean cafés are not just places to get coffee; they are destinations in themselves. From minimalist Scandinavian interiors to pink floral wonderlands, themed cafés are everywhere. You will find cafés that double as art galleries, photo studios, or places to spend time with cats, dogs, or even sheep. The drinks go well beyond standard espresso, sweet potato lattes, dalgona coffee, and elaborate fruit-based drinks are common. The coffee is excellent, the atmosphere is always unique, and you will quickly develop a list of favorite spots in your neighborhood. For many teachers, their local café becomes a second living room, a place to grade papers, decompress after work, or meet friends on a Saturday afternoon.

Dining Etiquette

Understanding dining etiquette helps you blend in and show respect at the table. In group meals, wait for the oldest person to begin eating first, as this is a sign of respect rooted in Confucian tradition. Use both hands when pouring drinks for elders, and receive drinks the same way. It is polite to refill others' glasses before your own, and you should never leave your chopsticks sticking vertically in your rice bowl, as this resembles a funeral rite. If you are ever unsure about what to do, observe your coworkers and follow their lead. Koreans genuinely appreciate when foreigners make an effort to respect cultural customs, and a little awareness goes a long way.

Metal chopsticks are standard in Korea, and they can be tricky at first since they are heavier and more slippery than wooden or plastic ones. The key is to hold them near the top to balance their weight. Keep the bottom chopstick steady, resting it in the crook between your thumb and index finger, and on the side of your ring finger; this one doesn't move. The top chopstick is the one you manipulate, held like a pencil with your thumb, index finger, and middle finger. To pick up food, keep the bottom one still and move only the top one up and down. Practice with small items like beans or pieces of kimchi to build control. You will know you have achieved chopstick mastery when you can pick up a quail egg without stabbing it.

Pro Tip

Learn a few Korean food phrases and use them at every meal. Say "jal meokkesseumnida" (잘 먹겠습니다, "I will eat well") before meals and "jal meogeosseumnida" (잘 먹었습니다, "I ate well") after. These polite expressions show gratitude and are considered good manners. They will earn you instant goodwill at any Korean table.

Pro Tip

Learn quickly how to use chopsticks, or don't be afraid to ask for a fork at first. But be warned, later, once you've become a chopstick master, you will feel mildly offended when a restaurant preemptively brings you a fork because you're a foreigner. It's a strange rite of passage, but it means you've arrived.

Weekend Trips and Cultural Experiences

Korea is small enough that you can reach almost any part of the country within a few hours, thanks to an efficient network of high-speed trains and buses. This makes weekend trips a realistic and affordable way to explore. Teachers often take advantage of their weekends and national holidays to visit new cities, participate in festivals, or discover Korea's natural beauty. Don't let a single long weekend go to waste; there is always somewhere new to see.

Seasonal Trips and Festivals

Spring is magical in Korea. Cherry blossom season draws crowds to cities like Jinhae, Seoul, and Gyeongju. The Jinhae Gunhangje Festival is one of the largest cherry blossom festivals in the world, with millions of blossoms creating a breathtaking canopy overhead. The weather is perfect for exploring, and the entire country seems to burst into color overnight.

Summer is all about the beaches. Busan's lively, social beach scene is hard to beat, but the quieter coastlines of Gangwon-do offer a more scenic and relaxed alternative. The Boryeong Mud Festival in July is a massive, multi-day party on Daecheon Beach, complete with music, giant inflatables, mud wrestling, and a truly unique atmosphere that draws visitors from all over the world.

Autumn offers the best hiking in the country. National parks like Seoraksan, Naejangsan, and Jirisan are transformed by breathtaking fall foliage, and the crisp, cool air makes it the perfect season to be outdoors. In the fall, the Andong Mask Dance Festival showcases traditional Korean culture, and the Jinju Lantern Festival, where thousands of lanterns float along the Namgang River, is one of the most visually stunning events in Korea.

Even winter keeps the country active. Snow festivals, light festivals, and seasonal street markets pop up across the country. Ski resorts like Yongpyong and Vivaldi Park are easily accessible from Seoul for a day or two of skiing or snowboarding. Korea doesn't have an off-season; every time of year has something worth experiencing. A great resource for planning is the Korea Tourism Organization's website at www.tour2korea.com.

Hanok Stays

For a truly immersive experience, many teachers enjoy staying in a hanok (한옥) guesthouse, a traditional Korean home with beautiful wooden beams, paper doors, and the unique floor-heating system known as ondol (온돌). These are especially popular in Jeonju and Gyeongju. Staying in a hanok is like stepping back in time; the serene courtyards, quiet evenings, and the feeling of warm floors beneath you offer a perfect escape from city life. Many hanok stays also offer activities like wearing a traditional hanbok (한복) for a photo shoot, participating in a tea ceremony, or learning calligraphy. This hands-on experience provides a deeper appreciation for Korea's heritage and is one of the most memorable things you can do during your time here.

Templestays

If you are interested in a deeper spiritual engagement, try a temple stay program. You can spend a night or a weekend living in a Buddhist temple, participating in traditional ceremonies, eating simple vegetarian meals, and meditating alongside monks. These programs offer a structured daily schedule that includes early morning chanting, communal meals served in silence, and opportunities for quiet contemplation. Available in English, they provide a powerful insight into Korea's spiritual traditions and an opportunity for self-reflection away from the noise of daily life. It is one of the most unique experiences available to you in Korea.

Teacher Story: The Monk's Robe

In my fifth year in Korea, I was working for the Korea Tourism Organization's head office in Seoul as a public relations manager. One day, my manager asked me to write a PR story about the Templestay program. I told her I had never done one before and wasn't sure what I could write about an experience I hadn't had. So she arranged for me to go to Busan and visit Beomeosa Temple for a full one-night, two-day Templestay.

The program started around three in the afternoon and finished around ten the next morning. In that short window, I lived an entirely different life. I changed into traditional Korean temple monk's clothing, practiced Buddhist martial arts, ate monastic vegetarian meals served in silence, learned the proper way to bow, attended temple ceremonies, and sat for a tea ceremony with a Buddhist monk who spoke through an English-speaking teenage helper serving as our translator. Our small group of expats sat cross-legged on the floor, sipping tea and listening to the monk share his thoughts on stillness and purpose. It was one of the most peaceful hours I have ever experienced.

The martial arts component hit me on a personal level. I had practiced martial arts my entire life, and to be standing in a centuries-old Korean Buddhist temple learning the movements that connected martial discipline to spiritual practice felt like something I had been moving toward without knowing it. It wasn't exercise, it was meditation in motion.

That night, the men slept in one large, shared room and the women in another, all of us on thin floor mats. It was not great for my back, but it added to the authenticity of the experience. There was no phone signal to speak of, no television, no distractions. Just silence, the sound of the temple bell, and the kind of stillness you almost never find in modern Korea.

We were woken up before dawn at 3:30 in the morning for the morning ceremony, then morning prayer, and a martial arts lesson, then a vegetarian monastic meal, and by the time I left Beomeosa at nine the next morning, I felt like I had been gone for a week. It was like Ajax for Seoul. The experience gave me more than enough material for the PR story my manager wanted, but it also gave me something I hadn't expected: a memory I still talk about years later and one of the experiences I most frequently recommend to friends, family, and every teacher I mentor. A few years later, I brought a group of 30 travel writers from the Midwest to the same temple for the same experience.

Takeaway: A Templestay is one of the most unique experiences available to you in Korea, and it is something you simply cannot replicate anywhere else. It strips away the noise of daily life and gives you a window into a spiritual tradition that has been practiced on Korean mountainsides for over a thousand years. Whether you are religious, spiritual, or neither, the experience of slowing down, eating simply, and spending a night in a Buddhist temple will stay with you long after you leave Korea.

Pro Tip

If sleeping on a thin mat in a shared room doesn't appeal to you, many temples offer a day-trip version of the Templestay that includes the key experiences, the clothing, the tea ceremony, the meditation, and the vegetarian meal, without the overnight stay.

This lighter version is a perfect introduction. You can find English-language information and book Templestay programs at www.templestay.com. Programs are available at temples across the country, and many are located in stunning mountain settings that are worth the trip on their own. If you stay the night, bring earplugs since you share the sleeping area with several other temple-campers.

Cooking Classes

One of the most delicious ways to engage with Korean culture is through a hands-on cooking class. These are offered in most major cities and let you learn to make classic dishes like kimchi from scratch, perfect your bulgogi (불고기), or assemble a beautiful bibimbap. Many classes include a trip to a local market to select fresh ingredients, which is a cultural experience in itself. You leave with a full stomach, a new skill, and a deeper appreciation for the ingredients and traditions behind the food you have been eating every day. Cooking classes also make for a great weekend activity with friends and are an experience you can bring home with you long after your contract ends.

Pro Tip

Make a habit of checking local tourism boards, travel blogs, and social media for upcoming festivals and events. Sites like VisitKorea, Trazy, and the Korea Tourism Organization offer English-language information and can help with booking experiences and tickets. Following expat groups on social media will also keep you informed about local events and spontaneous gatherings. The teachers who get the most out of Korea are the ones who actively seek out experiences rather than waiting for them to come along.

Final Thoughts

Living in Korea is a rare opportunity not just to teach, but to grow, explore, and experience life from an entirely new perspective. Your professional life in the classroom is beautifully complemented by a world of adventure waiting just outside the school doors. Each weekend is a chance to dive deeper into the country's heart, whether you are taking a high-speed train to a new city, trying a street food dish you can't pronounce, or hiking a scenic mountain trail. The memories you create will be woven from the bustling energy of Seoul, the tranquility of a temple stay, the laughter in your classroom, and the shared meals with new friends. Korea offers more than a teaching job; it is a launchpad for personal growth and cultural immersion, and it will give back as much as you are willing to discover.

Chapter 19: Making Friends and Building a Community

Chapter Summary

This chapter covers how to connect with both expats and locals to enrich your life in Korea, practical ways to join social groups, clubs, and hobby circles, language exchange and cultural immersion as tools for deeper relationships, dating culture in Korea, including honest tips and cautions, and how to build a sustainable support network for your time abroad.

Why This Chapter Matters

Teaching in Korea offers exciting opportunities for career growth and cultural exploration, but the social aspect of living abroad is just as important as anything that happens in the classroom. Your well-being, happiness, and long-term success are directly tied to your ability to create strong friendships and integrate into a community. Your social network becomes your support system, the people who give you advice on daily life, pull you out of your apartment when homesickness hits, celebrate holidays with you when your family is ten thousand miles away, and make the difference between a year you endure and a year you treasure. Whether you are looking for deep friendships, casual connections, cultural exchange, or romantic relationships, Korea offers a wide array of opportunities to build a fulfilling social life. You just have to be willing to take the first step.

Connecting with Expats and Locals

When you first arrive in Korea, it is natural to seek out other foreign teachers and expats who share your language and cultural background. These individuals can become an invaluable support system during your initial adjustment period. They understand the challenges of daily life, from navigating public transport to finding familiar groceries to dealing with a difficult director, and they can offer a sense of belonging when everything else feels unfamiliar. Many new teachers form lifelong friendships with their fellow expats, sharing travel adventures, celebrating holidays together, and supporting one another through homesickness and culture shock.

The best way to meet fellow expats is by joining online communities before you even arrive. Facebook groups such as "Every Expat in Korea," "Teachers in Korea," or city-specific groups like "Expats in Busan" are active with posts about meetups, events, housing, and job changes. Reddit forums like r/Korea and r/teachinginkorea are also useful for questions, networking, and staying informed. These online spaces are often the first place to find information on everything from visa renewals to restaurant recommendations. Once you arrive, participate in organized social events like trivia nights, foreign film screenings, or language exchange gatherings to start meeting people in person.

One of my teachers showed me exactly how to do this right. Before she even arrived in Korea, she had dinner meetups, hiking trips, and language exchange plans all lined up for her first week. I asked her how she managed it, and she said that since she had been placed in Bucheon, she joined the Bucheon Facebook page and simply posted: "Hi everyone. I'm from Los Angeles, California, and I'm new to Bucheon City. I arrive on Saturday, and I'd like to make some friends. Does anyone have time for coffee, sightseeing, shopping, hiking, or just hanging out?" She said several expats and a few Koreans messaged her directly, and she hit the ground running from the moment she landed. That kind of proactive energy is exactly what separates teachers who thrive socially from those who spend their first months feeling isolated.

Pro Tip

To make friends in Korea, you need to be proactive, even if that is not your typical character. The expat community is a pay-it-forward culture; everyone has been a newcomer at some point, and most people are genuinely eager to meet new faces. The best way to avoid homesickness or loneliness is to have an active lifestyle and meet as many people as you can in your first few weeks. Don't wait for invitations. Create them.

Building Relationships with Koreans

While it is comforting to spend time with other foreigners, building relationships with local Koreans will give you a far more profound and enriching experience. Koreans are generally warm and welcoming, especially toward foreigners who show respect and genuine interest in Korean culture. Many locals are also eager to improve their English or meet people from other countries, which creates a natural foundation for connection. These friendships can open a unique window into daily Korean life, helping you understand cultural nuances, discover hidden local gems, and feel more deeply rooted in your new home.

Some of the best Korean friendships start with simple gestures. Saying yes to a spontaneous dinner invitation, accepting help from a neighbor, or asking a coworker to teach you a Korean phrase can open doors you didn't expect. Attend school events like teacher dinners and cultural days, even if you are nervous. These are valuable opportunities to bond with coworkers and be seen as part of the team, and they demonstrate your commitment to the school's community in a way that Korean colleagues genuinely appreciate.

Pro Tip

Ask your Korean coworkers if they would like to do a language exchange with you for thirty to sixty minutes per day or a few days per week. Korean teachers love to share their language and culture with foreign teachers, and you can make the exchange even more enjoyable by meeting for coffee or a meal. These exchanges often evolve into genuine friendships that outlast your contract.

Language Exchange and Cultural Immersion

Language exchange is one of the most popular and mutually beneficial ways to connect with Koreans. You help someone practice their English while they help you learn Korean, and what starts as a structured arrangement often evolves into a real friendship. Apps and websites like HelloTalk, Tandem, Meetup, and Conversation Exchange are great places to find language partners. Universities and community centers also host language exchange events regularly, and these in-person gatherings tend to feel more natural and social than app-based conversations.

Participating in a language exchange goes beyond vocabulary. It allows you to understand cultural norms, learn slang, and develop empathy for what your students experience when they are learning English. Many teachers say that being a language learner themselves made them more patient and more effective in the classroom, because it reminded them how frustrating and humbling it feels to search for the right word and come up empty.

If you are serious about learning Korean, consider enrolling in a formal class. Many universities offer Korean language programs for foreigners, ranging from beginner to advanced levels, and evening and weekend classes are available for teachers working full-time. Online resources such as Talk To Me In Korean, How to Study Korean, and Duolingo can help you build a foundation at your own pace. Even a basic conversational ability in Korean will dramatically improve your daily life, your relationships with colleagues, and your confidence navigating the country.

The fastest way to improve your Korean, though, is to make a Korean best friend, boyfriend, or girlfriend. I watched countless friends — both expats improving their Korean and Koreans improving their English — make enormous progress in just a few months simply because they were spending so much time with someone who spoke the other language. There is no substitute for daily, natural conversation with someone you genuinely care about.

Immersing yourself in Korean life also means participating in holidays, festivals, and traditions. Celebrate Chuseok or Lunar New Year with your coworkers if invited. Try your hand at making kimchi during kimjang season. Attend a local harvest or lantern festival. These experiences help you understand Korean values, beliefs, and family dynamics in a way that no textbook or classroom can replicate, and they often create the stories and memories that stay with you long after you leave Korea.

Pro Tip

Start learning Hangul, the Korean writing system, before you arrive. It only takes a few hours to master, and it opens up access to signs, menus, and everyday communication. This simple step can dramatically improve your confidence and independence from day one.

Teacher Story: Building Bradley's Tennis Army

When I first came to Korea, I was the only expat at my school. That meant every friendship I made outside of work had to be intentional. Nobody was going to hand me a social life; I had to go build one. So, I joined a Hapkido hagwon and a hiking group through Facebook, both of which introduced me to people I never would have met inside my school bubble. Those early efforts taught me something I've carried through my entire time in Korea: your social network is the single largest factor in having a great experience here, outside of your work environment.

Years later, when I picked up tennis, I discovered Korea's open chat culture on KakaoTalk. I joined two open tennis chat groups in Incheon that each had over four hundred members. I started showing up to games three to five times per week, and quickly, I began seeing the same faces. Anyone who could speak English would gravitate toward me, and conversations that started at the net continued over meals and drinks afterward.

After a few months, I decided to start my own group. I created Bradley's Tennis Friends, a closed KakaoTalk group where I personally added players who were fun to play with, roughly 2.5-level or higher, and many of whom spoke little to some English. That group has grown to over one hundred and ten male tennis players, and it has become one of the greatest joys of my time in Korea. I play four to five times per week now, and the community I built through tennis has given me friendships, fitness, and a sense of belonging that goes far beyond the court.

This is exactly why we created the TEIK community dinners. Twice a year, in the spring and fall, we host dinners for up to sixty teachers per event specifically so that new teachers can meet like-minded people outside of their school bubble. When I came to Korea, that level of support didn't exist. I had to figure it out on my own. You don't have to.

Takeaway: Korea has an incredible number of sporting clubs, hiking groups, language exchanges, hobby circles, and social communities that anyone can join. The opportunities are everywhere — but they won't come to you. You need to make the effort to go out, be social, and interact with many different people. The teachers who build strong social networks are the ones who thrive in Korea. The ones who stay in their apartments waiting for friendships to happen are the ones who struggle with loneliness and homesickness. Be proactive from day one, and your social life will grow faster than you expect.

Pro Tip

Start with one group activity per week, a sport, a language exchange, a hiking group, anything that gets you out of the house and around other people consistently. Once you've found your rhythm, expand. Join a second group or start your own. The beauty of Korea's social culture is that people are genuinely open to meeting new faces, especially in expat and hobby communities. You just have to show up.

Social Groups, Clubs, and Online Communities

To build a fulfilling social life in Korea, take the initiative and join groups that align with your interests. Whether you are into hiking, photography, board games, yoga, volunteering, or religious study, there is almost certainly a group of like-minded people nearby. City-based clubs such as the Seoul Hiking Group, Busan Book Club, and Gwangju English Theater bring people together through shared passions and help newcomers connect quickly. Many cities also have expat-run sports leagues, including soccer, ultimate frisbee, dodgeball, and basketball. These are great for physical fitness and social bonding — group meals or drinks often follow weekend games, and most teams welcome players of all skill levels.

Volunteering is another meaningful way to connect while giving back to your host community. Organizations like Teach North Korean Refugees, Korea Animal Rescue and Education, and Habitat for Humanity Korea often seek help from English-speaking volunteers. Participating in community service expands your social circle and adds a sense of purpose to your time abroad that goes beyond the classroom.

Religious communities also offer strong networks for those who are interested. Korea has a sizable Christian population, and many churches offer English-language services and Bible study groups. Buddhist temples welcome foreigners for meditation, temple stays, and cultural education. Whether you are religious or simply seeking fellowship, these spaces often provide comfort and community during the times when you need it most.

Do not underestimate the power of online platforms for finding your people. In addition to Facebook and Reddit, apps like Meetup, KakaoTalk group chats, and Instagram hashtags make it easy to discover local events and connect with people who share your interests. It might feel awkward to reach out at first, but most people in these communities are open and eager to make new friends. Everyone in Korea's expat world was a newcomer once, and that shared experience creates an openness that you won't find in many other places.

Dating and Relationships in Korea

Many teachers in Korea are curious about or interested in dating Koreans. Romantic relationships can be one of the most rewarding aspects of living abroad, offering a unique opportunity to learn about cultural values, traditions, and communication styles on a deeply personal level. The Korean concept of jeong (정), a deep, almost familial affection that develops over time, often becomes a central part of serious relationships. At the same time, navigating dating in a foreign country requires sensitivity, respect, and honest communication.

Dating culture in Korea blends traditional values with modern trends. Public displays of affection tend to be more modest than in Western countries, and it is common for couples to celebrate monthly anniversaries, wear matching outfits, or share meals from the same plate. Dating apps like Tinder and Bumble are popular, but many relationships still begin through mutual friends, school connections, or chance encounters at social events. The path to meeting someone is often less app-driven and more community-driven than what you may be used to.

If you begin dating a Korean partner, expect conversations around family, job stability, and future plans to come earlier than you might be used to. Family approval is often a significant factor in serious relationships, and you may be invited to a formal dinner to meet the family sooner than you expect. Marriage-minded Koreans can be direct about their intentions, which can feel forward but is rooted in a culture where relationships are seen as serious commitments rather than casual explorations. That said, not all relationships follow this pattern, and many cross-cultural couples find a comfortable balance between traditions and shared values.

Teacher Story: The Co-Teacher Mistake

One of the teachers I mentored made a mistake in his second month with EPIK that I couldn't undo for him, no matter how much advice I gave afterward. He slept with his Korean co-teacher. When he told me about it casually, I asked the obvious question: "So are you a couple now?" He said no, he had no intention of dating her. It was just a hookup.

I did a facepalm and said, "You should start looking for a new job now."

He laughed it off. A week later, he called me, and he wasn't laughing anymore. Working with her had become unbearable. The awkwardness was constant. She was hurt, and she had every right to be. But the real problem was structural: she was the person who wrote his evaluation for contract renewal. Every interaction now carried a weight that hadn't existed before, and he didn't think he could tough it out for the remaining ten months of his contract. What had seemed like a harmless decision in the moment had fundamentally compromised his professional standing, his daily comfort at work, and his ability to get renewed.

I made the same mistake myself in my first year of teaching in Korea. I started dating Belle, the Korean art teacher at my hagwon. She was kind, eager to help me settle in, and offered to take me sightseeing on weekends. We started dating, only on Saturdays, as she wanted, but it went south quickly. Even though we didn't teach together, we shared a teachers' room with three other Korean staff members. The tension was visible and uncomfortable for everyone. It made my daily work life significantly harder for months.

The expat teaching community in Korea is not huge, and it is more interconnected than you think. A relationship that goes wrong with a colleague can have professional repercussions that extend well beyond your immediate school. School managers also dislike coworkers dating for exactly this reason, they've seen how it ends.

Takeaway: Do not date your co-teacher or coworker. It feels like common sense until you're the new teacher in a foreign country and the person helping you adjust is also the person you're spending the most time with. The proximity and the gratitude can easily be confused for something else. Keep those relationships professional and friendly, and build your romantic life outside of your workplace. If you do date a colleague despite this advice, at a minimum, keep it private and discreet, but understand the risk you are taking.

Pro Tip

If you're looking for romantic connections, build your social life outside of school first. Join social groups, attend expat events, use dating apps, or meet people through hobbies and sports. Korea offers endless opportunities to meet people, and none of them require you to complicate the one place where you need things to run smoothly every single day.

Teacher Story: The Sunday Lunch Ambush

Rachel, one of the teachers I placed in Suwon, met her Korean boyfriend Junhyeok through a language exchange group at a café near Suwon Station. They had been paired randomly for a conversation practice session, and what was supposed to be a one-hour English-Korean exchange turned into a three-hour conversation that closed out the café. They started meeting on their own after that, first for coffee, then for weekend hikes, and eventually for the kind of long, wandering walks through Hwaseong Fortress where neither of them was pretending the language practice was still the point.

About two months in, Junhyeok casually mentioned over dinner that his mother wanted to meet her. Rachel, who had been in Korea for about five months at that point, was caught off guard. In Canada, meeting the parents usually signals a serious, established relationship. She and Junhyeok had not even had the conversation about whether they were officially a couple. She called me that evening, slightly panicked, and asked what it meant.

I told her what I tell every teacher in her situation: in Korea, meeting the family can happen much earlier than you expect, and it does not always carry the same weight it does back home (but it can). Korean parents are often curious about the foreigner their child is spending time with, and the invitation can be as much about satisfying that curiosity as it is about evaluating you as a potential spouse. That said, it is never casual either. It means the relationship is being taken seriously enough to bring into the family's awareness, and how you handle it matters.

Rachel agreed to go. Junhyeok took her to his parents' home on a Sunday for lunch, and she described the experience as equal parts terrifying and heartwarming. His mother had prepared a full spread of homemade Korean dishes, far more food than four people could eat, which Rachel later learned is a common way Korean parents show care and welcome. The conversation was a mix of Korean and broken English, with Junhyeok translating back and forth. His father asked what her parents did for a living and whether she planned to stay in Korea, questions that felt intensely direct to Rachel but were completely standard for a Korean parent meeting their child's partner for the first time.

The moment she told me about afterward was the one that stuck with her. As they were leaving, Junhyeok's mother pressed a small envelope into Rachel's hand and said something in Korean that Junhyeok translated as: "Please take care of yourself. Korea is cold in winter." Inside the envelope was 50,000 KRW. Rachel tried to refuse it, but Junhyeok quietly told her that declining a gift from his mother would be more awkward than accepting it. She took it, bowed, and thanked her.

On the bus ride home, Rachel told me she started crying, not because anything was wrong, but because the warmth and generosity of the gesture hit her harder than she expected. She was thousands of miles from her own family, and this woman she had just met for the first time had treated her like she mattered.

Rachel and Junhyeok dated for the rest of her contract. They navigated the usual cross-cultural friction along the way. He thought she was too blunt when she disagreed with him in front of his friends. She thought he was too deferential to his parents about decisions that should have been theirs as a couple. They argued about how much time to spend with his family on holidays versus traveling together. But they also learned from each other. She became more attuned to the indirect ways Koreans express discomfort, and he became more comfortable with open, direct communication about what he wanted.

They eventually broke up after Rachel decided to return to Canada at the end of her second year, and neither of them wanted to attempt long distance. It was amicable. She told me later that the relationship taught her more about Korean culture than any class, book, or workplace experience ever could, and that the Sunday lunch with his family was still one of her favorite memories from her entire time in Korea.

Takeaway

Cross-cultural dating in Korea can be one of the most meaningful parts of your experience abroad, but it comes with dynamics you will not fully understand until you are in them. Family involvement happens earlier and more directly than most Western teachers expect. Gifts, meals, and personal questions are expressions of care, not intrusions. And the cultural friction that inevitably surfaces, around communication styles, family obligations, and future expectations, is not a sign that the relationship is failing. It is a sign that two people from different worlds are doing the real work of understanding each other. Go in with openness, patience, and respect, and even a relationship that does not last forever can leave you with some of the most important lessons of your time in Korea.

Marriage and Long-Term Relationships

Marriage between expats and Koreans is increasingly common, and if you pursue a long-term relationship that leads to marriage, it can open up new visa possibilities such as the F-6 spouse visa, which offers greater freedom in employment and residency. However, international marriage involves legal processes, paperwork, and sometimes cultural friction that you should be prepared for. Differences in gender roles, family traditions, and expectations around holidays can create tension if they are not discussed openly and early.

Korea has become less conservative over the past twenty years, but many Koreans remain traditional in their expectations around marriage and family. Be prepared to navigate these conversations with patience and respect. If you do get married to a Korean and have children, there are several excellent Facebook groups for expats with Korean spouses that offer support, shared experiences, and practical advice. Expat Dads in Korea is one that I personally recommend; it is a genuinely supportive community where members share their experiences and learn from the challenges and successes of others.

Pro Tip

Be honest with yourself and your partner about expectations, especially if your time in Korea is limited. Open communication helps avoid misunderstandings and protects both of you from building something on a foundation that one of you didn't agree to. Cross-cultural relationships are incredibly rewarding, but they require more intentional communication than relationships where both people share the same cultural assumptions.

Final Thoughts

Making friends and building a community in Korea is not just about staying social, it is about creating the emotional foundation that sustains you during your teaching journey. As you face the ups and downs of life abroad, having people to laugh with, learn from, and lean on becomes essential. You do not have to be an extrovert or fluent in Korean to build a meaningful life here. You only need to be open, respectful, and willing to take the first step. Every coffee shared, every new word learned, and every cultural custom embraced brings you closer to a sense of belonging.

A very special thing about teaching in Korea is the incredible diversity of people you will meet and become friends with. You will make lifelong friendships with people from all over the globe, Australia, New Zealand, the United Kingdom, Canada, South Africa, and of course, Korea itself. These friendships will outlast your contract, span continents, and become one of the most unexpected and cherished gifts of your time abroad. Whether you are here for one year or many, the community you build will likely become the thing you remember most fondly when you look back on your Korea experience.

A very special thing about teaching in Korea is the vast array of people you will meet and become friends with. You will quickly make life-long friendships, and you will make friends from all over the globe. I still have many friends in Australia, New Zealand, the UK, Canada, and of course, Korea.

Chapter 20: Managing Finances & Legal Matters

Chapter Summary

This chapter covers your tax obligations in Korea and how international tax treaties may benefit you, the process for applying for the two-year Korean income tax exemption, the most cost-effective ways to send money home and manage your accounts, how the National Health Insurance Service works and how to access healthcare, how the National Pension Service works and how to claim your pension refund, severance pay and what you are entitled to at the end of your contract, and how to stay organized with documentation to protect your legal and financial interests.

Why This Chapter Matters

Teaching in Korea is often framed as a cultural and professional adventure, and it absolutely is. But the financial and legal side of life abroad cannot be overlooked, because this is where the real long-term value of your Korea experience lives. From navigating Korean taxes to managing remittances, understanding health coverage, and ensuring your pension contributions are handled correctly, there are critical systems you must understand to protect your income and your future. Teachers who pay attention to this chapter leave Korea with substantial savings, a significant pension refund, and a financial foundation that makes the transition home comfortable. Teachers who ignore it leave with regret and empty pockets. This chapter walks you through everything you need to know.

What You Can Expect to Spend and Save

Before diving into the specifics of taxes, banking, and benefits, it helps to understand the financial landscape you are walking into. Korea offers one of the best savings opportunities for English teachers anywhere in the world, and the math is straightforward once you understand it.

Most teaching contracts provide free housing or a housing allowance, which immediately eliminates your single largest expense. Beyond rent, your major monthly costs will include utilities (typically fifty to one hundred dollars per month depending on the season), a mobile phone plan (around thirty to fifty dollars), groceries and dining (three hundred to five hundred dollars if you eat a mix of home-cooked meals and Korean restaurants), and transportation (a monthly transit card costs around forty to fifty dollars and covers buses and subway). Social life, coffee, and entertainment can vary widely depending on your habits, but Korea is remarkably affordable compared to most Western countries. A night out with friends for chimek might cost fifteen to twenty dollars. A weekend trip to Busan on the KTX can be done for under a hundred dollars, including food and accommodation.

On a typical teaching salary of 2,600,000 million won per month (roughly two-thousand dollars per month), teachers who are disciplined about their spending can realistically save between eight hundred and twelve hundred dollars per month without taking on any private classes. If a teacher makes money on the side, then the savings amount can be far greater. Over a twelve-month contract, that adds up to ten thousand dollars or more in savings, plus your pension refund and severance pay on top of that. The opportunity is real, but only if you are intentional about taking advantage of it.

What Your Paycheck Actually Looks Like

One of the most common questions I hear from teachers before they arrive is: "I know my salary, but how much will I actually take home?" It is a fair question, and the answer surprises most people because the deductions are smaller than they expect. Let me walk you through a realistic example using a monthly gross salary of 2,600,000 KRW, which is a competitive starting salary for teachers at established hagwons and a common figure for second-year renewals.

Your first deduction is National Health Insurance. The total premium is approximately seven percent of your gross salary, split evenly between you and your school. Your share comes to roughly 92,000 KRW per month. Next is the National Pension, where the total contribution is nine percent, again split equally, making your share about 117,000 KRW. You will also see a small deduction for employment insurance, which runs around 0.9 percent, or roughly 23,000 KRW. Finally, Korean income tax for a single filer at this salary level is modest, typically around 45,000 to 60,000 KRW per month under the progressive rate schedule. All told, your total monthly deductions come to approximately 280,000 to 295,000 KRW, leaving you with a net take-home pay of roughly 2,305,000 to 2,320,000 KRW, which is approximately 1,750 to 1,770 USD at recent exchange rates.

Here is where it gets interesting. If you are a citizen of a country with a bilateral tax treaty with Korea, such as the United States, the United Kingdom, or Canada, and you apply for the two-year income tax exemption discussed later in this chapter, your Korean income tax deduction drops to zero for your first two years. That puts an extra 45,000 to 60,000 KRW back in your pocket every month, which adds up to over a million KRW across two years, or roughly 800 to 1,100 USD. It is not a fortune, but it is free money that requires only a single application form, and many teachers never bother to claim it because they do not know it exists. You will know, because you read this chapter.

Now, from that take-home pay of roughly 2,310,000 KRW, here is what a typical month of living expenses looks like. Utilities, including electricity, gas, water, and internet, generally run between 60,000 and 130,000 KRW per month, with the higher end during winter when you are running your floor heating. A mobile phone plan costs around 40,000 to 60,000 KRW. Transportation on buses and subway using a T-money card is remarkably cheap, usually 50,000 to 60,000 KRW per month. Groceries and dining are your most variable expenses, but if you eat a mix of home-cooked meals and the affordable Korean restaurants near your school, budget between

400,000 and 600,000 KRW. Social spending, coffee, the occasional night out for chimek, weekend activities, and similar expenses might add another 150,000 to 250,000 KRW, depending on your lifestyle.

Add those up, and a comfortable but not extravagant month in Korea costs between 700,000 and 1,100,000 KRW, depending on the season, your city, and your habits. That means from a net paycheck of roughly 2,310,000 KRW, a disciplined teacher can realistically set aside between 1,200,000 and 1,600,000 KRW per month, which is approximately 920 to 1,220 USD. Over twelve months, that is 11,000 to 14,500 USD in pure savings from your salary alone.

But your salary savings are only part of the picture. When your contract ends, you will also receive one month's gross salary as severance pay, adding another 2,600,000 KRW. And if your country has a reciprocal pension agreement with Korea, your lump-sum pension refund will include both your contributions and your employer's matching contributions plus interest, which, after twelve months at this salary level, amounts to roughly 2,850,000 to 2,950,000 KRW. Combined, your severance and pension refund add approximately 5,450,000 to 5,550,000 KRW, or about 4,150 to 4,250 USD, on top of whatever you saved each month.

Put it all together, and a teacher who earns 2,600,000 KRW per month, lives comfortably, travels on weekends, and saves consistently can leave Korea after one year with 15,000 to 19,000 USD or more in combined savings, severance, and pension refund. That is not a theoretical number. I see teachers achieve it every single year. The ones who struggle financially are almost never the ones earning too little; they are the ones spending without a plan. Which brings me to the most important financial lecture I give.

Teacher Story: Dad Brad's Financial Lecture

At every TEIK dinner we host, there comes a moment when I turn into Dad Brad. The new teachers have been chatting, asking questions about schools and life in Korea, and at some point, the conversation turns to money. That's when I get blunt.

I tell them: Have fun in Korea. Travel. Go out. Experience everything you can. But if you don't save at least half of your pay, you're being foolish. I know that sounds harsh, and some teachers look uncomfortable when I say it. But I've watched too many teachers blow through their entire salary on clubbing, expensive trips, and weekend getaways, only to leave Korea after a year or two with nothing to show for it financially. The tragedy is that you can have an incredible time in Korea, an absolute blast, and still save half of your paycheck every month. The cost of living is low enough to make that entirely realistic. You just have to be intentional about it.

My advice is simple: pay yourself first. Every month or two, transfer money home. You can send up to ten thousand dollars to your home country without any extra documentation required. Set up a system and stick to it. Don't wait until the end of your contract to figure out your finances; by then, the money is already gone.

I learned this lesson the hard way, or rather, my wife taught it to me. About six months before we got married, my Korean wife sat me down and said, "I have a great idea. How about you let me take care of the finances? I'll make a detailed ledger, show you every month exactly what we earned, spent, and saved, and we'll each get a few hundred dollars in pocket money to spend however we want. The rest goes to our bills and savings."

I thought it sounded fantastic. No more worrying about bills, no more mental math at the end of the month. At the time, I was working at three part-time schools in addition to my main job, and each one paid me cash in a white envelope every Friday. After we agreed to my wife's system, I never saw another white envelope. She visited the schools before me to collect my pay. Every won went into the ledger.

Here's the thing: I was a spender. If the money was in my hands, it got spent. My wife was a dedicated saver. If you asked her today what we spent on any given day in the past fifteen years, she could pull out the ledger for that year and tell you down to the penny what we earned, what we spent, and what we saved. That system transformed our finances in ways I never could have managed on my own.

I'm not saying every teacher needs to hand their paycheck to a Korean spouse. But every teacher needs a system. Pay yourself first. Transfer money home on a schedule. Build a nest egg that will be waiting for you when your contract ends, whether that's for a down payment on a house, a car, paying off student loans, or simply having a financial cushion that makes the transition home comfortable instead of stressful.

Takeaway: The teachers who leave Korea in the strongest financial position aren't the ones who earned the most; they're the ones who saved consistently from day one. Korea gives you an extraordinary opportunity to build real savings while living abroad, but only if you're disciplined about it. Have the time of your life but pay yourself first every single month. Your future self will thank you.

Pro Tip

Set up an automatic transfer schedule. Every month or two, move a fixed amount from your Korean bank account to your home account. Treat it like a bill you have to pay, because in a sense, you're paying your future self. Once the money is out of your Korean account, you won't miss it, and you'll be amazed at how quickly it accumulates over a one- or two-year contract.

Teacher Story: Six Years of Taxes in One Afternoon

Here is a mistake I made that you can avoid entirely. When I moved to Korea, I assumed that because I was living and working in a foreign country, I didn't need to file taxes back home in the United States. I wasn't earning an American income, I wasn't living in

America, so why would I need to file? That logic seemed perfectly reasonable to me at the time.

It was wrong. American citizens are required to file federal tax returns every year, regardless of where they live or work in the world. I didn't know this, and nobody told me. For six years, I didn't file a single return.

The problem caught up with me when I needed to sponsor my Korean wife's fiancée visa to the United States. Part of the application process required me to demonstrate that I had reportable income for the previous years. Without filed tax returns, I couldn't prove it. So I sat down and filed six years of back taxes in one marathon session, scrambling to gather pay stubs, bank records, and documentation from years of teaching in Korea. It was stressful, time-consuming, and completely avoidable.

The most frustrating part? Once I finally understood the system, I realized I could have filed for free every single year just by downloading the 2555-EZ form from the IRS website. It is a two-page form. That's it. The Foreign Earned Income Exclusion allows American citizens working abroad to pay zero federal tax on foreign earned income up to a threshold that increases every year, for 2025 it is one hundred and thirty thousand dollars, and for 2026, it will be one hundred and thirty-two thousand nine hundred dollars. No teacher in Korea is earning anywhere near that amount, which means most American teachers owe absolutely nothing in federal income tax. But you still have to file the form.

Two pages. Ten minutes. Zero dollars owed. And I skipped it for six years.

Takeaway: If you are an American citizen, file your taxes every year, no matter where you live. The 2555-EZ form is free, fast, and will almost certainly result in you owing nothing. But failing to file can create serious problems down the road, whether it's sponsoring a visa, applying for a mortgage, or simply staying in good standing with the

IRS. Don't make the mistake I made. Set a reminder every year, download the form, and get it done.

Pro Tip

This advice applies beyond Americans. Citizens of many countries have tax filing obligations that continue while they live abroad. Before you leave for Korea, check with your home country's tax authority or a tax professional to understand what you need to file and when. A few minutes of research now can save you years of headaches later.

Pro Tip

Keep a digital folder of your pay stubs, tax statements, and all correspondence related to tax exemption applications. Having your documents organized will make filing far less stressful, both in Korea and back home. Cloud storage is your friend; upload everything as you receive it, so you never have to scramble.

Sending Money Home

Sending money to your home country is an essential part of your financial strategy in Korea. Whether you are saving for student loans, investing, supporting family, or just building a nest egg, choosing the right remittance method can save you significant money over the course of your contract.

The most common approach is to open a Korean bank account, receive your monthly salary, and then transfer money abroad. Major Korean banks like KEB Hana Bank, Shinhan Bank, and Woori Bank offer international wire transfer services that can be arranged in person at a branch or through their mobile banking apps. You will need the receiving bank's SWIFT code, account number, and the recipient's name. However, traditional bank transfers typically involve fees ranging from twenty-five to fifty dollars per transaction and often include unfavorable exchange rates that quietly eat into your savings.

A more cost-effective option is using international money transfer services such as Wise (formerly TransferWise), Remitly, or Western Union. These platforms allow you to link your Korean and foreign bank accounts, and their exchange rates are typically much better than those of traditional banks. Wise, for example, shows you the mid-market rate and charges a transparent transfer fee, often resulting in significant savings over time compared to a bank wire. To use these platforms, you will need to verify your identity by uploading copies of your passport, Korean ARC (Alien Registration Card), and Korean bank documents. Once set up, transfers can be completed in minutes through your smartphone. Keep in mind that many of these services have transfer limits, so if you are planning to send a large sum home at once, such as your pension refund, you may need to use a traditional bank wire or plan multiple transfers.

If you plan to return home eventually, maintain your home country bank account and use it for savings and debt repayment while you are abroad. Most Korean employers require a domestic Korean account for salary deposits, so you will need both accounts during your stay.

Pro Tip

When setting up your Korean bank account, ask about English-language banking support, mobile app access, and whether they provide remittance-friendly services. KEB Hana Bank is often preferred by expats for its user-friendly international transfer platform and English-language support. Having a bank that makes transfers easy removes one of the biggest friction points in getting your money home consistently.

Health Insurance

One of the most valuable benefits of working legally in Korea is enrollment in the National Health Insurance Service (NHIS). Under Korean law, full-time employees at educational institutions must be enrolled, and your monthly premium is split evenly between you and your employer. The premium is approximately seven percent of your salary, with half paid by your employer and the other half deducted from your paycheck. This coverage allows you to visit Korean hospitals, clinics, and dental offices at heavily subsidized rates.

The affordability of Korean healthcare is one of the pleasant surprises of living here. A routine doctor's visit may cost only five to ten dollars, and prescriptions are heavily discounted. Health insurance coverage includes general care, emergency services, dental care, and even some mental health counseling and rehabilitation. While there may be some language barriers at smaller clinics, many large hospitals in cities like Seoul, Busan, and Daegu have international clinics with English-speaking staff. You will receive a health insurance card after your ARC is issued, and you should carry this card with you whenever you visit a medical facility.

Pro Tip

If your school refuses to enroll you in health insurance despite being a full-time employee, this is a major red flag. It may indicate illegal employment practices or attempts to cut costs at your expense. You have the legal right to NHIS coverage, and the Ministry of Employment and Labor can help resolve disputes. Do not let a school tell you that health insurance is optional for foreign teachers; it is not.

National Pension Service

Along with health insurance, most foreign teachers are required to contribute to the National Pension Service (NPS). This is a shared contribution between you and your employer, currently around nine percent of your gross monthly salary, with each party paying half. The pension is essentially a retirement fund managed by the Korean government, and while it may feel like money disappearing from your paycheck each month, it can become one of the biggest financial windfalls of your entire Korea experience.

Citizens of certain countries, including the United States, Canada, and Australia, are eligible to receive a lump-sum pension refund when they leave Korea, provided they have contributed for more than one year and apply correctly. This refund includes both your contributions and your employer's matching contributions, plus interest. For many teachers, the pension refund amounts to several thousand dollars and arrives as a lump sum after departure, essentially a large bonus for completing your contract.

To claim your pension refund, you must visit a local NPS office before you leave Korea with your passport, ARC, final pay stub, and flight information. You can also apply via mail or online after departure, though the in-person process is typically faster. You will need to provide a foreign bank account for the funds to be transferred. Start researching the process well before your departure date to avoid delays. It is important to note that this lump-sum refund is only available to citizens of countries that have a reciprocal pension agreement with Korea. If your country does not have such an agreement, your contributions may not be refundable, so check your eligibility early.

Pro Tip

You and your school are both required to pay into the pension system by law, regardless of whether your country has a reciprocal agreement with Korea. If your school tries to avoid making pension contributions, report it. And if you are eligible for the refund, do not leave Korea without initiating the process. The money is rightfully yours, and it can be a substantial sum that makes a real difference when you return home.

Severance Pay

One financial benefit that many new teachers don't know about until they are close to finishing their contract is severance pay. Under Korean labor law, any employee who completes a full twelve-month contract is entitled to one month's salary as severance pay. This applies to foreign teachers at hagwons, public schools, and universities. Your severance is paid in addition to your final month's salary and is typically deposited into your Korean bank account within fourteen days of your contract end date.

Severance pay is not a bonus or a gift from your employer; it is a legal entitlement. If you complete your contract and your school does not pay severance, you have grounds to file a complaint with the Ministry of Employment and Labor. Combined with your pension refund, severance pay can add up to a significant sum of money waiting for you at the end of your contract, which is another reason to plan your finances and your departure carefully.

Pro Tip

When you add up what a full contract completion gives you, twelve months of savings, a pension refund including your employer's matching contributions plus interest, and one month's severance pay, the financial picture is compelling. A teacher who saves consistently, claims their pension, and receives their severance can leave Korea after one year with fifteen thousand dollars or more in combined savings and payouts. That is life-changing money for many young professionals, and it is entirely achievable if you pay attention to the details in this chapter.

Korean Income Tax and the Two-Year Exemption

In addition to your home country's obligations, you will also pay Korean income tax. Korea uses a progressive tax system, meaning the rate increases as your income rises. For most English teachers earning between two and three million KRW per month, the effective tax rate is relatively low, typically between three and six percent of your gross salary. Your school will deduct Korean income tax directly from your paycheck each month, so you do not need to file separately unless you have additional income sources.

However, there is an important benefit that many teachers either do not know about or fail to take advantage of: the flat-rate tax option for foreign workers. Under Korean tax law, qualifying foreign employees can elect to pay a flat nineteen percent tax rate on their gross salary instead of the standard progressive rate. For most English teachers, this is not advantageous because their progressive rate is already well below nineteen percent. But for teachers with higher incomes, such as those working at universities or international schools, it is worth running the numbers.

Far more relevant for the typical English teacher is the two-year income tax exemption available through bilateral tax treaties. Citizens of countries that have a tax treaty with Korea, including the United States, the United Kingdom, and Canada, may qualify for a full or partial exemption from Korean income tax for up to two years. The specifics vary by treaty. American teachers, for example, can claim an exemption under the US-Korea tax treaty for their first two years of teaching. To apply, you will need to submit a tax exemption application form to your school's payroll department, along with a certificate of residence from your home country's tax authority. Your school then processes the exemption through their payroll system, and the Korean tax withholding stops.

The key is timing. You must apply early in your contract, ideally within the first few months. Teachers who wait too long may miss the window or face difficulty recovering taxes already withheld. If your school's administrative staff is unfamiliar with the process, which is not uncommon at smaller hagwons, you may need to guide them through it or visit your local tax office for assistance. The savings over two years can amount to several thousand dollars, money that goes straight into your pocket rather than into the Korean tax system.

Final Thoughts

Managing your finances and legal obligations in Korea is not just about compliance; it is about maximizing an opportunity that most people never get. By taking advantage of available tax exemptions, using efficient remittance methods, saving consistently, and ensuring you are properly enrolled in health insurance and pension programs, you can leave Korea with significant savings and genuine peace of mind. The systems may feel bureaucratic at first, but with a proactive and organized approach, you will find them entirely manageable. Keep digital copies of all key documents, ask questions when anything seems unclear, and talk to experienced teachers who have been through the process before you. Think of this chapter as the blueprint for building a strong financial foundation while enjoying one of the most exciting cultural and professional experiences of your life.

Chapter 21: Preparing for What's Next

Chapter Summary

This chapter covers your options for renewing your contract in Korea and negotiating better terms, how to transition into other careers in Korea including educational administration, corporate positions, and entrepreneurship, how to market your teaching experience when returning home, planning post-contract travel around Asia, opportunities to teach in other countries using your Korean experience as a springboard, and the importance of networking, professional development, and legal planning for smooth career transitions.

Why This Chapter Matters

As your contract in Korea draws closer to completion, it is natural to start reflecting on what comes next. Whether you are planning to renew, pivot to a new career within Korea, return home, or travel through Asia before settling into your next chapter, the final months of your experience are an essential time for planning and decision-making. Teaching in Korea is more than a job; it is a transformative experience that opens doors, shapes your professional identity, and can launch you toward opportunities you might not have previously imagined. This chapter explores your options in detail and offers guidance to help you make informed, confident decisions about whatever comes next.

Contract Renewal and Career Advancement

If your teaching experience in Korea has been positive, renewing your contract is often the simplest and most rewarding path forward. Many schools prefer to keep experienced teachers rather than go through the costly and time-consuming process of recruiting, hiring, and training someone new from abroad. By renewing, you may gain access to better teaching hours, a raise in salary, or additional responsibilities such as curriculum development or mentoring new teachers. You already know the students, the staff, the systems, and the culture of your school, and that institutional knowledge has real value.

Before renewing, schedule a meeting with your director or head teacher to discuss any changes you would like. A raise of one hundred thousand won per month is the common industry standard for renewing teachers, since schools save money on recruiting fees and visa processing costs by keeping you. However, if your performance has been strong and you have built a positive relationship with your school, you may be in a position to negotiate for more. Some teachers have successfully negotiated raises of two hundred thousand won or higher by demonstrating concrete value, a high student retention rate, strong parent feedback, or a willingness to take on extra responsibilities. Housing and vacation terms are typically fixed policies and harder to adjust, but it never hurts to ask politely if you have a strong relationship with your director.

Some teachers use renewal discussions as an opportunity to transition into a more specialized role, such as head teacher or academic coordinator. These positions typically come with higher pay and greater responsibility. However, academic coordinator roles often require fluency in Korean, as a significant part of the job involves parent counseling and communicating with the local community. If you are interested in moving into leadership, start building your Korean language skills and expressing your interest to your director well before your renewal conversation.

It is equally important to recognize that not all contract renewals are in your best interest. If you have had persistent issues with your school, late payments, unclear expectations, a hostile work environment, or a director you cannot trust, you should reflect seriously on whether renewing is worth the stress. Loyalty to your students is admirable, but your well-being should always come first. You can always look at other schools for your second year, and switching schools often comes with a bigger pay raise and a location that better aligns with where you want to be. Many teachers accept positions outside of Seoul in their first year because they lack ESL experience, but with a year under their belt, schools in Seoul are much more willing to consider them, especially since you would be a visa transfer rather than a new hire from abroad, which simplifies the process significantly for the school.

Pro Tip

If you choose to renew, ask your school to provide the renewal agreement in writing well before your current contract ends. A verbal agreement is not enough. Get everything, salary, housing, vacation days, start date, documented and signed before you commit.

Teacher Story: The Thailand Negotiation

At the end of my first year in Korea, I wasn't ready to go home, but I also wasn't ready to jump straight into another twelve months of teaching without a break. Two of my Korean American friends and I, along with one of their Canadian girlfriends, had been talking about traveling to Southeast Asia for months. We all decided to sign on for another year at our respective schools, but instead of simply renewing, we each negotiated a month off between contracts. Our pitch was simple: we would commit to another full year, saving the school the cost and hassle of recruiting a new teacher, in exchange for four weeks of unpaid leave before the new contract started.

My school agreed, with one condition: I had to find a replacement to cover my classes while I was gone. So I did. I found another teacher who was happy to pick up the hours, briefed them on my classes, and left for three weeks in Thailand and one week in Malaysia with a clear conscience and a signed contract waiting for me when I returned.

That trip was one of the best decisions I made in my early years in Korea. Southeast Asia is incredibly inexpensive compared to Korea, and the four of us traveled comfortably for a month on just a few thousand dollars each. We explored Bangkok, island-hopped in southern Thailand, ate street food for next to nothing, and decompressed completely after a full year of teaching. By the time I came back to Korea, I was rested, recharged, and genuinely excited to start my second year.

Takeaway: If you are planning to renew your contract, use that leverage to negotiate for something you want — whether it's a raise, better hours, or time off between contracts. Schools would much rather accommodate a reasonable request from a proven teacher than go through the expense of hiring, training, and visaing a replacement from abroad. You have more bargaining power than you think, especially if your retention numbers are strong and your director is happy with your work. And if you can swing it, a month in Southeast Asia between contracts is one of the best investments you can make in your own well-being.

Pro Tip

Always plan your end-of-Korea trip to Southeast Asia well in advance. Countries like Thailand, Vietnam, Cambodia, and Malaysia are remarkably affordable, and you can travel comfortably for two to three months on just a few thousand dollars. Many teachers use this trip as a grand finale before flying home. If your school wants you to find coverage for your classes while you're away, start recruiting early; other teachers are often happy to pick up extra hours for the short term.

Transitioning to Other Careers in Korea

For some teachers, one or two years in the classroom is enough to spark curiosity about other career opportunities in Korea. Fortunately, Korea's dynamic economy, growing startup scene, and need for global-minded professionals create real possibilities for expats who speak English and understand Korean culture. The teaching experience you have built gives you a foundation that is more transferable than you might think.

One natural path is moving into educational administration. Larger hagwon chains, corporate training centers, and education-focused startups often need staff for curriculum development, academic coordination, or teacher training. These positions typically offer regular hours, higher pay, and a more structured career path than classroom teaching. For those interested in the university level, long-term career growth may include pursuing a master's or doctoral degree and applying for tenure-track positions at Korean universities.

Pro Tip

If you have a master's or doctoral degree, I strongly suggest applying for university teaching jobs during your first year of teaching in Korea. Most Korean universities do not hire candidates from outside of the country, and they typically require a minimum of two years of teaching experience. Being in Korea already and having classroom experience gives you a significant advantage over applicants abroad.

Another path is entering the corporate sector, especially in roles involving English content editing, digital marketing, customer relations, or international sales. If you are tech-savvy or entrepreneurial, consider roles in content creation, app development, e-commerce, or launching your own business. Some former teachers have built successful careers as YouTubers or bloggers sharing insights on life in Korea, while others provide translation services, write textbooks, or open tutoring academies and cafés.

Networking is crucial for making any career transition in Korea. Attend professional meetups, participate in language exchanges, and take part in business-focused events in cities like Seoul and Busan. Platforms like LinkedIn and Meetup.com are excellent resources for finding these opportunities. Upgrading your Korean language skills and obtaining certifications in areas like TESOL, digital marketing, or project management will also make your resume significantly more competitive for non-teaching roles.

Pro Tip

Changing careers in Korea often requires switching to a different visa, such as the D-8 business visa or E-7 specialist visa. Consult with an immigration lawyer or visa consultant well in advance to avoid legal complications. Visa transitions can take time, and you do not want to find yourself in a gap between your teaching visa expiring and your new visa being processed.

Your Final Month: The Exit Checklist

The last few weeks of your contract are exciting, but they are also when teachers make the costliest administrative mistakes. You are mentally checked out, dreaming about your next adventure, and the boring logistics of closing out your Korean life feel like they can wait. They can't. Handling these tasks before you leave will save you months of frustration and potentially thousands of dollars.

Start with your finances. If you completed a full twelve-month contract, you are entitled to one month's salary as severance pay, which your school is legally required to pay on your final payday. Confirm the exact amount and payment date with your director in writing at least two weeks before your last day. You are also entitled to a refund of your national pension contributions, which can be substantial after a year or more of deductions. You can apply for the pension refund at the airport on your departure day or submit a claim by mail after you return home, but the airport method is faster and avoids the headache of international paperwork. Bring your passport, ARC card, and a copy of your Korean bank details or your home country bank account information to the pension refund counter at Incheon Airport. Processing typically takes two to four months, regardless of which method you use, so do not count on that money being available immediately.

Next, handle your accounts and contracts. Visit your Korean bank in person to either close your account or convert it to a non-resident account if you plan to receive pension or severance payments after departure. Cancel your mobile phone contract and confirm there are no early termination fees; if you took over a plan from another teacher, make sure the account is transferred or closed properly so charges don't continue accumulating in your name. Settle all outstanding utility bills with your landlord or school, and take photos of your apartment's condition on your final day in case there are disputes about the security deposit later.

On your last day in Korea, you must return your ARC card at the immigration counter at Incheon Airport before passing through departure immigration. If you forget, it can complicate future visa applications. This step takes only a minute, but teachers who skip it sometimes face delays when applying for a new visa years later.

Finally, before you leave the building for the last time, collect written references from your director, head teacher, and any co-teachers you worked closely with. A reference from a Korean employer carries real weight with future schools and hiring managers, but once you are back home and six time zones away, getting someone to write and send one becomes exponentially harder. Ask in person, while you are still there, and walk away with the document in hand or in your email inbox.

Pro Tip

Create a simple timeline for yourself, starting thirty days before your contract ends. Week one: confirm severance amount and pension paperwork. Week two: give notice to your bank and phone provider. Week three: settle utilities and collect references. Week four: photograph your apartment, pack, and return your ARC at the airport. Teachers who follow a schedule like this leave Korea cleanly. Teachers who wing it spend months chasing paperwork from the other side of the world.

Returning Home: Marketing Your Teaching Experience

Whether you are planning to return home after one year or five, you may wonder how your time teaching in Korea will be viewed by future employers. The answer depends entirely on how you present it. Teaching abroad can be a powerful asset on your resume if you frame it strategically, or it can look like a gap year if you don't.

Start by emphasizing the transferable skills you developed. Teaching in Korea builds communication, public speaking, time management, conflict resolution, cross-cultural competence, and adaptability — skills that are highly valued across industries from education and nonprofit work to sales, marketing, and international business. Employers want candidates who can work with diverse teams, think on their feet, and solve problems in real time. Your classroom experience provides direct, concrete evidence of all of these abilities.

On your resume, treat your teaching experience the way you would any professional position. Use quantifiable achievements whenever possible. Instead of simply listing "English teacher in Korea," write something like "Taught over three hundred students per semester using communicative methods and game-based learning techniques, resulting in improved language scores and a ninety-five percent student retention rate." Highlight any curriculum development, leadership roles, mentoring of new teachers, or extracurricular involvement. If you created materials, trained colleagues, or took on administrative responsibilities, those belong on your resume.

During job interviews, speak positively and specifically about your time abroad. Share how it broadened your worldview, improved your resilience, and shaped your long-term goals. Most interviewers will be genuinely interested, and you can position yourself as a candidate with a unique perspective and a proven ability to thrive in unfamiliar environments. When answering behavioral questions, draw directly on your Korea experience — describe a specific situation you faced, what you did, and what the result was. Your classroom stories are full of exactly the kind of problem-solving and adaptability that hiring managers are looking for.

Pro Tip

Before you leave Korea, reach out to your supervisors, co-teachers, and even parents of students you taught for LinkedIn recommendations or written references. These add credibility to your resume and demonstrate your impact beyond the classroom. A glowing recommendation from a Korean director or head teacher carries real weight with future employers, especially if they can speak to your professionalism, reliability, and ability to work across cultures.

Traveling Around Asia Before Returning Home

Many teachers take advantage of Korea's central location and excellent flight connections to travel through Asia before returning home. With Korean budget airlines like T'way, Jeju Air, and Jin Air offering low-cost routes across the region, and carriers like AirAsia and Scoot connecting you to Southeast Asia, the opportunities for affordable travel are extraordinary.

Popular destinations include Japan, Vietnam, Thailand, Cambodia, Indonesia, the Philippines, Taiwan, and Malaysia. Each offers unique cultural experiences, natural beauty, and vibrant city life at a fraction of the cost of traveling from North America or Europe. Many former teachers plan a one-to-three-month backpacking trip as a grand finale to their time abroad. A common route is the Southeast Asia loop — Thailand, Laos, Vietnam, and Cambodia — as these countries are easy and affordable to travel between, with well-established backpacker infrastructure and visa-free or visa-on-arrival entry for most nationalities.

When planning your trip, consider the season, your budget, and entry requirements for each country. Some countries allow visa-free travel for up to thirty days, while others require e-visas or advance planning. Purchase travel insurance before you leave, research any health precautions you need to take, and book accommodations during peak travel months well in advance. Apps like Skyscanner, Agoda, and Rome2Rio make it easy to compare prices and build a flexible itinerary.

Pro Tip

If you plan to travel long-term after your contract ends, have your pension refund and final paycheck sent to your home country bank account or an account you can access from anywhere. Store copies of all essential documents, passport, ARC, contract, pay stubs, and pension paperwork in cloud storage so you can retrieve them from any device. You don't want to be tracking down paperwork from a beach in Thailand.

Teaching in Other Countries: Where to Go Next?

Many teachers find that their time in Korea is only the beginning of their international teaching journey. With your experience, you will be a strong candidate for positions across Asia, the Middle East, Europe, and Latin America. Schools in other countries value applicants who have experience teaching in structured environments, especially if you have taught multiple age groups, created your own lesson plans, and worked in the fast-paced world of Korean private academies.

Some teachers transition to countries with similar demand for English instruction, such as Japan, Taiwan, Vietnam, or China. Others explore positions in the Middle East — the United Arab Emirates, Saudi Arabia, and Oman often offer tax-free salaries, free housing, and generous vacation time. European countries such as Spain, Poland, and the Czech Republic are popular with teachers who hold EU passports or have advanced TESOL qualifications. Each destination has its own culture, pay scale, and teaching environment, and your Korean experience gives you the credibility and the classroom skills to be competitive in almost any market.

To pursue international teaching jobs, start by upgrading your credentials if you haven't already. A 120-hour TEFL course with a practicum component is a solid foundation, and a CELTA or DELTA certificate will open doors to more competitive markets. Update your resume to reflect the skills and experience you gained in Korea, join teaching job boards like TeachAway, Dave's ESL Café, and International TEFL Academy, and attend virtual job fairs to connect directly with schools that are hiring.

Pro Tip

If you loved the experience of living and working abroad, do not feel pressured to return home permanently. Many teachers build long-term careers as global educators, moving from country to country, gaining new skills, and living fulfilling lives while seeing the world. Korea may have been your first stop, but it doesn't have to be your last.

Teacher Story: The Recruiter in Lakewood

I never planned to come to Korea. There was no grand strategy, no five-year plan, no carefully researched decision. A Korean recruiter was holding a meeting near Pacific Lutheran University in Lakewood, Washington, and something told me I should go. It felt like serendipity, a door opening that I hadn't been looking for but couldn't ignore. So I walked through it, and just like that, I was in Korea.

That spur-of-the-moment decision changed the entire trajectory of my life.

I came to Korea as a young guy with no teaching experience, no real plan, and no idea what I was getting into. What I found was an adventure that kept evolving, changing, and getting better with every turn, personally, professionally, and financially. I met my wife in Korea. I worked for the Korean government in Seoul and later in Chicago. I came back to Korea to become a university professor. And all the while, starting in 2006, I was building the business that eventually became TEIK and this book you are holding now.

None of that was in the plan when I sat down in that recruiter's office in Lakewood. All of it happened because I said yes to an opportunity I didn't fully understand and then stayed open to wherever it led me.

Most teachers who come to Korea stay for a year, maybe two or three. Some, like me, stay for the long haul. There is no wrong answer. Whether you spend twelve months here or twenty years, the experience will shape you in ways you can't predict right now. You will learn things about yourself that you couldn't have learned at home. You will build friendships that span continents. You will develop skills in the classroom and out of it that will serve you for the rest of your career. And you will carry Korea with you wherever you go next.

Takeaway: I don't need to tell you how much coming to Korea changed my life. By now, you've read the stories. But I do want to tell you this: your Korea experience will be exactly what you make of it. Come with a positive attitude, keep your eyes open, look for the good even when things get hard, and celebrate the experience for what it is — a rare opportunity to grow, meet extraordinary people, and expand your understanding of this corner of the world. Say yes to the things that scare you. Be kind to your students. Save your money. Make friends from everywhere. And when the time comes to decide what's next, trust that the skills, memories, and relationships you built in Korea will carry you further than you ever imagined.

This book exists because I walked into a recruiter's office on a whim more than twenty years ago. Your story starts now.

Pro Tip

If you loved the experience of living and working abroad, do not feel pressured to return home permanently. Many teachers build long-term careers as global educators, moving from country to country, gaining skills, and living fulfilling lives while seeing the world.

Final Thoughts

The end of your teaching contract in Korea is not an ending. It is a pivot point. Your time here has equipped you with valuable skills, a broadened perspective, and a depth of experience that will serve you for years to come, whether you choose to renew, move into a new role, return home, or set off on a new adventure entirely.

Every classroom you walked into made you a better communicator. Every cultural misunderstanding you navigated made you more adaptable. Every student who smiled at the end of your lesson reminded you why this work matters. And every friendship you built — with fellow teachers, Korean colleagues, and students — gave you a connection to this country that distance and time cannot erase.

This is your chance to reflect, realign, and set intentional goals for the next chapter of your life. Approach the transition with curiosity, confidence, and a willingness to embrace change, and you will find that your Korean teaching experience becomes a powerful stepping stone toward an even more rewarding future. You are no longer just a teacher. You are an international professional, a cultural bridge, and a storyteller with memories and lessons to last a lifetime.

This book exists because I walked into a recruiter's office on a whim more than twenty years ago. Your story starts now.

For an excellent video summary of the entire process of moving to and teaching in Korea, from the initial visa application to what to expect on your first day, visit: https://youtu.be/S52LIxsRDfQ.

Bonus Resources

This section is your toolkit. Everything here is designed to be practical, ready to use, and directly tied to the advice in the chapters you have just read. Whether you are polishing your application, preparing for your first class, or trying to order lunch without pointing at the menu, these templates, scripts, and cheat sheets will help you stand out, stay organized, and feel more confident from day one. Keep this section bookmarked; you will come back to it often.

Sample Resume and Cover Letter

Sample Resume Overview:

When applying for teaching positions in Korea, your resume should be clear, professional, and tailored specifically to ESL education. Korean directors are not looking for flashy graphic designs or a comprehensive history of every job you have ever held. They want to see your education, your TEFL certification, any teaching or mentoring experience, and a professional photo. That last part surprises many Western applicants, but every school in Korea will require you to submit a passport-style or lifestyle-type photo with your application. It is standard practice, not optional.

Your photo matters more than you might think. Korean directors will look at it before they read a single word on your resume. Take the photo during the day with natural lighting, using a plain white wall as your background. Smile naturally. Wear business casual attire, a blouse for women or a collared shirt without a tie for men. Avoid excessive makeup, visible piercings beyond small studs, and casual clothing. If you have tattoos, cover them for the photo. Keep facial hair very short or shave cleanly, as Korean professional culture generally favors a clean-shaven appearance. You can always express your personal style later once you have the job, but the application photo should be polished and professional.

On the resume itself, lead with your education and certifications, followed by any teaching, tutoring, mentoring, coaching, or childcare experience. Volunteer work counts. Babysitting counts. Sunday school teaching counts. Anything that demonstrates responsibility for guiding or mentoring others, especially children, should be included. Keep the format simple, clean, and easy to scan. Here is an example of what a strong application resume looks like:

Sample Resume Format:

Jane Smith

123 Main Street, Toronto, ON, Canada

Jane.smith85@gmail.com | +1-555-123-4567 | Teams   ID: jane.smith85

Objective

Enthusiastic and certified English teacher with a Bachelor of Education and 120-hour TEFL certificate. Experienced in teaching young learners and passionate about creating engaging, student-centered learning environments. Eager to contribute to a dynamic Korean school community.

Education

Bachelor of Education – University of British Columbia, Vancouver, Canada

Graduated: June 2020

Certifications

120-hour TEFL Certificate – GoTEFL.com, Completed May 2025

Teaching Experience

Volunteer ESL Tutor – YMCA Language Exchange, Vancouver, 2020–2021

• Taught conversational English to adult learners in weekly group sessions

• Designed interactive games to support vocabulary acquisition

Student Teaching Practicum – Lincoln Elementary School, 2019

• Led 3rd-grade reading and writing lessons

• Integrated classroom technology and peer activities

Skills

• Lesson Planning • Classroom Management • Google Workspace • Storytelling Techniques • Phonics Instruction

Pro Tip

Be sure to use a business casual portrait-style photo. Do not wear excessive makeup, piercings, or too casual attire. A blouse for females or a collared shirt with no tie is recommended for men. If you wear a nose ring, only wear a small stud earring. If you have any tattoos, make sure to cover them up (for now).

Pro Tip

Be sure to list any volunteer work, teaching, mentoring, coaching, babysitting, etc. All of these activities show responsibility in mentoring and teaching children.

Sample Cover Letter

Your cover letter should be brief, professional, and enthusiastic. Korean directors receive dozens of applications, and they do not have time to read a full-page essay about your life philosophy. Three short paragraphs are ideal: who you are and what you bring, what your teaching approach looks like, and a polite closing. Let your personality come through, but keep it concise. Here is an example:

Dear Hiring Manager,

I am writing to express my interest in the English teaching position at your school. As a certified teacher with a Bachelor of Education and a 120-hour TEFL certificate, I am confident in my ability to create engaging and effective learning experiences for your students.

I have classroom experience working with children of various ages and backgrounds. My approach to teaching emphasizes interactive lessons, clear communication, and fostering a positive, respectful classroom culture. I am highly adaptable, a strong team player, and excited to immerse myself in Korean culture and contribute to your school's community.

Thank you for considering my application. I look forward to the opportunity to speak with you and share how I can support your program.

Sincerely,

Jane Smith

Pro Tip

Keep your cover letter to one page or less. Directors want to see that you are professional, enthusiastic, and qualified. They do not need your autobiography. If your resume and photo are strong, the cover letter just needs to confirm that you can communicate clearly and that you genuinely want the position.

Self-Introduction Video Script

Most schools will ask you to submit a short self-introduction video as part of your application. This is your chance to show your personality, your comfort in front of a camera, and your ability to speak clearly and engagingly, all of which are critical skills for a classroom teacher. The video should be sixty-to-ninety-seconds long, filmed in a well-lit and quiet space, and it should showcase your enthusiasm and warmth.

Film during the day to take advantage of natural sunlight. Position a light source behind the camera, not behind you. Keep the camera at eye level in a fixed position, do not hold your phone. Smile, speak at a moderate pace, and let your personality come through. Do not read from a script. Directors can tell immediately when someone is reading, and it defeats the purpose of the video. Instead, review the key points you want to cover and speak naturally. Here is an example of the kind of content to include:

> Hello! My name is Jane Smith. I am from Toronto, Canada, and I have a Bachelor of Education and a 120-hour TEFL certificate. I have experience teaching young learners, and I love creating fun and interactive lessons using songs, games, and storytelling.

> I am excited to start teaching in South Korea because I love working with kids. I have always enjoyed teaching and mentoring my younger siblings, cousins, and children that I babysat for. I have always been fascinated by Korean culture, music, and of course Korean food, and I cannot wait to

experience Korea firsthand and make an impact on my students' education.

In my free time, I enjoy hiking, learning about different cultures, and trying new foods. I am really excited about the opportunity to teach in Korea because I want to gain valuable teaching experience and have fun while doing so.

Thank you for watching, and I look forward to meeting you soon!

Pro Tip

This script is just an example — do not memorize it and do not read from a teleprompter. Directors want to see the real you, not a rehearsed performance. Speak naturally, cover the key points (your name, qualifications, why you want to teach in Korea, and something personal about yourself), and let your energy and warmth come through. To watch a dozen excellent one-minute teacher self-introduction videos, sample lessons, and teacher interviews, visit https://www.teachenglishinkorea.org/videos.

Sample Lesson Plan Template

A well-structured lesson plan helps you maintain flow, timing, and engagement in the classroom. As we covered in Chapter 15, the five-phase structure — warm-up, presentation, guided practice, independent activity, and wrap-up — is the foundation of an effective lesson. Korean directors appreciate teachers who come prepared, and having a clean lesson plan template ready to go will make your first weeks significantly smoother. Here is an example of what a complete lesson plan looks like for an elementary class:

Lesson Title:

Daily Routines

Level:

Elementary (Ages 7–10)

Objective:

Students will be able to describe their daily routines using the simple present tense.

Materials:

Flashcards, whiteboard, daily routine worksheet, digital clock printouts.

Warm-Up (5 minutes):

Greet the class and play a short game of "What time is it?" using clock flashcards. This gets students focused and activates prior knowledge about numbers and time.

Presentation (10 minutes):

Introduce six daily routine verbs with flashcards: wake up, brush teeth, eat breakfast, go to school, do homework, and go to bed. Model pronunciation clearly and have students repeat each word several times as a class and then in pairs.

Guided Practice (15 minutes):

Students work in pairs to match images to verbs. Follow this with a sentence-building game where students create simple sentences like "I wake up at seven" and "I eat breakfast at eight." Circulate the room and offer gentle corrections.

Independent Activity (10 minutes):

Each student draws their daily routine on a worksheet and writes one sentence for each activity using the target structure. Volunteers present their routines to the class.

Wrap-Up and Game (5 minutes):

Play charades with the routine verbs. One student acts out the verb while the class guesses. Reinforce vocabulary while ending the lesson on a fun, high-energy note.

Assessment:

Informal assessment based on participation, pronunciation accuracy, and sentence construction during the independent activity and wrap-up game.

Pro Tip

This template follows the five-phase structure from Chapter 15. Once you have used it a few times, you will be able to build lesson plans quickly without even looking at a template. The structure becomes second nature, and you will start adapting it instinctively to different topics, levels, and class sizes. Keep a few blank copies of this template handy during your first weeks — it will save you time and keep your lessons organized.

Teaching Jobs and Resources

Finding the right teaching position starts with knowing where to look. The following resources are the most trusted and widely used by teachers applying to work in Korea.

Teach English in Korea (www.teachenglishinkorea.org) is the companion website to this book and offers in-depth visa guidance, job search support, teacher videos, and community resources specifically for teachers heading to Korea.

GoTEFL (www.gotefl.com) offers affordable, accredited TEFL certification including a 200-hour course and a Korea-specialized program. A TEFL certificate is required for most teaching positions, and GoTEFL's programs are well-regarded by Korean schools and recruiters.

Dave's ESL Café (eslcafe.com) is one of the longest-running job boards and teacher forums for ESL teachers worldwide. The Korea-specific job listings are updated frequently, and the forums are a good place to research schools and ask questions.

Gone2Korea provides job placement support with a focus on matching teachers to schools that fit their preferences for location, age group, and school type.

Korean Horizons is a recruitment agency that offers job listings and placement assistance for teachers looking for hagwon, public school, and university positions across Korea.

WorknPlay is a recruiting platform with blog content, job listings, and resources for teachers navigating the application process and life in Korea.

General Expat Resources

Beyond job boards, these resources will help you navigate daily life, connect with other expats, and stay informed about visa, legal, and housing matters.

Korea4Expats is one of the most comprehensive resources for expats living in Korea, covering visa information, legal guidance, housing, and practical tips for daily life.

Expat Women in Korea (Facebook Group) is an active community offering support, resources, and Q&A for female expats living and working in Korea. It is a welcoming space for asking questions and connecting with others.

KakaoTalk is Korea's main messaging app, used for both work and social communication. Download it before you arrive; your school, your coworkers, and your new friends will all use it to communicate with you. Think of it as Korea's equivalent of WhatsApp, but with more features and near-universal adoption.

Papago (파파고) is the single most useful app you will download in Korea. Developed by Naver, it is a translation app that handles Korean-to-English translation far better than Google Translate. It includes text translation, voice translation, image translation (point your camera at a sign or menu), and conversation mode. Install it on your first day and use it constantly.

Korean Survival Phrases Cheat Sheet

Learning even a few key Korean phrases will dramatically improve your daily life. You do not need to be fluent — even basic greetings and simple requests show respect, smooth out interactions, and earn you goodwill from nearly everyone you encounter. The phrases below are organized by situation so you can find what you need quickly. Practice the romanized pronunciations, but also start learning to read Hangul as soon as you can — it only takes a few hours to learn and will make these phrases much easier to remember.

Basic Greetings and Politeness

> **Hello** — 안녕하세요 (Annyeong haseyo)
>
> **Thank you** — 감사합니다 (Gamsahamnida)
>
> **Excuse me / I am sorry** — 죄송합니다 (Joesonghamnida)
>
> **Goodbye (when you are leaving)** — 안녕히 계세요 (Annyeonghi gyeseyo)
>
> **Yes / No** — 네 / 아니요 (Ne / Aniyo)

At a Restaurant

I would like this — 이거 주세요 (Igeo juseyo)

Is this spicy? — 매워요? (Maewoyo?)

Not spicy, please — 안 맵게 해 주세요 (An maepge hae juseyo)

Water, please — 물 주세요 (Mul juseyo)

I am vegetarian — 저는 채식주의자예요 (Jeoneun chaesikjuuijayeyo)

Daily Life

Where is the bathroom? — 화장실 어디에요? (Hwajangsil eodieyo?)

How much is this? — 이거 얼마에요? (Igeo eolmaeyo?)

I do not speak Korean well — 한국말 잘 못해요 (Hangukmal jal motaeyo)

Help, please! — 도와 주세요! (Dowa juseyo!)

Taking a Taxi

Please take me to [destination] — [장소]로 가 주세요 ([Jangso] ro ga juseyo)

Please use the meter — 미터기 켜 주세요 (Miteogi kyeo juseyo)

I want to pay with a card — 카드로 계산할게요 (Kadeuro gyesanhalgeyo)

Asking for Directions

Where is the subway station? — 지하철역이 어디에요? (Jihacheol yeogi eodieyo?)

Is it far from here? — 여기서 멀어요? (Yeogiseo meoreoyo?)

Please show me on the map — 지도에서 보여 주세요 (Jidoeseo boyeo juseyo)

Visiting a Shop or Convenience Store

Do you have this in another size? — 이거 다른 사이즈 있어요? (Igeo dareun saijeu isseoyo?)

Where is the fitting room? — 탈의실 어디에요? (Taruisil eodieyo?)

Can I return this? — 이거 환불 돼요? (Igeo hwanbul dwaeyo?)

Opening a Bank Account

I want to open a bank account — 계좌 만들고 싶어요 (Gyejwa mandeulgo sipeoyo)

Do you have English service? — 영어 서비스 있어요? (Yeongeo seobiseu isseoyo?)

I need an ATM card — 현금카드 필요해요 (Hyeongeum kadeu piryoh haeyo)

At the Doctor or Hospital

I do not feel well — 몸이 안 좋아요 (Momi an joayo)

I have a fever — 열이 있어요 (Yeori isseoyo)

Do you speak English? — 영어 하세요? (Yeongeo haseyo?)

I need a prescription — 처방전 필요해요 (Cheobangjeon piryoh haeyo)

At the Immigration Office

I need to apply for my ARC — 외국인등록증 신청하고 싶어요 (Oegugin deungnokjeung sincheonghago sipeoyo)

Here are my documents — 서류 여기 있어요 (Seoryu yeogi isseoyo)

When will it be ready? — 언제 나와요? (Eonje nawayo?)

At the Phone Store

I want a prepaid SIM card — 선불 심카드 원해요 (Seonbul simkadeu wonhaeyo)

I need unlimited data — 데이터 무제한으로 주세요 (Deiteo mujehan euro juseyo)

Can I use this phone in Korea? — 이 폰 한국에서 사용할 수 있어요? (I pon hangugeseo sayonghal su isseoyo?)

Public Transportation

Does this bus go to [destination]? — 이 버스 [장소] 가요? (I beoseu [jangso] gayo?)

Where do I get off? — 어디에서 내려요? (Eodieseo naeryeoyo?)

How do I get to [place]? — [장소] 어떻게 가요? ([Jangso] eotteoke gayo?)

These phrases are designed to make your daily life smoother and more confident from the moment you arrive. You will find that most Koreans appreciate even a few words of Korean and will respond warmly to your effort. For pronunciation support and vocabulary building on the go, download Papago and Naver Dictionary. Talk To Me In Korean is also an excellent free resource for structured lessons that will take you well beyond survival phrases if you want to keep learning.

Pro Tip

Start learning Hangul, the Korean writing system, before you arrive. It was designed to be easy to learn and can be mastered in just a few hours. Once you can read Hangul, signs, menus, subway maps, and even text messages become accessible to you in a way that romanized pronunciation guides cannot replicate. It is the single best investment of your time before you step on the plane.

Glossary of Korean Terms

Education & Work

Term	Hangul	Meaning
hagwon	학원	Private academy/cram school
hoesik	회식	Company or staff dinner outing
gongchaek	공책	Notebook/journal (student communication book)
TOPIK	토픽	Test of Proficiency in Korean
Suneung	수능	Korean college entrance exam
Taekwondo	태권도	Korean martial art

Food & Drink

Term	Hangul	Meaning
kimchi	김치	Fermented vegetable side dish
dak-ttongjip-twigim	닭똥집튀김	Fried chicken gizzards
bibimbap	비빔밥	Mixed rice bowl with vegetables and sauce
bulgogi	불고기	Marinated grilled beef
samgyeopsal	삼겹살	Grilled pork belly
galbi	갈비	Grilled short ribs
galchi	갈치	Hairtail fish (often grilled)
jjigae	찌개	Stew
sundubu	순두부	Soft tofu
tteokbokki	떡볶이	Spicy rice cakes
banchan	반찬	Small shared side dishes
mandu	만두	Dumplings
pajeon	파전	Savory green onion pancake
hotteok	호떡	Sweet filled pancake
haemultang	해물탕	Spicy seafood stew

maeuntang	매운탕	Spicy fish stew
yangnyeom	양념	Seasoned / marinated
gochujang	고추장	Red chili pepper paste
doenjang	된장	Fermented soybean paste
chimek	치맥	Chicken and beer (치킨 + 맥주)
maekju	맥주	Beer
soju	소주	Korean distilled spirit
makgeolli	막걸리	Unfiltered rice wine
dongdongju	동동주	Unfiltered rice wine (lighter style)
Geonbae	건배	Cheers / drinking toast

Culture & Daily Life

Term	Hangul	Meaning
Hangul	한글	Korean writing system
Chuseok	추석	Korean harvest festival
Joseon	조선	Joseon Dynasty (1392–1897)
hanok	한옥	Traditional Korean house
hanbok	한복	Traditional Korean clothing
ondol	온돌	Underfloor heating system
noraebang	노래방	Private singing room (karaoke)
PC bang	PC방	Internet / gaming café
pojangmacha	포장마차	Street food tent / stall
jeong	정	Deep emotional bond / affection
jeonse	전세	Lump-sum deposit rental system
wolse	월세	Monthly rent system

Apps & Services

Term	Hangul	Meaning
KakaoTalk	카카오톡	Korea's main messaging app

Naver	네이버	Leading Korean search engine / portal
Papago	파파고	Naver's translation app
T-money	티머니	Rechargeable transit card
Kyobo	교보	Major Korean bookstore chain

Travel & Experiences

Term	Hangul	Meaning
Templestay	템플스테이	Overnight Buddhist temple experience
Olle	올레	Jeju Island walking trail system

Final Thoughts: Your Journey Begins Now

When I started writing this book, I had one goal: to give you the guide I wish someone had handed me when I walked into that recruiter's office in Lakewood, Washington, more than twenty years ago. Nobody told me how to read a Korean contract. Nobody warned me about the rainy season or explained what a hoesik was. Nobody sat me down and said, "Save half your paycheck" or "Don't date your coworker" or "Learn Hangul before you get on the plane." I figured all of it out the hard way, through mistakes, through trial and error, and through the kindness of colleagues and friends who took the time to share what they knew.

This book is my way of doing the same for you.

Throughout these chapters, I have walked you through the entire process, from preparing your application materials and understanding your visa options to managing your first classroom, adapting to Korean work culture, navigating finances, and building a meaningful life outside of school. I have shared real stories from my own experience and from the teachers I have mentored, detailed explanations of paperwork that nobody makes easy, sample documents you can use immediately, classroom strategies that actually work, and cultural advice drawn from more than two decades of living and working in Korea.

Teaching in Korea is more than a job. It is an opportunity to grow as an educator, immerse yourself in one of Asia's most vibrant and generous cultures, and make a lasting impact on students who will remember you long after you leave. It is also a chance to discover things about yourself, your resilience, your adaptability, your capacity for patience and humor, and your connection that you simply cannot discover by staying home.

I hope this guide helps you feel more confident, more informed, and more prepared to begin your adventure. I hope the stories made you laugh, the Pro Tips saved you from a few avoidable mistakes, and the practical details gave you the clarity to move forward without unnecessary stress. Most of all, I hope you arrive in Korea knowing that someone who has been exactly where you are right now is cheering for you.

Thank you for reading. The next chapter of your life starts now. Go forward with curiosity, openness, and enthusiasm. Korea is waiting for you, and it is going to be worth it.

Warm regards,

Bradley S. Brennan, Ph.D., MBA, B.Ed.

Professor of Hospitality and Business, Inha University | Founder and Principal of TeachEnglishinKorea.org

About the Author

Dr. Bradley S. Brennan has dedicated nearly three decades to the intersection of education, international tourism, and cultural exchange in South Korea. His journey as an educator began at Pacific Lutheran University, where he earned his B.Ed. in Secondary Education. Driven by a lifelong passion for teaching and a desire for global experience.

Dr. Brennan's decision to teach abroad was shaped well before his first classroom in Korea. During his final years at university, he became an exchange student at Lancaster University in the United Kingdom. What was initially planned as a one-year experience extended into two and a half years, during which he traveled extensively throughout the UK, Ireland, and on a month-long European trip, often backpacking with American and British classmates. Between academic terms, he also spent several months living in Regensburg, Germany, experiences that heightened his sensitivity to how mobility, place, and everyday cultural encounters shape identity, perspective, and ignited his desire to travel and live abroad.

After returning to the United States from Europe, he completed his student teaching at Rogers High School in Washington State, yet found himself unwilling to settle into a conventional career path. He was actively seeking another meaningful international experience when the opportunity to teach in South Korea emerged in an unexpected and almost cinematic moment of chance. While sitting in a local coffee shop, he was on the phone lamenting that he had missed the application deadline for the JET Program in Japan. A woman seated nearby overheard the conversation, tapped him on the shoulder, and asked if he had ever considered teaching in Korea. When he replied that he had not, she handed him a business card for a Korean American recruiter she had met earlier that same day. He contacted the recruiter immediately, met him in person that afternoon, and within a week was on his way to Korea to begin teaching. What initially appeared as a fortunate coincidence would later become a defining reference point in his academic work, shaping his interest in tourism, cultural exchange, and the everyday moments through which international mobility and life-changing decisions often unfold.

Academic and Professional Evolution

Before transitioning into high-level administration, Dr. Brennan committed to advancing his business acumen, completing MBA coursework at Syracuse University, followed by an MBA with a Marketing Concentration from Sejong University in Seoul. This rigorous academic foundation paved the way for his appointment as the National Public Relations Manager for the Korea Tourism Organization (KTO) in their Seoul headquarters, where he worked closely with government stakeholders, international partners, and global media to shape Korea's tourism image abroad.

His success in Seoul at the KTO head office led to a leadership role abroad as the Midwest Regional Marketing Manager for the KTO in Chicago for the twenty Midwestern states. In this capacity, he managed large-scale promotional campaigns and forged strategic partnerships to increase international travel to South Korea. Despite his success in the corporate world, Dr. Brennan remained dedicated to supporting the expat community, and in 2006, he founded www.teachenglishinkorea.org (TEIK) to provide a comprehensive resource for aspiring educators who wished to work abroad, help Korean children, and to enjoy traveling the world.

Academic Research and Leadership

In Spring 2012, Bradley returned to his roots in academia, joining Inha University as an Assistant Professor in the College of Business. Today, he continues to serve as a full-time faculty member, balancing his leadership of the TEIK program with a robust research agenda.

Dr. Brennan is a published scholar in high-impact SSCI and KCI-indexed journals, with specialized expertise in Smart Tourism and

Technology, Sustainable and Cultural Tourism, Consumer Behavior, and Marketing.

Outside of his professional work, Dr. Brennan enjoys a balanced and active family life in Korea. He is married to his wife, Yumi, and they have a 12-year-old son, Jae. In his free time, he is an avid tennis player and golfer, finding both sports to be an important outlet alongside his academic work. He continues to enjoy writing academic research papers and remains deeply curious about culture, travel, and education, often combining these interests through family travel and long-term living abroad.

Beyond formal titles and credentials, Dr. Brennan's work is grounded in lived experience. Over the years, he has personally mentored thousands of prospective teachers, reviewed countless contracts and visas, mediated school and teacher conflicts, and helped educators navigate both the opportunities and challenges of life in Korea. His approach blends academic rigor with practical realism, emphasizing cultural understanding, adaptability, and long-term success rather than short-term placement alone. This book reflects that philosophy, offering not just instructions, but perspective earned through decades of firsthand involvement in Korea's education system.

With a Ph.D. in Hospitality and Tourism from Kyung Hee University and decades of experience navigating the Korean professional and educational systems, Dr. Brennan is uniquely positioned to guide the next generation of teachers through the rewards of living and working in South Korea.

Resources & Links Index

This index lists every online resource referenced in this book, organized by chapter. For the most up-to-date links, visit www.teachenglishinkorea.org.

Chapter 5: Preparing Your Application Materials

Teacher self-introduction videos and sample lessons: https://www.teachenglishinkorea.org/videos

Chapter 6: Finding the Right Job

Country-specific visa processing guides: https://www.teachenglishinkorea.org/blog/categories/e2-teaching-visa-process-for-korea

Chapter 16: Teaching Different Age Groups

GoTEFL certification programs: www.gotefl.com

Chapter 18: Exploring Korea: Travel, Food, and Fun

Research article on the Jeju Olle Trail: https://www.mdpi.com/2071-1050/18/3/1540

Research article on Korean Templestay experiences: https://www.mdpi.com/2071-1050/17/14/6483

Templestay program information and booking: www.templestay.com

Korea tourism and travel planning: www.tour2korea.com

Chapter 20: Managing Finances & Legal Matters

IRS Form 2555 (Foreign Earned Income Exclusion):
https://www.irs.gov/forms-pubs/about-form-2555

Chapter 21: Preparing for What's Next

Video overview of the teaching-in-Korea process:
https://youtu.be/S52LIxsRDfQ

Teacher self-introduction videos and interviews:
https://www.teachenglishinkorea.org/videos

Teaching Jobs and Recruitment

Teach English in Korea (companion site to this book):
www.teachenglishinkorea.org

GoTEFL (TEFL certification): www.gotefl.com

Dave's ESL Café (job board and forums): www.eslcafe.com

Gone2Korea (job placement): www.gone2korea.com

Korean Horizons (recruitment agency): www.koreanhorizons.com

WorknPlay (job listings and resources): www.worknplay.co.kr

General Expat Resources

Korea4Expats (visa, legal, housing info): www.korea4expats.com

Expat Women in Korea, Search "Expat Women in Korea" on
Facebook

KakaoTalk (messaging app), Available on iOS and Android app
stores

Papago (translation app by Naver), Available on iOS and Android app stores

VisitKorea (Korea Tourism Organization): www.english.visitkorea.or.kr

Trazy (experience booking platform): www.trazy.com

Talk To Me In Korean (language learning): www.talktomeinkorean.com

TEACH ENGLISH IN KOREA:
A Complete Step-by-Step Guide

Everything You Need to Know — From Someone Who's Done It for Over 20 Years

Every year, thousands of people dream about teaching English in South Korea. The pay is good, the housing is free, and the adventure of a lifetime is waiting. But between the dream and the departure gate, there are visa applications, contract negotiations, background checks, apostilles, interviews, and a hundred other details that can overwhelm even the most determined candidates — or worse, land them in the wrong job.

This book exists so that doesn't happen to you.

Written by Bradley S. Brennan, PhD, the founder of TEIK (Teach English in Korea) and a university professor in South Korea, this is the most comprehensive guide available for aspiring English teachers. Drawing on more than two decades of recruiting, mentoring, and placing teachers across Korea, Bradley S. Brennan, PhD walks you through every step of the process — from deciding whether Korea is right for you, to landing in Incheon, to thriving in your classroom and building a career you're proud of.

This isn't generic advice pulled from internet forums. This is hard-won knowledge from someone who has lived it, built a career on it, and helped hundreds of teachers navigate the same journey you're about to begin.

The complete process, start to finish: visa types, document preparation, TEFL certification, job applications, interviews, contract negotiation, and arrival logistics, all in one book.

Real teacher stories throughout — dozens of firsthand accounts from teachers who made mistakes, found solutions, and learned lessons you can benefit from before you even board the plane.

The Golden Circle — the single most important framework for long-term success in Korean private academies, explained by someone who used it to build a 20-year career.

Cultural fluency, not just classroom tips — how to navigate Korean workplace hierarchy, build trust with your director, and avoid the cultural missteps that derail promising teachers every year.

Written by an insider — Bradley S. Brennan, PhD has been a teacher, a recruiter, a government PR manager, and a university professor in Korea. He knows the system from every angle.

Bradley S. Brennan, PhD is an Assistant Professor at Inha University's College of Business Administration in South Korea and the founder of TEIK (Teach English in Korea). Over the past two decades, he has recruited, mentored, and supported hundreds of English teachers throughout their Korean journeys. He has worked as an ESL teacher, a public relations manager for the Korea Tourism Organization in Seoul, a regional marketing manager at the KTO's Chicago office, and a published academic researcher specializing in Korean tourism. He lives in South Korea.

www.teachenglishinkorea.org

$24.99

ISBN 979-8-234-00638-7

52499>

9 798234 006387